PRAISE FOR THE "BREVIARY OF FIRE"

"The Letters written by Mère Mectilde de Bar to Madame de Châteauvieux have been treasured by the Benedictines of the Perpetual Adoration of the Blessed Sacrament since the seventeenth century. Published in 1989 with useful introductions, notes, and comments, they are now elegantly translated into English for the first time.

In this rigorous teaching permeated with maternal love, the great values of the Benedictine *Rule* are rendered into the language of the French school of spirituality. Humility becomes *anéantissement*; the centrality of Christ is affirmed. Pride of place is given to the liturgical and sacramental life which, together with a prudent asceticism, provides solid foundations to the quest for 'pure love'—what St Benedict called 'perfect charity.'

Directing a soul is like painting a portrait—or writing an icon. By little touches of light and grace, encouragement and correction, the soul of the reader is slowly cleansed and enlightened. One's life changes, and as the Holy Spirit more and more takes the leading place in the soul, the true image of God is slowly restored.

A sure guide for serious souls who take God and His love seriously."

—ABBOT XAVIER PERRIN, OSB

"No woman in the French *Grand Siècle*, or in any other time, has been as inspirational as Mother Mectilde of the Blessed Sacrament (Catherine de Bar, 1614–1698) in giving the Church a profound understanding of the Real Presence in the Eucharist. She knows how to express its constantly astounding depth as a permanent Sacrifice offered by the Son in the power of the Holy Spirit through the Church to the Father. The Sacrifice that heals all, the Victim whose *kenosis* saves all of Creation. Saint Catherine of Siena reminds priests that they are Ministers of the Blood; Saint Brigid of Sweden gives us the giant monstrance for Adoration; and, as so often in Christian history, many other women reveal to us the mysteries of the Faith which, albeit unspeakable, are by them made speakable. The principal Mystery, that of His Divine and Human Presence in its total self-giving and self-emptying is here described by the Venerable Mother Mectilde to another woman, the Countess de Châteauvieux, but in reality to all of us. May we all learn to truly love more the Sacrament of Love through this text, now after more than three centuries finally available in English. The great authoress teaches us that this Sacrament is new every day and that we are to live it as such so that we may live already on this earth in the Triune God, even as we will forever in Eternity."

—MSGR KAREL KASTEEL

"In her 'Breviary of Fire,' French Benedictine Mother Mectilde of the Blessed Sacrament provides a tender, motherly yet precise guide through the path of the sacraments into an increasingly deeper dying to self which opens to an ever-deeper intimacy with Christ. Drawing her spiritual daughter, the Countess of Châteauvieux, into the interior dispositions of the mysteries of Christ, we find in her letters one of the clearest applications of the spirituality of Saint Francis de Sales and the French School."

—**FR THOMAS ACKLIN**, OSB

"Having read the first volume of this series of writings of Mother Mectilde de Bar published in English, *The Mystery of Incomprehensible Love*, I was glad to see this next volume appear. Mother Mectilde is one of those chosen souls who give themselves to God in Christ without holding anything back. Her spirit burns with the fire of total devotion, and she expects all those who are inspired by her words to do likewise. There are no half-measures or partial responses in her view of the Christian soul dedicated to God. She aims at perfection, trusting completely in God's grace to accomplish this miracle."

—**DR ELLEN GRYNIEWICZ**, Obl.OSB

"Mother Mectilde was so aflame with the love of God that her whole life was a sacrifice to Him. To read her letters is to be filled anew with the desire to give oneself to God."

—**P. EDMUND WALDSTEIN**, O.Cist.

The "Breviary of Fire"

The "Breviary of Fire"

Letters by
MOTHER MECTILDE
OF THE
BLESSED SACRAMENT

Chosen & Arranged by
MARIE DE LA GUESLE
COUNTESS OF
CHÂTEAUVIEUX

Translated by
AN OBLATE OF
SILVERSTREAM PRIORY

Angelico Press

First published in French as
Une amitié spirituelle au grand siècle (Téqui, 1989)

First published in the USA by Angelico Press 2021

For information, address:
Angelico Press, Ltd.
169 Monitor St.
Brooklyn, NY 11222
www.angelicopress.com

ppr 978-1-62138-714-5
cloth 978-1-62138-715-2
ebook 978-1-62138-716-9

Book and cover design
by Michael Schrauzer
Cover image: Vermeer, "Lady with Her Maidservant
Holding a Letter" (detail), ca. 1667

TABLE OF CONTENTS

[illegible]

TRANSLATOR'S PREFACE

MOTHER MECTILDE OF THE BLESSED SACrament (Catherine de Bar, 1614–1698) was the foundress of the Benedictines of Perpetual Adoration of the Blessed Sacrament.[1] Born in Lorraine, she exhibited early in life an attraction to the Holy Eucharist and a deep devotion to the Blessed Virgin Mary. After a short period in the Order of the Annunciation, she transferred to the Order of St. Benedict. Her gifts and holiness were quickly recognized and, despite her reluctance, she accepted the office of Prioress. Forced to relocate during the upheavals of the Thirty Years' War, she settled with her nuns in Paris. There she was approached about beginning a house devoted to perpetual adoration. Despite many bitter trials, she was faithful to this call and went on to found seven monasteries during her long life. In the midst of her many duties she served as spiritual guide, teacher, and confidante to many people, both lay and religious. Among these was Marie de la Guesle, the Countess of Châteauvieux.

Having come to Mother Mectilde's temporary dwelling for a charity visit, Marie de la Guesle, a prominent woman in Parisian society, was struck by the Prioress's supernatural insights. She returned several days later to talk of spiritual matters, about which she was extremely curious.[2] She opened her soul to Mother Mectilde, having found in her new friend a wisdom she had seen nowhere else. The Prioress soon began to direct the Countess, leading her in the paths of faith, self-renunciation, prayer, and the pure love of God. At the same time, the Countess of Châteauvieux and her supportive husband set to work assisting the future foundress. Marie gave not only financial resources to Mother Mectilde's foundation, but her very self as well: on the day after her husband's death, she withdrew from the world into the monastery she had helped to build at rue Cassette.

---

1 The most complete biography in English to date is that of Canon G. A. Simon, "Mectilde of the Blessed Sacrament and Her Times," in *The Mystery of Incomprehensible Love: The Eucharistic Message of Mother Mectilde of the Blessed Sacrament* (Brooklyn, NY: Angelico Press, 2020), 113–51.

2 *Documents Historiques*, 81.

The friendship which grew ever deeper between the Benedictine Prioress and the grand lady left a permanent testament in their candid and multifaceted correspondence, conducted over a period of about a dozen years. The Countess later arranged the Prioress's letters into a volume which she affectionately called her "breviary of fire." Benedictine in its fundamental principles, Mother Mectilde's teaching reflects and contributes to the French School, which included such luminaries as Pierre de Bérulle, St. John Eudes, and Jean-Jacques Olier, while drawing freely on other sources, especially St. John of the Cross and St. Francis de Sales. Her gifts of psychological penetration and practical mysticism are fully evident in the advice she gave to Marie de Châteauvieux.

As was typical in the era of its composition, most personal references and particular dates were removed when the letters were selected and rearranged, in order to make the advice they contained suitable for anyone who might read them. Mother Mectilde herself reviewed the collection and allowed her nuns who so desired to copy it for their own use. For over three centuries, these copies were handed on from one generation of Benedictine nuns to the next as part of the precious inheritance of their foundress's teaching, until they were published under the auspices of the nuns of Rouen in 1989. In this French publication, the nuns include the following note:

> The manuscript we are publishing bears the title:
>
> *Breviary of Fire*
> *Madame the Countess of Châteauvieux*
> *—original of our Mother Institutrice—*
> *who gave that Lady many instructions*
> *according to her spiritual inclination*
>
> According to the most ancient copies known in our Institute, this collection of letters addressed by our foundress Mother Mectilde of the Blessed Sacrament de Bar (1614–1698) to the Countess of Châteauvieux, was gathered and selected by the recipient herself. The plan for it was chosen by her. Our archives possess many other letters to the Countess of Châteauvieux; those we are presenting are

> organized according to a logical plan and we believe it was approved by Mother Mectilde herself, given the rapid diffusion of these texts in our monasteries, even while our foundress was alive.
>
> The rich personality of the Countess of Châteauvieux is very endearing. She was a devoted collaborator and a friend for Mother Mectilde. Many pages of Mother Mectilde's biography are from her niece, Mademoiselle de Vienville, a boarder at the monastery of rue Cassette and therefore an eyewitness of the reported facts, which makes them trustworthy. It is the same with the *Mémoires*, which is both a biography of Mother Mectilde and a history of the foundation of our Institute and of the first four monasteries. These memoirs, from the pen of some close collaborator of Mother Mectilde, were published under our auspices under the title of *Documents Historiques* in 1973.[3]

In addition to the letters to the Countess, this volume contains three important essays. In the Introduction, Fr. Paul Milcent, CJM, a specialist in St. John Eudes, unfolds the spiritual thought of Mother Mectilde, highlighting four characteristic features of it: our baptismal insertion into the life, death, and resurrection of Jesus Christ; our knowledge of God in the "luminous darkness" of faith; the extinction of our self-love and the awakening of pure love of God; the liberty of the children of God who are moved by His Spirit. In Appendix I, Fr. Michel Dupuy, PSS, a specialist in seventeenth-century spirituality, sets the *Breviary* in the larger context of the French School and outlines its shared and unique elements. In Appendix II, Msgr Charles Molette, sometime president of the Archivists of the Church of France, presents a short history of the author, recipient, and manuscript history of the work. The three essays taken together serve as an admirable overview of the scope of Mother Mectilde's spiritual theology and its ongoing fruitfulness for serious seekers after God. As Dom Jean Leclercq says, her "message has value not only for the

3 The essay by Fr. Michel Dupuy in Appendix I cites all of these historical documents, some still in manuscript form.

seventeenth century, for Benedictine nuns, but for Christians of all times and of our time."[4]

One may go a step further: the *Breviary* has a special relevance for believers in the twenty-first century, who often suffer from the same difficulties the Countess initially did: a tendency toward activism and the loss of the priority of prayer, preoccupation with self, doubts and anxieties over one's state of soul. To all of these problems, Mother Mectilde brought a deep insight and a compassionate heart. May this volume make her still better known in the English-speaking world, and may it lead souls into a deeper relationship with Our Lord Jesus Christ, sublimely present in the Most Blessed Sacrament and present, too, in the soul of every faithful Christian.

Feast of St. Frances of Rome
Patroness of Benedictine Oblates
March 9, 2021

---

4 *Catherine de Bar: à l'écoute de Saint Benoît*, Benedictines du Saint Sacrement (Paris: Téqui, 1988), 10.

A NOTE ON THE TRANSLATION

ALONGSIDE THE SPIRITUAL WISDOM AND PSYCHOlogical insight to be found in the *Breviary of Fire*, there are potential difficulties for modern readers. During the *grande siècle* hyperbole was the norm; extreme rhetoric was the way to present one's point. A certain "translation" has to be made so that an accurate view is gained. Accordingly, two key ideas in the *Breviary* need a word of clarification (for a more in-depth treatment, see the Introduction as well as the first Appendix).

Mother Mectilde frequently uses the Bérullian term *anéantissement* and its various forms such as *s'anéantir*. The background of this concept is St. Paul's teaching on *kenosis*, the self-emptying of the Son of God in becoming man to redeem us, and His giving Himself totally on the cross. Unfortunately, a strict translation of *anéantissement* as "annihilation" would carry misleading connotations for modern English readers. It is not what Mother Mectilde meant; there are variations in meaning which depend on context, especially when applied to Christ. No English word conveys directly and simply this idea of death to one's self, utter humility, and self-emptying. Therefore *anéantissement* has been left in French, while the verb form is usually translated as "reduce to nothing."[1]

The use of the terms "victim" and "victimhood" may also cause confusion or distaste in some readers. In theology a victim (*hostia* in Latin) is one wholly made over to God in sacrifice. In Catholic spirituality, the word "victim" does not refer to a person to whom something bad has happened, but to a person to whom something *good* has happened—to whom, indeed, the very best thing has happened: communion with Jesus Christ, specifically in the mystery of His eternal self-offering to the Father.[2] As Dom Mark Kirby comments:

> She [Mother Mectilde] uses the word *victim* in the same way the texts of the sacred liturgy use it. One could cite

1 See also the introduction by William M. Thompson to *Bérulle and the French School* (New York: Paulist Press, 1989), 35–46.

2 Fr. Dupuy's treatment of this concept is very helpful: see below, p. 280.

> here any number of Secrets and Postcommunions from both the Temporal and Sanctoral Masses. A victim is a living being made over to God alone in so radical and irrevocable a way that she no longer has any life outside of life in God, for God, and by God. The liturgical use of the term *victim* makes it very clear that this is the ordinary state of anyone who receives Holy Communion consciously and devoutly. By being atoned (at-oned, joined) to the Divine Victim, the Lamb of God, one becomes a single *victim* with Him, that is, an offering made over to the Father in a holocaust of love.[3]

Two other terminological notes are in order. The Prioress often uses the term *fond* or *fonds*, sometimes translated here as "ground" and at other times as "depth/depths." Jean Leclercq explains the provenance of the term: "This is an echo of what the Rheno-Flemish mystics — whose influence on the French School is well known — had called the *Grund*: that is, the center of ourselves, where our egoism is situated and which, emptied, purified, can become the place of the divine Presence."[4]

Mother Mectilde speaks of *amour-propre*, a common enough term in French, but not easy to render into English. In modern French, it can have a positive meaning (self-esteem, properly understood) or a negative one (pride, vainglory). The religious use of the term in *grand siècle* literature is generally negative, amounting to an excessive attachment to one's self-image, passions, prejudices — something closer to self-absorption or self-centeredness, a preoccupation with self that is hypersensitive and easily wounded. In a journal entry from 1823, philosopher Maine de Biran wrote: "self-love [*l'amour de soi*], which is only the instinct to live, differs from *amour-propre*, which concerns the ideas one has acquired, the comparisons that arise between oneself

3 Introduction to "On the Solemnity of Thursday," in *Mystery of Incomprehensible Love*, 13–14.

4 Dom Jean Leclercq, "Una Benedettina nel suo secolo: M. Mectilde de Bar (1614–1698)," in *Deus Absconditus: Primo centenario dell'Istituto delle Benedittine dell'Adorazione Perpetua del SS. Sacramento in Italia, 1880–1980*, Supplement to *Deus Absconditus* 71 (1980), 72–81; English translation by a monk of Silverstream Priory.

and others." *Amour-propre* is an obstacle to moral and spiritual progress. As Emmanuel Mounier noted in 1946: "Spiritual writers have always made *amour-propre* out to be the foremost and most rebellious adversary of moral striving." In these pages the term is usually translated "self-love" or "pride," depending on context.

Like all spiritual masters, Mother Mectilde was steeped in Scripture, which she frequently cites or paraphrases, in Latin or in French, often prompted by the Mass of the day. She seems to be drawing from her memory and does not pause to "get the exact quote"; for this reason, the notes herein avoid adding "cf.," which should simply be understood to be the case. Psalm references are given in both forms: the traditional Septuagint/Vulgate numbering and the Hebrew numbering.

INTRODUCTION

The Spiritual Theology of Mother Mectilde of the Blessed Sacrament

PAUL MILCENT, CJM

AS WE SURVEY THE LETTERS OF MOTHER Mectilde of the Blessed Sacrament to the Countess of Châteauvieux, we may experience a first impression of asperity, of austerity—we admire it, but isn't it perhaps a little too sublime? This happens especially since the first few pages offer little for the imagination to grasp, at least in the present condition of the letters: the recipient doubtless eliminated all that seemed to her to be too personal and that would, on that account, have moved us. However, if we persist, we are gripped by the astonishing presence of this woman of strong personality, lively, warm, deeply sensitive and spontaneous, prompt with sympathy—and who expresses herself in beautiful, vigorous language, without any monotony but with an innate sense of rhythm.

These letters had as their only goal to offer an initiation into the spiritual life. In them we discern a strong and coherent concept of Christian holiness—though with some areas of emphasis which can seem today excessive or debatable. This teaching has nothing cold or theoretical: it is entirely imbued with a very sublime idea of God, or to put it better, with a pure and fervent experience of the search for God, of life with God.

We summarize Mother Mectilde's teaching here in four sections:

1. "The profession of Jesus Christ we made in baptism, to live from His life and to be animated by His Spirit."[1]

2. God known in the "luminous darkness" of faith.

---

1 n. 2404, p. 140. The first number refers to the item number attached to each letter by the editors of the French manuscripts of Mother Mectilde; the second number is the page in this volume where the letter in question appears.

3. A desire for *anéantissement* (that is, being reduced to nothing), of which the other name is "pure love."

4. A path of liberty, "very docile to the movements of Jesus's Spirit."[2]

Perhaps Mother Mectilde would say to us, smiling, just what she wrote to her "very dear daughter": "Read this lesson attentively, not once, but several times, gently, without effort or strain. Receive what it will please Our Lord to bring about in you."[3]

I. "THE PROFESSION OF JESUS CHRIST WE MADE IN BAPTISM, TO LIVE FROM HIS LIFE AND TO BE ANIMATED BY HIS SPIRIT"

Mother Mectilde quite frequently directs the attention of her correspondent to the sacrament of baptism and to the promises made to God in baptism.[4] When she wanted to give the Countess a complete and coherent doctrine of baptism, she opened Fr. Eudes's book, *The Life and Kingdom of Jesus in Christian Souls*,[5] and she copied some pages from it.

This sacrament is a benevolent initiative of God in our regard; it obligates us to the perfection of the gospel. In the account of baptism the Father, the Son, and the Holy Spirit are there, "laying hold of us and conforming and consecrating us to Himself in an entirely special manner, imprinting His divine character and image within us. . . . "[6] More precisely, baptism joins us to Christ: in it we make "a profession to have only one life, one spirit, one heart, one soul, one will, one thought, and one and the same disposition and devotion" with Jesus.[7] He causes us to enter into the mystery of His divine filiation and into His human birth, into His death and His resurrection.

From then on, all throughout the letters, we hear the call to "renounce ourselves in order to cleave to Jesus."[8] There are a multitude of formulations inspired by St. Paul, but also by Bérulle, Olier, and above all St. John Eudes, repeated in a thousand ways. "Live like Jesus Christ since through baptism you are clothed with

---

2 n. 421, p. 229. 3 n. 674, p. 52. 4 n. 1947, p. 5.

5 We are using (as did Mother Mectilde) the edition made in Paris in 1670 with Frederic Leonard.

6 n. 195, p. 7. 7 n. 2408, p. 8. 8 n. 1653, p. 10.

Him."[9] Did the Countess want to know how to receive in a Christian way the services rendered her by her domestic servants? "Remember that it is not yours, or for you, rather it is for Jesus Christ in you."[10] Therefore, everything she does should "continue the life of Jesus Christ."[11] The nun invites her correspondent to live in such a way that only Jesus is seen in her; her thoughts the thoughts of Jesus, her word the words of Jesus, her actions the actions of Jesus. . . . [12]

This will not happen without difficulty, since we must accept seeing everything in us which is not Jesus Christ destroyed. Suffering, trials, contradictions come to the aid of this labor: "O cross, O affliction, O loss, O disaster, how beneficial you are!"[13] We think we hear Bérulle again when the counselor writes, "In this state of *anéantissement*, the soul has become a pure capacity for God."[14]

Henceforth, there are no other virtues than Jesus Christ's virtues which God produces in us. Strength, for example, is in us "the strength of Jesus" and can indeed coexist with our own weakness.[15] Cultivating the virtue of poverty will mean first of all "to give oneself to the Spirit and the grace of Jesus Christ, the poor one."[16] Faith itself consists in this, that we must no longer see anything "except through the eyes of Jesus Christ."[17] Christ's mysteries, which the liturgy makes us re-live, are inscribed in us, they take hold of us and transform us. For they remain present in a hidden way and are active in the Mystical Body. Certainly, Bethlehem is past: "The temporal birth of Jesus will not happen again, but the grace of His birth will last eternally. And He is born mystically in our souls continually when there is no opposition to this on our part."[18]

Mother Mectilde intended to truly cooperate in God's work in the one she was accompanying: "It is Jesus Christ Himself that I would like to introduce into your heart and tear out all the rest!"[19] Does this Benedictine want to summarize "all Christian perfection"? She says it consists, first, in considering Jesus Christ, and then in cleaving to

9 n. 996, p. 19.
10 n. 674, p. 51.
11 n. 2054, p. 66.
12 n. 530, p. 120.
13 n. 2054, p. 67.
14 n. 312, p. 97.
15 n. 120, p. 212.
16 n. 1819, p. 171.
17 n. 3086. The expression is from St. John Eudes, *Life and Kingdom* (1670), p. 77.
18 n. 1389, p. 210.
19 n. 1389, p. 171.

Him, in submitting to His plans. "Everything is contained in these two points."[20]

We should note that belonging to the Body of Christ removes the Christian from his isolation; he becomes part of the Church.[21] Henceforth his prayer is always the prayer of the Church. If his own limitations sometimes overwhelm him, he will find his joy again in thinking that all the spiritual treasures of the other members of the Body are his. In the Church each member shares in the grace of all the others, and each member contributes, perhaps without knowing it, to the grace of others.[22]

Some practical counsels flow directly from these ideas about faith. Thus, the call to "give yourself to Jesus" and "to expose yourself to Jesus" are familiar formulas. "Take up the devotion, which I saw practiced for a long time by a certain soul, of exposing yourself often in spirit to Jesus, to receive into yourself His grace and virtue... I would like you to take a quarter of an hour in your day, when you are free, to expose yourself to Jesus Christ according to your needs."[23]

Moreover, Mother Mectilde lived herself what she was advising. She writes at the beginning of one of her letters, "I give myself to Our Lord Jesus Christ to speak to you about holy baptism."[24] Jesus is her love and her whole life: "I confess to you that I take a singular pleasure in speaking to you of Jesus Christ."[25]

This, then—a luminous teaching on baptism, the sacrament of incorporation into Christ—is the place of entry into Mother Mectilde's spiritual direction.

2. GOD KNOWN IN THE "DARK LIGHT" OF FAITH

"As soon as you are awake, you will raise your mind to God, not only as to the one who is present in you, but as the immensity in which you come to rest."[26] For Mother Mectilde, God is an intense reality; He exercises a formidable enticement over her, He rouses in her a burning affection: "I write these things to you on my knees, prostrate before the adorable majesty of my God, who gave all of these to me, as well as many other things to tell you...."[27]

20 n. 2826, p. 71.
21 n. 1324, p. 105.
22 n. 1191, p. 136.
23 n. 2054, p. 68.
24 n. 996, p. 17.
25 n. 674, p. 45.
26 n. 844, p. 91.
27 n. 9, p. 42.

Nonetheless, she says and repeats with rare energy that God is unknowable, that He is above every feeling and every thought, and that it is only in learning to know nothing that we can approach Him. "Strip yourself of all your ideas and all your tastes, all forms, all images and appearances. God is a pure spirit; He desires to be adored by you in spirit,[28] stripped of all sensible representations. Faith teaches you that everything which meets the senses and comes into the human comprehension is not God. No, no, my dearest daughter, everything you feel, everything you taste, and everything you see is not God. It may be some effect of His grace, but it is not God, the source of grace."[29] She concludes: "Through a simple ignorance of all things, you must remain by faith in God."

Very consciously, she professes—according to the great tradition familiar to the Eastern churches—a "negative theology." Faith, she says, "raises the soul to a holy ignorance of all affirmatives."[30] Then let us be blind, "as will please God's Spirit."[31] Everywhere this is the background to a brief and dense formula like the following: "Faith is the sight of the soul."[32] For her faith is "luminous darkness"[33] or "dark light."[34] Progress in faith thus lived does not happen without a painful impression of emptiness, *anéantissement*. It is necessary to go forward in "the secret paths of faith where the human intellect loses the way."[35] We should desire this emptiness, and initiate it inasmuch as it depends on us, by detaching ourselves from all that occupies the senses and the mind, by patiently, obstinately separating ourselves from "the din of creatures."[36]

We must consider a little this logic of *anéantissement*, which is like the thread of her teaching, so often expressed, about being on guard against creatures. Even in its role as part of a certain pedagogical dramatization, we can ask if her nothingness is not too absolute. It is connected, at least in part, with a pessimistic vision of human nature tainted by sin, and of our false relationship to created things. This

28 Jn 4:23.
29 n. 9, p. 42.
30 n. 2054, p. 64.
31 n. 307, p. 241.
32 n. 1391, p. 34.
33 n. 1389, p. 210.
34 n. 1014, p. 82. In French: *ténèbre lumineuse* and *lumière ténébreuse*.
35 n. 167, p. 125. And because she likes to place herself very clearly within the great Benedictine tradition, she adds here, "This spirit of death is the true spirit of St. Benedict."
36 n. 275, p. 28.

climate of thought marked her whole century. Mother Mectilde wrote, "Our life is nothing but sin and corruption through the continual inclination we have toward creatures."[37] Creatures divert us and stop us on our path . . . they lay waste our interior depths, profaning our grace and drawing us away from God."[38] "When will it be that we have enough strength and courage to destroy and annihilate them? Or to put it better, to allow grace to cause their destruction in us."[39] Such is the very rigorous teaching that turns up so frequently under her rapid pen.

We might too hastily conclude that for her, nature, insofar as it is nature, is definitely corrupted and that God's creatures cannot be for man anything but idols or traps. Actually, some texts open the way for a more positive conception of creation and respect more the coherence of created things, their role of mediation in God's plan. For example: "There are two ways in which you love God in creatures and creatures in God: seeing them in God and seeing God in them. Both the one and the other are good." "To see all creatures in God is to see them engulfed in His divine essence. This is to go beyond creatures in order to see them in that immensity where they have their being and their conservation in being, and outside of which they have no subsistance."[40] Correctly situated, creatures become word and parable, they speak of God. "Voices, voices, voices everywhere, in heaven, and on earth. An attentive soul listens only to the voices which invite it to love, adore, and glorify the One who is."[41] No, in reality, creatures are not necessarily rivals to God in our hearts. There is a way to regard them "according to Jesus Christ's estimation of them"[42] and to use them with gratitude and liberty.

In conclusion let us emphasize two stimulating aspects about the conception of faith which Mother Mectilde affirms. First is the good news that we can be truly faithful to God even if we do not have any palpable experience of Him and His presence, any felt experience. "The hidden remembrance of God which is in the depth of the soul shows it clearly that it is not separated from Him. But inasmuch as it does not see Him or experience Him, it does not believe it. You must become habituated to exercising a pure and detached faith: this

---

37 n. 996, p. 18.
38 n. 3086, p. 155.
39 n. 3086, p. 153.
40 n. 421, p. 234.
41 n. 2549, p. 166.
42 n. 3086, p. 156.

is your path."[43] This is the path of many—and certainly, faith here is more "pure and detached" in that it is less felt and experienced. These reflections are comforting and liberating.

The second stimulating point is the dazzling affirmation of the beauty of the being who lives from God. Certainly, "in virtue of Adam our misfortunes are shocking." But we have Jesus Christ! And, "in virtue of Jesus Christ, you are a daughter of God, bride of Jesus Christ, clothed with Jesus Christ, and renewed by His grace. You are a member of His Body and you bear His image and likeness. You are the beloved of the Holy Trinity."[44] Yes, such is our reality when understood in faith. This is the way that Mother Mectilde envisions the unfathomable reality of God and His work in us.

3. A DESIRE FOR *ANÉANTISSEMENT*: PURE LOVE IS ITS OTHER NAME

"Be inexorable toward nature's complaints; there is no longer any mercy for it: it must die."[45] This theme returns ceaselessly in the letters of the nun from Lorraine. As deep as her affection was for Madame de Châteauvieux, her dear daughter, she seems pitiless in her regard. Removed from their context, certain formulas would cause us to shudder: "You must find it good that I am helping in your destruction according to the grace God has given me."[46] "You must suffer differently: you have only begun."[47] The brave disciple didn't allow herself to be thrown off by such words. On the contrary, she who was so lively, so spontaneous, so eager to understand—she carefully gathered all these exhortations and it is thanks to her that we have them. She found her life in them. This suggests to us, moreover, that she could understand them.

This invitation to *anéantissement* does not rest solely on a pessimistic concept of our corrupted nature. It has also another foundation: a certain conception of sacrifice as "being reduced to nothing" which, from the first, conjures up the name of Fr. de Condren. Mother Mectilde could have gotten it from Jean de Bernières, her friend and teacher, or indeed from their common friend and spiritual father,

43 n. 307, p. 241.
44 n. 3041, p. 193.
45 n. 844, p. 93.
46 n. 1435, p. 39.
47 n. 3057, p. 84.

Fr. Chrysostom de St.-Lô, regular of the Third Order of St. Francis. We could formulate it thus: God the creator alone is *the one who is*; to proclaim His glory, the creature aspires to disappear, to be immolated.

Let us hear this prayer of Mother Mectilde's, for example, which she sent to her correspondent. She addresses God like this: "All that You desire of me is that I remain immersed in the center of my nothingness, where, ceasing to be, I confess and proclaim in silence that You are, O my God, the One who is, and the only One worthy of being eternally. Amen."[48]

She gladly has recourse to the whole of a rather realistic vocabulary of sacrifice: the victim must be bound, slain, thrown into the fire, consumed...[49] In the Christian life, she said, "everything tends toward nothingness and the destruction of yourself."[50] This way of *anéantissement* is "the pure and holy state which you vowed in baptism."[51] Often she tied this way of immolation to the celebration of the Eucharist, which associates us with the "state of victimhood which Jesus has in the Most Blessed Sacrament."[52] Prayer is an expression of our sacrificial offering. "When you enter into your oratory, you are entering into... the place where your sacrifice should be brought to completion. In this spirit, kneel in order to immolate and completely abandon yourself to the pure and holy Spirit of Jesus Christ.... You are not there to enjoy some consolation, but to bring about your destruction."[53]

We might contest the claim that the creature must be destroyed to glorify God: did not God create it that it might exist and sing His glory by its very existence? In reality, what the nun expressed in this way, utilizing the received ideas of her period at their best, is perhaps something else more fundamental.

First, certainly, the conviction that the proprietary instinct, which is incorrigible, falsifies our relationship to the things of this world.

48 n. 2826, p. 72.

49 A juridical conception of sin and redemption sometimes interferes with this teaching: as sinners, we are culpable and must undergo a punishment to God's justice; as we are incapable of bearing this, Jesus the Son of God substituted for us: he died in our place. Mother Mectilde utilized the theological schemas current in her epoch. They can be disconcerting to us today.

50 n. 1191, p. 134.

51 n. 2258, p. 148.

52 n. 3022, p. 123.

53 n. 844, p. 91.

Even if they are good, our freedom, by its spontaneous movement, egotistically appropriates things and its own life.... In reflecting too much on your own activities, said the Mother to her disciple, aren't you seeking to appropriate them as your own, thus robbing them of "the glory they should give to God? You must distrust your malicious subtlety which steals everything, pollutes everything, and appropriates everything for itself."[54] "Everything must be sacrificed to Jesus Christ: your husband, your children, and your friends. You must not become their owner."[55]

She herself, the advisor, knew what it cost to renounce every possession. To this young woman to whom God had connected her as she never had been united to anyone, she wrote: "After all, I must be deprived of you according to God's good pleasure. You are more Jesus Christ's than mine. I do not want to... become the owner of someone who is a prize of Jesus's blood, whom His providence entrusts to me. I hold you and I do not hold you.... Alas! Would I be so wicked as to profane the temple of the Holy Spirit, to take the place of the divine Master in your heart, and appropriate what ought to be uniquely His?"[56]

More profoundly still, the language of *anéantissement* is the language of love. All genuine love has a sacrificial aspect: it is participation and gift; it is a fire which consumes; it implies service and even servitude. "Allow yourself to be bound and tied down with the chains of pure love."[57] We may take it that love, in what it has of the oblative and consuming, is the highest meaning of this sacrificial and victimal terminology which she so frequently used: "That divine fire must purify us, and nothing is worthy of God if it has not passed through its flames."[58] The soul that loves "does not consider whether it is pleased, because it does not act for itself, but only for its uniquely adorable Jesus Christ."[59] The soul knows it will have to suffer; it has already experienced it, because if "pure love" has not yet already finished its work of "destruction," "it has already sent its quartermasters to prepare its dwelling."[60]

---

54 n. 421, p. 238.
55 n. 2985, p. 177.
56 n. 2258, p. 150.
57 n. 1374, p. 74.
58 n. 2531, p. 56.
59 n. 1014, p. 79.
60 n. 1712, p. 81.

But watch out! To love does not mean *feeling* that one loves. It isn't a question of the love which affects the feelings: "I mean the more purity there is in your soul's depth, that is, if you have an intention which is more purified and tends toward acting uniquely for and through the love of God, then there is more grace and consequently, more merit."[61] When love is understood this way, it "does not leave a soul at rest unless it has effected a complete overthrow. It is without pity and without mercy: it shatters everything, it destroys everything. It goes even further, since it consumes everything."[62] It is precisely this love beyond what is sensible that, with Jean de Bernières (and before Fénelon) she calls "pure love."

And she invites us to contemplate this pure love in Mary: "The most holy Mother of God when on earth merited more through one turn of the spindle than all the saints through their penances and extraordinary austerities—because she had more love than all the angels and saints together.... It is the purity of love which gives the weight."[63] *The purity of love gives the weight.* This is also why the call, frequently renewed, to sacrificial *anéantissement* of self makes sense.

4. A PATH OF LIBERTY

Lively, brilliant, curious, ever in motion, the Countess of Châteauvieux had some trouble and much to lose in becoming "blind, deaf, and mute"... "Your natural understanding is delighted when it does not remain fasting";[64] "your mind is insatiable: it devours everything"; "if you search too much, you will find little."[65]

On that long path of detachment and death, it was important that this Christian lady be patient with herself, that she accept what she was: "Your poor nature suffers ... it is not necessary to crush it entirely."[66] "I recommend patience with yourself. Beware of your natural activity and being overly zealous for perfection. You must die to everything, even to desires which are too eager for this...."[67] Was the need for activity sparked by some startling event? To do violence to oneself, to tense up in order to reestablish peace, this would not be true fidelity. Instead: "Humbly await the return of your calm, which God will

61 n. 307, p. 251.
62 n. 1014, p. 81.
63 n. 307, p. 252.
64 n. 1391, p. 36.
65 n. 966, pp. 187–88.
66 n. 1819, p. 170.
67 n. 725, p. 185.

restore to you soon after this little tempest.... Do not make so much effort to stop it, for that would be a double fault you commit."[68]

Mother Mectilde, patient too, taught her discernment little by little. First, don't desire to be like others, even if their accomplishments seem enviable. Vocations are different. "Each soul must remain in its own path and stay within its degree, without wanting to enter into those that appear to us fine and pleasing in other people."[69] Did the Countess feel more or less guilty? Did she experience reproaches in herself? She had to discern if those reproaches came from God or from another source, perhaps from the Tempter. In order to know, she had to observe the habitual effects of grace, "which are contrary to those of nature: since grace humbles without disturbance, it abases without discouraging, it casts you into a holy horror of yourself without making you impatient; and finally, little by little, it reduces you to nothing and makes you leave your self-regard in order to surrender without reserve to Jesus Christ."[70] This peace and trust in the midst of humiliation are also the signs of the Spirit.

How does the disciple bear her suffering, when a trial overtakes her? "Does this sorrow cause secret anxiety?"[71] Then it was some subtle egotism finding itself wounded... Learning to recognize in oneself the weight of a hidden pride demands much vigilance and finesse. "What makes you recognize your pride so little is the fact that you have always been on its side!"[72]

For this lay woman seeking God, discernment applied to the tasks and relationships of everyday life; it was important to recognize God's calls in them. "You must take care of your household affairs and it would not be a virtue to neglect them."[73] And even: "If they are urgent, you may put them before your prayers." If you try to preserve when doing them "the interior spirit which ought to accompany you in all your actions, then in doing them you will find that you perform your duties with a spirit of prayer.... Everything is for God."[74]

But what about the case where the Christian has to make human choices by her own lights? Don't such decisions escape from the

68 n. 1879, p. 112.
69 n. 1191, p. 133.
70 n. 725, p. 184.
71 n. 3057, p. 86.
72 n. 356, p. 189.
73 n. 2033, p. 194.
74 n. 307, p. 251.

"loving submission" she owes to Christ? Not at all. "Although they are at your liberty, you must always and only do them out of obedience to Jesus Christ who inspires you."[75] In fact, why shouldn't we also say it of our human reflection carried on in a humble and disinterested fashion? "Eat . . . sleep . . . work . . . relax out of obedience."[76] Interior and loving obedience to Jesus Christ.

Married love itself—Mother Mectilde dares to talk about it—exists within this complete fidelity. The Count of Châteauvieux was sick and his wife was grieving. She should live that spontaneous compassion fully, but she should live it in God, respecting God's plans concerning her husband's body and soul. She should offer him to God in a loving sacrifice, because, as the Mother explained, your husband is "part of yourself through the sacrament which united you."[77]

We could gather up from her words a whole treatise on prayer. Here are some bits and pieces: "There is a great difference between meditation and mental prayer."[78] What is mental prayer then? It is a very "stripped" prayer, above every image, every feeling and every conceptual thought. "Learn to pray in faith, without reasoning in your mind . . . in this way lovingly putting all things into God's hands."[79] "Interiorly enter your soul, to be occupied with this simple and loving gaze toward God."[80] We see that Mother Mectilde willingly uses the word "loving" to characterize our most stripped-down relationship with God, past the level of feelings. The body, too, has its place in prayer. "Entering into your oratory, you will prostrate yourself on the ground. . . . "[81] Mother Mectilde taught her disciple to use her distractions and powerlessness well: "It is a great infidelity for a soul in this state to try to leave it; we must let ourselves be reduced to nothing."[82]

Beware of "an excessive desire to do well"![83] And regarding principles applied with too much rigidity, let us learn freedom! "In the end, we should pray as God causes us to pray. . . . We should not be attached to our interior practices."[84] This is because an essential disposition for prayer is "exposing yourself to the divine power."[85] Prayer is not only the time set apart for God. It is also, throughout all activities,

75 n. 307, p. 251.
76 n. 2531, p. 56.
77 n. 353, p. 53.
78 n. 2613, p. 95.
79 n. 1324, p. 104.
80 n. 389, p. 226.
81 n. 844, p. 94.
82 n. 312, p. 97.
83 n. 2804, p. 217.
84 n. 1324, p. 104.
85 n. 2613, p. 94.

a "continual regard toward God, but very simple and loving."[86] "A remembrance of God in faith, namely, without images."[87] In fact, all of life must be a life in the Spirit: having been baptized we are "born of the Spirit." This calls us to a great inner freedom, to a kind of secret cooperation with the Holy Spirit who wants to speak within our life, "in the secret of the heart" which is carefully kept for Him who dwells there.[88] If the Christian is faithful, his or her life becomes "pure abandonment to the guidance and Spirit of Jesus,"[89] "entirely full of His divine Spirit."[90] "Allow yourself to be led in the manner that will please Our Lord. Be very pliant to the touches of His Spirit."[91]

This life in the Spirit is a path of childhood: "May He grant you the grace to be like a little child, entirely submissive and simple toward His holy guidance."[92] Mother Mectilde returns to this theme in many variations. Above all, it is a path of liberty: "You will have an inner freedom so holy that you will be amazed.... Yes, my dearest daughter, the freedom you love so much and which your pride fears to sacrifice will be given you doubly. That is, you will be more free and nothing will imprison you anymore."[93]

In this collection of letters, Mother Mectilde doesn't speak much about the Virgin Mary. But she has some very telling ideas on that subject. For example, for the feast of Christmas, regarding the Child Jesus, she says, "Remain at the feet of His most holy Mother in the stable; and as she has the power to give Jesus to the world, ask her humbly to give Him to your soul and to give your soul to Jesus. It is through her ministrations that we enter into the holiness of the interior life."[94]

BRIEFLY SYNTHESIZED, SUCH IS THE SPIRITUAL TEACHING which Mother Mectilde of the Blessed Sacrament gave to the Countess of Châteauvieux, in the course of the long years of their epistolary relationship. The whole edifice rests on a powerful doctrine of baptism, the sacrament of entry into the Body of Christ, and into the holiness of Christ. At the center of everything is faith,

---

86 n. 1379, p. 29.
87 n. 307, p. 244.
88 n. 1946, p. 5.
89 n. 1391, p. 35.
90 n. 2258, p. 149.
91 n. 844, p. 92.
92 n. 1391, p. 37.
93 n. 674, p. 48.
94 n. 1389, p. 208.

a faith beyond what is sensed and beyond reasoning, a faith which deprives us of our knowledge in order to open us to the One who is beyond everything; and a love likewise stripped, the "pure love" which experience identifies with *anéantissement* of self, in communion with Christ's complete gift of self on the cross. And this path opens into supple docility to the Spirit who makes us completely little and free.

After having imparted this wisdom to us, Mother Mectilde takes her leave of us. Perhaps she says to us, as she wrote to her disciple at the end of one of her missives, with words and images which are so much her own: "*Adieu,* to God, in God for the eternity in which I lose you and immerse you, withdrawing to the center of my nothingness."[95]

95 n. 389, p. 227.

The "Breviary of Fire"

Letters by
MOTHER MECTILDE
OF THE
BLESSED SACRAMENT

Chosen & Arranged by
MARIE DE LA GUESLE
COUNTESS OF
CHÂTEAUVIEUX

Holy Baptism[1]

BAPTISM IS A MYSTERY FULL OF TRUTH wherein a certain consecration is made of souls to God, which dedicates them by the interior unction of grace and the presence of His Spirit. The soul has only a passive power with regard to effecting this mystery. It does not contribute to the working of the sacrament, but receives it as the establishment of a new being and the preparation for a new life, which causes St. Paul to call baptism an interior renovation,[2] and Jesus Christ, in St. John, calls it a pure and spiritual birth,[3] which God alone causes in the persons whom He has destined to be His children and the coheirs with His only Son.[4]

Through baptism we remain obligated to be God's and to live for God, following the movements of the grace He gave to us, which do not fail, from the beginning of the age of reason, to urge our heart to go to Him. If at that time grace is victorious over concupiscence and it has its effect, which is to unite us to God voluntarily, to whom we were united only passively (which God had caused in us without us), we [now] carry it out in Him and with Him, ratifying the promises which the holy Church made in our name, swearing that we will belong to God, live in God, and die for God. And we consecrate and vow ourselves to His service, through the inspirations of that precious charity which separates the soul from all that is not God and unites it to God by [a permanent] state.

In order to secure the ways of your predestination, you must renew the first state of holy baptism as often as you can and revive this first spirit which established you in the adoption of the children of God; you must purify your soul by the tears of an unreserved and loving

---

1 These headings, suggested by the major themes according to which the letters have been arranged by the Countess, have been introduced for this edition. No change has been made in the sequence of texts, which range freely over many topics, as befits the genre of correspondence.

2 Rom 6:2–7. 3 Jn 3:1–8. 4 Rom 8:15–17.

penitence, ceaselessly asking Our Lord to receive you into the number of His own, renouncing any contrary spirit, and renewing the promises which the holy Church made for you, namely, to adhere to Jesus Christ and His cross; and thus you must begin to live as a true Christian, living the original and first life which consists, as Our Lord says,[5] in a resemblance to the Holy Spirit Himself in His way of acting, through three similarities which must be constant in the life of Christians.

In the third chapter of the Gospel of John, Our Lord says that to be spiritual to the degree that we must be, and to enter the kingdom of God and the school of Jesus Christ His Son, each Christian must, for the conduct of his life, according to his state, have a threefold resemblance to the Holy Spirit. Here are His words: "The Spirit blows freely where it pleases Him," because He is free in His operations; "He makes Himself heard," and this, by the words and actions of those who possess Him and who are His spokesmen, and yet we do not see Him, since He is hidden within; "one does not know whence He comes or whither He goes"—through where He enters, by where He leaves, we know not how He acts. "*Hic est omnis qui natus est ex spiritu*": every person who has been born of the Spirit is of the same kind.

The first resemblance we must have to the Holy Spirit is a perfect interior liberty which consists in: 1. Not being constrained to follow the foreign inspirations of a concupiscence which casts souls into this evil, until baptismal grace has caused sin to die in them. 2. Being able to do without hindrance all that the law of conscience shows we must do, and this by means of a victorious charity which strengthens the human heart so much that nothing hinders its service of God. 3. Doing nothing except through love, because Christian liberty comes from the nobility of the Spirit, who inspires in those whom He animates a sentiment worthy of God's children, to whom, therefore, it is in no way fitting to act through fear, like hirelings, nor from selfish expectations, like mercenaries, but through a holy desire and a right intention for the glory of their Father.

The second resemblance which the spiritual person must have to the Holy Spirit is to show that she is spiritual by words and deeds, in such a way that the interior grace and gifts of the Holy Spirit, though

5 Jn 3:5–9.

not seen by the eyes of the body, sanctify her behavior so much that one sees how beneficial the state and disposition of the new man is, since in her life there is only what is spiritual and divine.

The third resemblance is to preserve the secret chamber of the heart with so much reserve that there is nothing in it but God alone and those whom He destines to assist the soul in its paths, who understand its purity and know how to guide it.

Here, then, is something in general about the state of the Christian. For the individual, this applies to each soul according to its own path, grace, and vocation, and can be discerned only within the secret of each one's particular conduct and disposition. (n. 1946)

WHAT BAPTISM REQUIRES OF US

Baptism binds us to a high perfection, which is that of Christianity, because it conforms us to the death and the new life of Jesus, and it imprints His character and likeness on our souls, wherein all our grace and perfection consists, because He is the entrance to the law of grace, which is a law of love and perfection, contrary to the old law which was a law of fear and slavery. "For the law was given through Moses; grace and truth were brought by Jesus Christ."[6]

In short, baptism is a spiritual birth which makes us children of God. Further, since it belongs to children to imitate their fathers, we are bidden by the Son of God to be perfect even as our heavenly Father is perfect.[7] And here is our first obligation, which is engraved so deeply in us with the character of the sacrament of baptism that it can never be effaced.

Baptism obliges precisely to perfection. But the other states of life in the Church, such as those of the religious, obligate a person to the means of perfection rather than to perfection itself; for they require the observance of vows which mark out for us the path to it and they make it easier for us to arrive at it; but they suppose the obligation which we have through baptism.

Moreover, the religious give God their wills, but by baptism God chose us by His authority. The first do this through their profession, which depends on human freedom; and the latter [do so] by the

---

6 Jn 1:17. 7 Mt 5:48.

spiritual regeneration which is independent of us. Therefore, your first grace, to which you owe fidelity, is that of Christianity, a grace of the evangelical law and of Jesus Christ our Lord. This is a state and an order higher than Adam's original grace and above that of the angels, being proportionate to the One who is its author and subject; a grace we received in baptism and which requires the perfection of the gospel and ties us to the Son of God in the character of a perpetual servitude.[8]

Your first intention must be to revive this grace, which is in us, but often as if dead and without a sign of life; we must renew it when it seems to be failing or the watchman is drowsy; we must light this fire which Our Lord came to bring to the earth[9] when it is extinguished in our hearts and restore the primitive spirit of the first Christians of the newborn Church, which often dwells in us as if imprisoned and ineffectual; we must apply it, put it to use, increase and perfect it; we must enter into a zeal for the poverty and holiness which belong to the gospel of Jesus Christ and renew our first servitude toward Him.

I have again sketched some thoughts about truths concerning baptism and afterwards drew up an act of renewal of the profession we make therein. I do not intend to oblige you to recite it as I have written it; I want to leave you to the Holy Spirit to form it in you according to His good pleasure: but I have drawn it up in this way to reveal to you more in depth what you and I are obligated to. You will notice in this what you are pledged to and the obligation you have to renew yourself in that holy and pure spirit. You will see how you are baptized in the name of the Most Holy Trinity, and what this means.

I had in mind still to explain to you the ceremonies of baptism, but I think I have said enough and I do not know if something of what we have written to you will be useful; I abandon the whole to Providence, keeping for myself only the pure nothingness in which I must be immersed. I do not know or understand how you make me leave it so often in order to produce some fruits from darkness and ignorance. (n. 1947)

---

8 This idea of perpetual servitude was a common theme among the thinkers of the French School. For example, the *Total Consecration* of St. Louis-Marie de Montfort, familiar to many, culminates in a promise of perpetual servitude to the Blessed Virgin Mary.

9 Lk 12:49.

WE ARE BAPTIZED IN THE NAME OF THE MOST HOLY TRINITY[10]

We are baptized through Our Lord Jesus Christ, as was said; but it is in the name and in the power of the Most Holy Trinity that we are baptized, because the three divine Persons are present at holy baptism in a particular manner. The Father is there engendering His Son in us and engendering us in His Son, that is, giving us a new being and a new life in His Son. The Son is there, taking on birth and life in our souls, and communicating His divine filiation to us, in virtue of which we are made children of God, as He is the Son of God. The Holy Spirit is there, forming Jesus in the bosom[11] of our souls, just as He formed Him in the Virgin's womb.

The Father, the Son, and the Holy Spirit are there, separating us from all things, conforming and consecrating us to Himself in an entirely special manner, imprinting His divine character and image within us and dwelling in us, as in His living temple, His holy tabernacle, as on His holy throne, and as in His heaven, mansion, glory, kingdom, and life. After which, if our sins do not cause any obstacle to it, these three divine Persons dwell always in us in a particular and ineffable manner; in us He would glorify Himself wondrously and would live there with a life completely holy and divine: as also after this we belong to God, as a thing wholly consecrated to Him and which, consequently, must not be employed in any other work except that of His glory and service. (n. 195)

RENEWAL OF THE PROFESSION WE MADE IN HOLY BAPTISM[12]

O Jesus, my Savior and my God! Humbly prostrate at your feet, I adore you as my Head whom I must follow and imitate in all things, according to the solemn and public profession I made in baptism: for then I promised and made profession, through the mouth of my godfathers and godmothers, before heaven and earth, to renounce Satan entirely, his works and pomps, that is, sin and the world, and

10 This text is borrowed, with small variations, from St. John Eudes, *The Life and Kingdom of Jesus Christ in Christian Souls.*

11 In French, the word *sein* signifies both bosom and womb.

12 Also from St. John Eudes, in the same work, part 7, paragraph XIII. He entitles it: "Elevation to Jesus for renewing the profession that we have made in baptism."

to adhere to you as my Head, and to give and consecrate myself totally to you and to abide in you forever.

This promise and profession is great and obliges me, in the capacity of a Christian, to a very great perfection and holiness: for in making profession to be one with you, as the members form one [body] with their head, this is to make profession to have but one life, one spirit, but one heart, one soul, one will, one thought, and one and the same disposition and devotion with you. In this way it is not only to make a profession of poverty, or chastity, or obedience, it is to make a profession of *yourself*, namely, of your life, your spirit, your humility, your charity, your justice, your poverty, your obedience, and all the other virtues which are in you: in a word, it is to make the same profession which you made before the face of your heavenly Father, at the moment of your Incarnation, and which you most perfectly fulfilled through your whole life—namely, it is to make a profession to never do one's own will, and thus to put all one's consent into doing what God wills; to be in a state of perpetual servitude, with respect to God and to creatures out of love for God; and to be in the state of a host and a victim continually sacrificed to God's pure glory. This is the vow and the profession I made at baptism.

Oh, how holy and heavenly is this profession, and how it obligates me to a holy and heavenly life! Oh, how remote my life is[13] from this holiness and perfection! How much I am opposed to you, O my most adorable Jesus, and how much I have ruined and spent fruitlessly your grace and profaned your gifts by the pride, vanity, and satisfaction I have taken in creatures and in myself! My past life was nothing but a constant opposition to the holiness of your designs. How great is the wickedness of my ground to have so many times destroyed your grace, stolen your glory, and trampled your Blood underfoot. In short, I have been contrary to you my whole life, in every way perpetrating infidelities against a profession so holy and sacred. Please forgive me, my most adorable Lord. O my divine Redeemer and reparator, make reparation for me, I beg you, for all my failures and sins, and in satisfaction offer to your Father all the

13 The next several sentences belong to Mother Mectilde. It becomes St John Eudes's text again at "make reparation for me."

honor which you gave Him in your whole life, through the perfect accomplishment of the profession which you made to Him at the moment of your Incarnation.

O Jesus, in honor of and in union with the greatest love and all the other holy dispositions in which you made that same profession, I desire to do now in my own person what I did through others at my baptism, that is, through the mouth of my godfathers and godmothers. For this reason, in the power of your spirit and your love, I renounce forever Satan, sin, the world, and myself. I give myself to you, O Jesus, to cleave to you, to abide in you, and to be only one with you, in heart, and spirit, and life. I give myself to you that I may never do my own will, thus putting all my happiness in doing your most holy will.

I give myself, I vow and consecrate myself to you, in a state of perpetual servitude, with respect to you and to every kind of person for love of you.

I give myself again, I vow and consecrate myself to you, in the state of host and victim, in order to be wholly immolated for your pure glory, in every way that will please you.

O divine Jesus, please give me the grace, through your very great mercy, to accomplish perfectly this holy profession: but accomplish it yourself in me and for me, or rather, for yourself and for your pure joy, according to all the perfection you desire, since I offer myself to you in order to do and to suffer everything that will please you for that intention. (n. 2408)

EXPLANATION OF THE PROFESSION OF BAPTISM

"I adore you as my Head whom I must follow and imitate in all things."

In baptism you regard Jesus Christ not only as your master, but as your Head whom you must follow and imitate. Now, if Jesus Christ is your head, it is necessary that you are one of His members and that He does in you what the head does in the human body.

The head infuses life into the body; and all our ability for thought, understanding, and will, resides in our head. However, if you take away the head, you take away the life. Likewise, if Jesus withdraws from your soul, it loses its life of grace; since Jesus, its Head, infuses life and virtue into the soul, without Him it does not have a single ability. The soul is under His power the way the parts of your body are under the control of your head: if your hand moves, it is by order of your mind, it is by the command of the head. Likewise, if your soul acts, this must be only in obedience to Jesus who is its Head. The soul must follow Him, that is, it must not have any other disposition than the one He gives to it and in this be so submissive that it never turns away from His good pleasure and never acts according to its own understanding.

The soul must follow Him everywhere, to the cross and to death, even as He was most perfectly submissive in all His conduct and dispositions. It must imitate Him in His patience, in His charity, in His humility, in His sufferings, in His fidelity, in His love, in His constancy, in His innocence, in His simplicity, in His perseverance — in short, in His perfection.

Here is the first step that you make to enter into the spirit and grace of your baptism.

"I promised by the mouth of my godfathers and godmothers to renounce Satan and to cleave to you as my Head." I think that this article has no need of an explanation. You understand it sufficiently, because our own wickedness demonstrates to us our need to renounce ourselves to cleave to Jesus. But because this is a promise or legal notice which you make to God in the presence of heaven and earth, it is most necessary that you understand its weight and importance — especially since the promises we make to God are not like those we make to men, because the inconstancy of some and the infidelity of others make them break or change their promises. With respect to God, however, things do not work in that way: it is necessary to die for Him in order to keep inviolably the fidelity promised in baptism, and nothing can dispense us from this. That is why we must renounce Satan, in reality as well as in words. We must do the same with regard to the world and sin. We must abhor diabolical suggestions, we must give up sin, and the maxims of the world, flee from creatures, falsehood, the vanity of the senses, and our pride.

You have promised God to not cling to the temptations of the world, of the devil, of yourself, and thereby to cleave to Jesus Christ as your Head. And then you gave and consecrated yourself completely to Him to dwell in Him forever. Weigh these last words: to dwell *in Him*.[14] That is, to dwell in His grace, in His love, and in His divine will, with respect to thoughts, words, and works. With respect to thoughts, through a simple and loving attention in His holy presence. With respect to words, in speaking the truth and what is for His glory; that is, speaking in order to produce Him and glorify Him in souls or out of obedience to His guidance. With respect to actions, this means to work for His love, for Him alone, without considering creatures or your interests. This is what it means to dwell in God according to the promise you have made to Him. Now there are still other kinds of abiding in God; but since they are produced in the soul in another special manner, I leave them aside, in order to continue to show you what you are bound to by your baptismal profession.

"A very great promise and profession . . ." Yes, truly very great, and so great and so sacred that you cannot receive from God a higher grace than that of baptism. For it makes you a child of God, makes you a member of His body, makes you a bride of Jesus, and you share with Him in the eternal inheritance. In brief, it gives you a likeness to Jesus Christ, unites you and transforms you so perfectly that He is, in a certain manner, completely suffused into you and fills you with Him, giving you life in Him, but a life of grace, a life completely holy and divine. A very great profession, which causes you to be wholly dedicated and consecrated to the divinity, and makes you live completely from Jesus Christ. What does it mean to "live from Jesus Christ"? It is to live from His grace, His spirit, His love. We no longer live from a [merely] human life, from the animal life, from the life of sin, from the impure life of the senses and creatures; instead, we live from the life of Jesus: a pure life, a detached life, a life reduced to nothing, a life which longs for nothing but pure love. In a word, it is to live like Jesus Christ and to act from His Spirit and for the interests of His glory. The whole intention of our soul must be to live for Him and to honor Him as He honored His Father.

14 Jn 15:4.

"A profession very great which obliges you to have only one life, one mind, one heart, and only one will with Jesus Christ, only one thought and one same disposition. . . . " These words do not need to be further expanded. For to have only one life, one mind, one heart, and one will with Jesus is to be animated more from Jesus than from yourself, it is to be transformed into Him, not to see yourself, not to have your own will, and thus to have a will completely submissive and conformed to His, to have a heart which loves Jesus Christ and which loves like His, which has no more love for self or creatures. To have only one life with Jesus Christ means that you must live now only for Him, and your life must be conformed to His. In brief, one must see in you, in your soul, in your heart, and in all that you are only Jesus Christ, and He must live in you more than you do in yourself.[15]

For a Christian soul who desires to live by faith, this is easy to do. For truth teaches you that Jesus Christ is in you. You must believe it without doubt and allow Him to be in you all that pleases Him, always having a disposition of love, submission, and reverence toward His action; becoming accustomed to see nothing outside of His commands or His good pleasure; referring everything to Him, being concerned about nothing but Him, preferring nothing to Him.[16] He must be all in all for you,[17] being assured by the truth of faith that there is nothing worthy of love or esteem except Him, nothing firm, nothing permanent, nothing solid, nothing true, nothing perfect, nothing precious, nothing adorable, nothing divine, and nothing holy except Him. Oh, the terrible blindness of the Christian soul who does not want to know Jesus and does not find Him sufficient to satisfy and content it!

"It is to make profession of yourself, O divine Jesus." It is to make profession to be by grace what you are by nature. "Because to make profession of Jesus Christ is much more than the profession of poverty, chastity and obedience." It is to make profession of the perfection with which Jesus Christ was perfect on earth. In a word, it is to make profession of *Him*: namely, to be as much as possible for you,

15 Gal 2:20.
16 *Rule of Benedict* [RB] 4:21.
17 1 Cor 15:28.

through His grace, another self for Him,[18] through the imitation of His virtues. But this is to make profession to be so united to Him that He is more you than yourself.[19]

"It is making profession of your spirit, of your humility..." You make profession of Jesus's virtues and of His Spirit, that is, you must act only by His Spirit, and all the virtues you practice you must see as Jesus Christ's virtues operating in you. If you are humble, it is the humility of Jesus Christ; if you are charitable, it is the charity of Jesus, and likewise with the others.

"Finally it is to make profession with the same profession that Jesus Christ made at the moment of His Incarnation," where He dedicated Himself in such a perfect and divine way to the glory of His Father that He was consumed for His interests. From that precious moment His holy soul was so turned toward God through the hypostatic union that it never withdrew from Him. It is necessary that, as you are wholly consecrated to God through Jesus Christ in your baptism, you dwell united to God and never depart from His love and the interests of His pure glory in yourself and all creatures. Jesus Christ perfectly fulfilled this divine profession throughout the whole course of His holy life. In order to imitate Him and follow Him as your Head, you must be faithful and never abandon the practice of such a sacred profession. You must never do your own will, thus taking as your only pleasure and happiness the accomplishment of the divine will.

You must be "in a state of perpetual servitude with respect to God and creatures" for love of God. But to fulfill this obligation well, you must view Jesus Christ as the one most reduced-to-nothing of men. He said of Himself, through His prophet, "I am a worm and no man, the disgrace of men and the outcast of the people."[20] He was reduced to such a point of subjugation and servitude, you can see it in His whole life. He was in everything and everywhere most humble and obedient. He became the servant of all men, and not

18 Aristotle and Cicero, among other ancient Greek and Roman authors, used the phrase *alter ipse*—"another self"—as a pithy definition of an intimate friend.
19 Cf. St. Augustine, *Confessions* 3.6.11: "Tu autem eras interior intimo meo, et superior summo meo" (But You were more within me than what is most inward in me, and higher than what is highest in me).
20 Ps 21:7 (22:6).

only the servant, but the slave of men and the captive of their passions, when they robbed Him of life on the cross. Is He not in every way most perfectly subjugated to His Father? Does He not come to accomplish the works of His glory and of our salvation in the capacity of a servant?[21] Thus, in imitation of Him, and in homage to and union with His divine slavery with respect to His Father and with respect to all men for love of His Father, you must enter into a spirit of servitude, firstly with respect to God, and then with respect to His creatures for His love.

You must take a singular pleasure in being God's servant. Bear this title with a great respect and regard yourself as very unworthy of it. Do not take it up in vain or out of vanity. Do not profane it, it is a very precious title. In the world, one takes pride in being the king's servant and working in his court. Oh, how much must we esteem, as beyond compare, our servitude in regard to Jesus Christ!

St. Paul says that to serve God is to reign.[22] In consequence, all God's servants are kings. O noble servitude! Therefore, honor the title that you bear as servant of God and faithfully fulfil your duties with respect to the charges He has entrusted to you. Be faithful to Him in the use of His gifts: in short, be faithful to Him in every way and, above all, in respect for and obedience to His commandments. The servant must do the will of his master. Therefore, be obedient to God in all that He desires of you, even to dying like Jesus Christ on the cross.

Also, be obedient to creatures for love of Him. Firstly, believe that all creatures are purer and better than you, that sin reduced you to being lower than all and put you into servitude with regard to all. It is necessary to dwell in this captivity, not because sin has placed you there, but through a disposition of the deepest humility, seeing your unworthiness, and that through sin you made yourself a slave, and that it makes you unworthy to have a place among rational creatures.

---

21 Mk 10:45; Phil 2:6–8.

22 Mother Mectilde takes this formulation from *The Life and Works of St. Catherine of Genoa* by Jean Desmarets, published in Paris in 1662 (ch. 34, p. 174)—a book of which we possess a copy inscribed by Mother Mectilde herself. The phrase is also found in the postcommunion prayer for the Mass of St. Irenaeus.

You will also bear your servitude with regard to creatures in honor of and homage to the subjugation of Our Lord Jesus Christ to the executioners who crucified Him. You can also bear it by seeing all persons as members of Jesus. You can regard them as the living temples of the divinity,[23] in short, as Jesus Christ on earth, and with this view, be subject to them for love of Jesus.

Still, when you reprove your household servants, you do not leave your servitude for this; on the contrary you are exercising it, because you assist their souls by setting them right and showing them their duty. The head of a family, the superior in a religious house, is the servant of all. Alas! How harsh a servitude is authority! Our Lord has made me feel it deeply! But it is necessary to consent to it with an act of servitude and obedience to Jesus Christ. It is always better for us to obey than to command; but when Our Lord fixes us in this subjection, we must humbly submit to it. So, when you are obliged to command, do it in the power of Jesus Christ, because considered in yourself, you do not have any right of authority or commanding: you have lost it by sin and you are unworthy to be obeyed. But Our Lord Jesus Christ alone is worthy to command since He has this power from His Father, and He has redeemed us all.

Therefore, have a spirit of servitude with respect to all souls, that is, be willing to serve them all and to see yourself as the least of all. For the one who calls herself handmaiden is pronouncing herself inferior to the smallest of all. And whatever graces Our Lord gives you, if He wanted to give them to someone else, you must consent to it through the esteem you must have for souls and the belief that they will make a better use of them than you. And your delight must be, not to be great in the graces and gifts of God, but to see Him well loved, well served, and properly glorified. And if another person does better than you, you must be glad, in order to avoid the spiritual envy which so often reigns in the minds of those who are too little humbled and too little reduced to nothing.

The handmaiden has nothing that must not be in the power of her mistress. If you bear the state of servitude with regard to all souls, you will be anathema like St. Paul, for the sake of their sanctification:[24]

23 1 Cor 2:27. 24 Rom 9:3–4.

that is, you would deprive yourself of your most treasured consolations to contribute to their salvation, and indeed be stripped of your good works in order to clothe others in them; it is perfect charity which produces these results in our hearts.

I end with the quality of victim, with which you are given to God in your baptism. The victim is chosen: Jesus Christ chose you. The victim is bound: Jesus Christ bound you with the bonds of His love and the obligations of your baptism. The victim is conducted to the place appointed for the sacrifice: Jesus Christ leads you by the secret paths of His *anéantissante* grace which brings you to the place of death and sacrifice. The victim is slain: mortification for Jesus Christ and the renounced life which you lead every day slay you. The victim is cast into the fire: and Jesus Christ casts you into the fire of suffering and trials. Finally, it is consumed: and Jesus Christ consumes you by transforming you into Himself through the powerful effects of His most ardent charity. Pure love brings about in the soul the final operation which prepares the soul for eternal joy, when she has thus perfected her sacrifice.

O blessed victim, may it please God that you know your excellence! Do you know what makes you most noble? It is that you are thus sacrificed for the pure glory of God. Self-love and creatures have no part in such a sacrifice. God alone must be the only reason for our immolation. I pray Him that it may be so in the working of our consummation.

Here is enough teaching on your baptismal obligation. I ask Our Lord Jesus Christ to give you His Holy Spirit in order to comprehend it and to imprint it on your heart, and that He grant you the grace to fulfill it perfectly in yourself, through Him and for His pure glory. In Him I am most eager for your sanctification and to see you truly adorned with the Christian grace which you have received in baptism. That is where you must begin in order to know yourself, to know Jesus Christ, and our obligations.

Pray for me and receive Communion today in the octave to honor the baptism of Our Lord Jesus Christ, uniting yourself to all the mysteries it contains. Desire that He renew in you the grace of your baptism. (n. 1653)

ON THE CONSECRATION OF OUR SOULS EFFECTED BY JESUS CHRIST IN THE HOLY SACRAMENT OF BAPTISM

I give myself to Our Lord Jesus Christ to speak to you about holy baptism as I told you I would, corresponding to your desire.

Baptism is a consecration of our souls made by Jesus Christ to the Most Holy Trinity. And in order to live according to your Christian obligation, you must live according to the dignity you received in baptism. Now, from all eternity, God looked upon you and chose you to be consecrated to Him through baptism; and at the time of your birth on earth, Jesus Christ made the consecration. You know what this word means, I will not explain it; but I will only tell you that your soul and your whole existence being connected to God through your baptism, you are not your own and you cannot live for yourself.[25] Your soul is a temple dedicated to the three divine Persons and Jesus Christ effected its dedication and sacred anointing with the unction of His grace in baptism.

But since physical temples are now no longer used for any profane purpose, rather for sacrifices and oblations which are offered daily to the Most Holy Trinity, likewise your soul must not be profaned by any small sin, or defiled by creatures. You must regard your soul as a consecrated temple; and with this in view, keep it pure and spotless, since it must be the sacred resting place of the divinity. The soul is under obligation to be separated from all the profane uses for which it could employ its faculties. It must remain in constant recollection and in very reverent attention to the greatness that it contains in itself. Oh, if all Christians really understood their high dignity, could they ever lower themselves to the offenses and abominations, if I dared to speak of them, which we see every day? Oh, terrible profanation of the living temples of the Most Holy Trinity! No respect for the divinity who is present holds back these miserable people! What an obligation you have to the goodness of God who gives you the opposite sensibilities and who shows you the greatest mercy by taking you out of your errors, to make you attentive to the dignity of your soul; what an obligation you have to preserve, as much as is possible for you, the purity which it received through baptism, or to try to recover it if through some misfortune you have lost it.

---

25 1 Cor 6:19; 2 Cor 5:15.

Therefore, consider your soul not only as something sacred, but as something consecrated: that is, as something which is not its own, being dedicated. And all the uses you make of yourself which are not related to God are profane uses; you dishonor the divinity in you and profane His holy temple. Understand this truth properly and henceforth do not allow your soul or its faculties to be used for the sake of creatures, your senses, or your self-love. God alone must reign in His temple; and if you serve creatures, may it be for His pure love; may the temple of your soul receive continual sacrifices, immolations, victims presented to God in an odor of sweetness. This is what your soul must serve, and not be a den of thieves, as Our Lord says in the Gospel, or a place of trade, or admit anything unworthy of His greatness, for fear of obliging His Majesty to take up a whip again to drive them out and to deprive you of His holy presence on account of the lack of respect you have for Him.[26]

It is necessary that you conceive anew the intentions of Jesus in your baptism. What I will tell you contains one part, since you see that His plan was to relate you entirely to His Father's glory, to adopt you as His child, to associate you with Jesus Christ so as to share in the eternal inheritance. In short, to unite you so much to Christ that your life might be nothing but a continuation of His life.

Here are Jesus's intentions in your baptism and you are obliged to enter into them through love and submission, and never deviate from them.

If a child at his baptism were capable of understanding what Jesus does in him, how He consecrates him and dedicates him to the glory of the Most Holy Trinity, and this child united himself to the intentions of Jesus Christ in the baptism and consented to all His plans without turning aside through sin, he would have no need to renew His intentions. For the renewal is only to make up for the many ruptures of intention, straying after creatures, and returns to ourselves through self-love, such that we can say quite boldly that our life is nothing but sin and corruption through the continual inclination that we have toward creatures. This is the reason that obliges a soul who desires to be God's to renew it, not only once a year, but at every

26 Mt 21:12–13, Mk 11:15–17, Lk 19:45–46, Jn 2:14–17.

moment, if she were able, since we are so inclined to the uncleanness of our senses that we are polluted at every moment.

It is true that we are very wretched because of Adam our first father, but we have a worthy reparator in Jesus Christ. Baptism restores us to favor and makes us children of God and brothers of Jesus Christ, as it says in Scripture.[27] What we have to do is properly understand our Christian obligation and bind ourselves to its perfection.

There is no need of great intelligence to be holy, but it requires true faith and much love. We see few learned people who are truly spiritual. St. Paul wanted to know nothing but Jesus Christ and Him crucified.[28] You know your obligations and the dignity of your Christian state well enough; you must live in conformity with that knowledge, and practice great fidelity and purity of life, since the grace you received in baptism obliges you to this.

Live like Jesus Christ, since through baptism you are clothed with Him.[29] Do not think that by the power of reasoning in your mind you can really understand Jesus Christ: He is not known in this way. A deep humility of heart and a great submission of mind do more than knowledge. Faith is the true light of the Christian soul. It is a torch which was given to you in baptism in order to illumine your whole life, and to show you the knowledge and doctrine of Jesus Christ, learned in the practice of humility, simplicity, and so on.

Our Lord says in the Gospel, "If you can believe, you will be saved."[30] He does not say "if you can see," but "if you can believe," in order to teach us that our path in Christianity is a path of faith, and the one who believes is able to receive the grace of baptism. Also, in the rites of baptism, the *Credo* is said by our godfathers and godmothers in our name. They say it for us and we say it in them, since they are our guarantee. When we have the use of reason, we are bound to confirm and ratify our belief through acts of faith, since our godfathers and godmothers are pledged for us only until that time.

Thus, let us renew our faith every day in order to make up for our insufficiency and inability in that state of infancy. Let us ask Jesus Christ to repair all those times and the time we spend every

27 Rom 8:15–17, Gal 3:26–27.
28 1 Cor 2:2. 29 Rom 13:14. 30 Mk 16:16.

day in an infinite number of things opposed to our Christian grace. Comprehend, then, what we are telling you.

Faith is absolutely necessary in order to be a Christian. You have no obligation to understand the depth of our holy mysteries, or the infinite grandeurs of God, or the secret workings of Jesus Christ, but you are required to believe them and submit to them.

Three things are given in baptism in virtue of the three divine Persons: first, faith; second, hope; third, charity. Faith is appropriated to the Father, hope to the Son, and charity to the Holy Spirit. With these three gifts, which are infused into you at baptism, you are capable of entering into the highest sanctity and perfection. What is it that makes saints? Faith, hope, and charity.

Faith establishes the soul in the knowledge of God and of Jesus Christ and His holy mysteries, not by human arguments, but by a simple belief in the truths which are revealed to us in Sacred Scripture and by the Church. We submit our judgment to this without wanting to examine these things minutely and by submission we reverence them and bind ourselves to the grace they contain, our minds being completely subject to them.

Hope causes us to remain firm in the faith and gives us a full trust in God through Jesus Christ, remaining confident by the truth of His holy words. Hope detaches us from earthly things and makes us long for those which are eternal, which we await, as St. Paul says.[31]

Charity unites us to God and makes us one with Him. It makes us love divine things, binds us to the cross, and separates us from creatures and ourselves, in order to transform us into Jesus Christ.

Thus, see if in baptism you have not been endowed with divine powers and heavenly gifts, without the use of which you cannot be saved. If you complain of your weakness in combating your enemies, here are the weapons Jesus Christ gives you in baptism, which are [both] offensive and defensive:[32] you have only to make use of them. See what St. Paul said about this.

Accordingly, to make use of the grace of your baptism, you must practice these three virtues; they are called the theological virtues because they have God as their immediate object. From this moment

31 Col 3:2; Phil 3:20; 2 Cor 5:2.

32 2 Cor 6:7.

begin to practice them and you will see that they will produce very good results in you. (n. 996)

ON THE GRACE OF BAPTISM

My dear sister, if only Our Lord Jesus Christ would give me the grace and ability to express to you what His light causes me to understand concerning the holy baptism you have received through Jesus Christ! Never, never will you be able to comprehend the dignity and excellence of the grace to which baptism raised you. This is not the grace our first father had, it is not the grace of the angels or the seraphim; rather it is the most precious and wholly divine grace of Jesus Christ. If grace is the Holy Spirit, you must thus acknowledge that the Holy Spirit is completely in you through Jesus Christ from the time your baptism filled you completely with His grace, and renewed you entirely in Him. O grace, O incomprehensible mercy!

In your baptism, you receive two lives in Jesus: His life of death, and His resurrected life. St. Paul says, "You are dead and your life is hidden with Christ in God."[33] You receive a life of death: that is, a crucifixion in your senses, in your passions, in your will, in your desires and in your inclinations; in short, all that you are which comes from Adam. Your baptism is an expression of the death of Jesus on the cross and of His resurrection. Therefore, you must have a likeness to and union with them. Thus you must continually die to yourself and to creatures: this is the likeness to the cross. And you must walk, as St. Paul says, "in newness of life."[34] This means that your soul must be separated from the things of earth and everything that could sully you. Your baptism being a renewal, Jesus Christ also made everything new in you; He gives you an entirely new being and an entirely new grace.[35] Therefore, live with a heart and mind renewed,[36] and amend your life.

What must we do to live the resurrected life of Jesus? We must live a life wholly withdrawn from creatures and the senses; we must no longer have any claims on the world, or on all its possessions; we must renounce the affection and esteem of creatures. In short, we

---

33 Col 3:3. 34 Rom 6:4. 35 Rev 21:5.
36 Rom 12:2.

must be detached from all that can defile us and not have anything but God in the depth of our hearts.

Your soul must be mystically clothed with the four marriage portions[37] of the blessed, namely: impassibility, agility, subtlety, and clarity.

Impassibility means no longer dying through sin or clinging to temptation or our passions; to leave behind our senses and natural affections.

Agility means being so prompt in obedience to God and those who command us on His behalf, that we never admit any delay.[38] It means that you are most diligent in corresponding to grace. Agility does not know what slothfulness is. The soul must always be agile to obey God and continually give itself totally to Him.

Subtlety means that we penetrate so deeply into temporal things that we discover the divine essence in order to be united to it; that we go beyond all creatures; that nothing earthly can stop us or imprison us for a moment. A soul with spiritual subtlety surpasses all things in order to be united constantly to God.

Clarity means having a pure and right intention toward God, remembering the words of Our Lord, "if your eye is simple, your whole body will be luminous."[39] A soul with clarity is living in the faith which discloses divine truths to us.

Oh! How beautiful it is to see a soul clothed with these four dowries of glory! To be impassible, to be agile, to be subtle, to be clear! I pray that Jesus Christ, who has given these to you spiritually or mystically in your baptism, will renew them in you. When He has granted you the grace to bear their fruits, we will tell you more about them and show you, if He grants us the capacity, how a prayerful soul is arrayed in marvelous manner with these four marriage portions of glory and how it is transformed into Jesus Christ.

At present, let us be content with this little lesson and try to learn it well and surrender ourselves truly to Jesus Christ. I desire this for you with all the affection which He has given me to love your soul.

---

37 The word in French is *douaire*, dower, marriage settlement. St Thomas, following the scholastics before him, speaks of the four properties or characteristics of the bodies of the glorified (see, e.g., *Summa theologiae*, *Supplementum*, qq. 82–85; *Summa contra gentiles* IV, 86).

38 RB 5.

39 Mt 6:22.

Do not draw back from your resolution; make it your study to truly understand the grace of your baptism, your dignity and your lineage as a Christian, and the obligation you have to live in accordance with that high state. Oh! How plebian is earthly nobility and how very abject in comparison with the noble lineage of being children of God, brethren of Jesus Christ, and indeed being God Himself by the union of grace, being Jesus Christ![40] Oh, who can comprehend this! As for me, I am lost in this mystery and I confess that everything created is unworthy of our thoughts.

We must be consumed by love for a God so infinitely loveable and who loved us so ardently. Let us be pierced with it and die of love! Forever may we burn with it and be reduced to ashes by the holy flames of pure Love. (n. 2477)

APPLICATION OF BAPTISM[41]

Since all things which are outside of God have their idea, exemplar, and archetype within God, so also our baptism has for archetype and exemplar four great mysteries which are in God. These are: first, the mystery of the eternal birth of the Son of God in the bosom of His Father; second, the mystery of His birth in time from the womb of the Virgin; third, the mystery of His death and burial; and fourth, the mystery of His resurrection.

The mystery of His eternal birth, because, as His Father in His eternal generation communicated to Him His being, His life, and all His divine perfections, in virtue of which He is the Son of God and the perfect image of His Father; likewise through holy baptism, He communicates to us the being and the divine and heavenly life He received from His Father, and imprints in us a living image of Himself and makes us children of the Father of whom He is the Son.[42]

---

40 Here Mother Mectilde draws on the traditional doctrine of man's deification or divinization: by our baptismal union with Christ we are made partakers of the divine nature (cf. 2 Pet 1:4), the soul becoming by grace what God is by nature: "God became man that man might become God" (St. Athanasius).

41 Also from St. John Eudes, *The Life and Kingdom of Jesus Christ in Christian Souls.*

42 Speaking of the Son vis-à-vis the Father, Mother Mectilde writes "communicated" and "received," but it is clear she is not referring to a past event but to

The mystery of the temporal birth, just as at the moment of His Incarnation and His origination within the Virgin, He unites our nature to Himself and Himself to it, filled it with Himself and is clothed in it, so also, in the holy sacrament of baptism He united Himself to us and we are united and incorporated into Him; He is formed in and, so to speak, incarnated within us[43] and we are clothed and filled with Him, according to the words of the Apostle, "All you who are baptized into Jesus Christ have put on Jesus Christ."[44]

The mystery of His death and His burial, since St. Paul proclaims to us, "All we who have been baptized into Christ have been baptized into His death," and that "We are buried with Him in His death through baptism."[45] This does not mean anything other than what is expressed by the same Apostle in different words, "You are dead and your life is hidden with Christ in God,"[46] namely: you have entered by baptism into a state which obliges you to be dead to yourself and to the world, and no longer to live except in Jesus Christ and with a life that is completely holy and divine, and which is hidden, buried, and absorbed in God—and so much so that it is the life of Jesus Christ.

The mystery of the resurrection, because the Son of God through His resurrection entered into a new life, a life entirely separated from the earth, and completely heavenly and spiritual. Also, the holy Apostle teaches that "we are buried with Jesus Christ through baptism so that, as he rose from the dead and entered into a new life, so through baptism we walk in newness of life."[47] (n. 275)

---

an ever-present reality. She is emphasizing that what the Son always is by nature, the Christian is made to be on earth and in heaven.

43 Gal 4:19. 44 Gal 3:27. 45 Rom 6:3–4.

46 Col 3:3. 47 Rom 6:4.

Reverence for God's Holiness

TU AUTEM IN SANCTO HABITAS, LAUS ISRAEL.[1] This morning upon waking, I found myself saying these holy words of the prophet: "O Lord, You dwell in holiness and all creatures praise You." If Providence had given me time this morning, I would have talked with you about what is going on in my soul with regard to the feast we are celebrating today,[2] and my desire was to apply you to the holiness of Jesus Christ.

Would to God that you are able to understand what I wish to be able to say about that infinitely adorable holiness! Revere what you cannot understand and know that today's feast is the feast of Jesus's holiness, which produces effects in all the saints. These are the words of the Church from the holy Mass, "You alone are holy." Yes, in truth, God alone is holy and nothing is holy except by participation in His divine holiness.

Therefore, at your Communion today, adore the emanations of the divine sanctity in all the saints and say often with the Church, *Tu solus sanctus*, "You alone are holy." O my God, I rejoice in Your divine sanctity, I rejoice that all the saints are the effects of it. Expose yourself to the divine sanctity so as to have some share in it, but remember that it causes a marvelous purity in souls, for in order to be holy it is necessary to bring about the destruction of all the impurities which are in us.

Our Lord causes you to have in your present condition some effects of His divine holiness, but you do not know them. Know, then, that He dwells in His holiness. God is in you, withdrawn into Himself. He dwells in His holiness; adore Him in it and think about your miseries as little as you can.

Holiness is the most austere, rigorous, and abstract of all the divine perfections. Moreover, there is nothing in God which is so much His, and which is so remote from what is not God, as His holiness.

---

1 Ps 21:4 (22:3). But thou dwellest in the holy place, the praise of Israel.

2 A letter for the Feast of All Saints.

To love His holiness is to love Him very purely for Himself, without any interest and without any regard to oneself. The smallest perfections in God—if we can speak of something more or less great in Him—are those which have to do with us, such as mercy, since this has nothing to do with Himself. Moses, who was a mortal man, and viewed God in connection with creatures, magnified God's mercy and cried, "*Misericors, clemens, patiens et multae misericordiae.*"[3] But the seraphim, who are pure spirits, detached and completely consumed in God, celebrate His holiness and sing, "*Sanctus, sanctus, sanctus.*"[4] And it is the superiority of the New Law established through Jesus, to consider God, not according to our interests, but according to those of His greatness and glory. It is our obligation to honor and extol His sanctity along with the seraphim; to love Him not only as good and merciful toward us, but also as holy and for Himself.

In His agony Jesus properly bore God's justice, but in the forsakenness of the cross, He bore God's holiness. That is why for the sake of expressing the harshness of His forsakenness and the depths to which the divine holiness reduced Him, after saying, "My God, My God, why have You forsaken Me, I cry night and day and You do not hear me," He adds, "*Tu autem in sancto habitas, laus Israel.*"[5] As for you, You will dwell and abide in Your holiness: that is, God, with respect to His Son on the cross, withdrew Himself into the highest solitude and most distant retreat of His holiness, and left Him entirely forsaken in His sufferings.

God is so holy, so incomprehensible, and so mysterious that we can truly say that He is a hidden God, "*Deus absconditus.*"[6] He is so deeply hidden that He is above everything our minds can think. He is a God hidden from our senses, He is a God hidden from our understanding, in short, He is the *Deus absconditus* in an infinite number of ways. And if we adore Him hidden under the sacramental species, how much more must we adore Him in the mystery of Himself, or rather, in His incomprehensibility and hidden in His divine sanctity.

3 Ex 34:6. Merciful and gracious, patient and of great mercy.

4 Is 6:2–3.

5 Ps 21:2–4 (22:3–5). In keeping with Catholic tradition, Mother Mectilde understands Christ on the cross to be reciting the whole of Psalm 21.

6 Is 45:15.

Oh! If you understood the dignity and excellence of a hidden God, you would take a singular delight in the retreat that God makes in Himself within you. But what prevents you from living in this truth, which is nevertheless a dogma of faith, is that when He does not pour out the sweetness and consolations of His graces into your soul, you suppose that God has withdrawn from you.[7] Oh! How great is our blindness and how terrible is our presumption! Why do you want God to lower Himself so far as to please your senses? You must learn to find God in Himself and to take your satisfaction in the delight He finds dwelling in His holiness.

All the retreats God makes into Himself are holy and adorable and you must love and unite yourself to them. When you find in your soul that God makes Himself inaccessible, you must remain hidden in your nothingness, hiding yourself in such a way that the divine Majesty will cast His holy gaze on you and take delight in seeing you reduced to nothing in homage to His retreat in Himself within you.

It is presumption for the soul to want to understand something about God; it is not for us (poor little wretches that we are) to fathom the divine ineffability. We must do as the seraphim do: veil our faces, and cry out with profound reverence and love, *Sanctus, sanctus, sanctus*! Oh, how holy God is, how great God is, how immense God is, how powerful God is! Oh, how inaccessible and incomprehensible God is! I have a very great and profound joy in my soul to see that God can be comprehended only by Himself. We must be overwhelmed and lost in Him, not scrutinize His divine qualities. And it seems to me that we know God in a way that is much more pure when we know nothing at all through our intelligence but solely by the light of faith.

Our manner of thinking about God demeans His grandeurs, but the practice of pure faith raises us to Him and causes us to find Him in our soul's center, where He makes His abode, which makes us to say with Jacob, "Truly God is in this place and I knew it not."[8] Yes, God lives in us, "*et habitavit in nobis*,"[9] and you do not know it. He rests in Himself in the highest point of your soul, where He has established His dwelling, as He did in the past on the holy [mountain]

---

7 The first part of this sentence (until "dogma of faith") is not found in all manuscripts.

8 Gen 28:16.

9 Jn 1:14.

Zion. In that place He rests as on a throne of peace, as David says, "*Et factus est in pace locus eius.*"[10] Oh, how blessed is the soul that is led into this region of peace and is not disturbed by the impurity and din of creatures and its senses! In this profound solitude, the soul understands the marvelous lesson: "Be holy, for I am holy."[11] God desires you to be holy; it is by His divine mouth that He commands it. O holy and divine mandate! Since God orders you to be holy, it is a dogma of faith that He will give you the graces for it.

But what must we do, according to our small capability?

You must labor to empty yourself of yourself as much as you can, and walk in the presence of God. This point alone, faithfully practiced, is capable of making you live in the holiness which is God Himself. There is nothing so powerful for the right ordering of a soul as the continual presence of God; it vivifies, it purifies, and it sanctifies. That is why God says to Abraham, "*Ambula coram me, esto perfectus.*" Walk in My presence and be perfect.[12] Believe that God is saying these same words to you; receive them out of obedience as from His divine mouth, and open your heart to be filled with the virtue of faith, so that by the pure use of it you may persevere in it.

I wish you in faith the highest of all blessings and the grace of perseverance, or rather, being consumed in the love of Jesus. (n. 88)

About God's Presence Through Faith

I observe a small light in the depth of your mind, by which you begin to understand, but still in a rather confused way, that withdrawal from creatures puts into us a capacity to find God. This light is in the truth and I ask Our Lord to grant you the strength and courage to go beyond all creatures so that you can taste and experience Him in your soul.

You are at a loss as to how one can be and live in the presence of God through a simple gaze of faith. A soul who is a bit familiar with the maxims of pure love does not have much trouble understanding it. But seeing that the senses and human reason are always dominant in us, we cannot fathom other ways. I hope that one day, if you are

---

10 Ps 75:3 (76:2). And his place is in peace [and his abode in Sion].

11 Lev 19:11. 12 Gen 17:2.

faithful, you will understand this truth perfectly: since God is in you, you have need only of respect, love, attention, and submission in His divine Presence; respect for His greatness and sovereignty, love for His goodness, His holiness, attention to His divine will and to the prompting of His divine Spirit, and submission to accomplish it willingly and perfectly.

Your regard toward God must be continual, but very simple and loving. And when He gives you some prompting to renew your sacrifices or to make some act of reverence, or love, or abandonment, do these very simply, being content when you are not entirely distracted from experiencing this disposition in your soul, leaving yourself to God in the sentiments He impresses on you. But when you are not in prayer, or at holy Mass, or occupied with important business, you can give your mind a little freedom to reflect on some particular mercy of God toward you, or occupy yourself with some Christian truth, or with the things in which you have been instructed. And if you see that this has carried you away too far into useless digressions, withdraw from it gently and put yourself in God simply and without strain, but quietly and humbly, abasing yourself before His incomprehensible grandeur. Calm your mind with a simple act of reverence and remain in silence for a time, indeed until the Spirit of God moves you to speak. Do the same with your mind's wanderings during your prayer time. In your actions, it is enough to raise your mind from time to time to God who is present and to act with a mind detached from yourself and what you are doing or what you must do.

In no way will your senses establish you in the real and true presence of God. Rather, it will be faith, purely and fervently practiced. It is often necessary to renew yourself in this divine presence by a simple and loving belief, to accustom yourself to this exercise. This is a bit of work for those who are beginning, but the blessings which accompany its progress give a great strength to the soul.

Work a little at your own expense (you have done enough of it in the past at God's expense), for His pure glory and His interests; you are not yet convinced of this, but you will be one day and you will regret it. (n. 1379)

ON THE ESTEEM AND RESPECT WE MUST HAVE FOR GOD

Turning over in my mind before Our Lord the various dispositions of your soul so as to offer them to His Majesty, I was concerned at the sight of that species of slackness you are beginning to feel, which you call drowsiness—and which I call a slackness, interior as well as exterior, since it demonstrates a disposition which shows that your soul is not animated by the respect it must have for God.

Oh! How I pity the blindness of souls who do not know God, who are weary and bored in His holy presence, who are not moved to reverence by His greatness! "*Pleni sunt caeli et terra Majestatis gloriae tuae*," the heavens and the earth are full of the majesty of His glory and we do not think about it. We do not give ourselves to that adorable fullness in order to have a share in it.

What pains me most is that during the most precious moments of our lives, those for prayer, we allow our souls to remain without attention, without respect, without vigilance, and without love toward a Majesty so adorable. Alas! If we were before an earthly monarch, what would our disposition be? But for a God of infinite greatness, holiness, and majesty we do not have the fortitude to wait in His divine presence for one hour with reverence. If we knew the importance of the loss we bring about through our fault, we would weep tears of blood. But we are in the darkness, our senses cast us into blindness, and our faith is as if annihilated. What will we do in eternity if one hour of prayer wearies us?

Let us awaken our spirits by faith, which makes us understand the esteem we must have for God, and humble ourselves before His grandeur. The seraphim and all the blessed in heaven are so full of loving reverence that the former veil their faces, not being able to bear the weight of His grandeur, and the latter reduce themselves to nothing in His divine essence, in order to render Him the most reverent worship. Why do we on earth do less than the celestial spirits in heaven? Is it not the same God? Is it not the same divinity? And since we have Him truly present in our souls as He is with the blessed on the throne of His glory, why do we not pay our respects to Him just as all the heavenly hosts do in heaven?

I know well that the turmoil of the present life makes us unable to cry with the celestial choir, "*Sanctus, Sanctus, Sanctus,*"[13] without intermission or interruption; but at least for the time given to us for personal prayer, let us come before God with the love and reverence of the seraphim, who exclaim in the most profound silence, "*Sanctus.*" Let us come before God, say I, in profound humility and if we do not see His grandeur with our bodily eyes, we must see it more purely and more truly with the soul's eyes by a simple conviction of faith. Alas! If a damned soul had one hour of our time to be converted, what use would be made of it before God? Let us lower ourselves utterly and sink into the depths of hell, because we are unworthy to glorify God.[14] (n. 2646)

ON THE CREATION OF THE SOUL

My dearest sister, the Apostle says, "You have nothing you have not received, and if you have received it, why do you boast as if you had not received it?"[15] Your soul came forth from God, the faith teaches you this; it is in no way from you or yours. It is loaned to you in order to merit eternity, and at death you must return to God as to the source whence you come, and give yourself to Him perfectly through Jesus Christ who came into the world in order to be the way by which we go to His Father.

Now, your soul, with all the excellences described to you, adorned with its three powers, through which it has a likeness to the three divine Persons, is nevertheless created from nothing.[16] And it is in this truth that the soul establishes the origin of its nothingness, from which it must never depart.

---

13 Rev 4:8.

14 This sentence may be best understood by connecting it to the mystery of the *kenosis* of Christ; He descended into the lowest place. For Mother Mectilde, this is a call to join Christ's humility and reverence before the Father. One might understand her to be saying: "Let us cast ourselves into the very lowest place. Let us put ourselves in that desolate and unlovely place that is the center of hell, in order to be delivered out of it by the strong arm of Christ, in whom alone we can glorify God worthily."

15 1 Cor 4:7.

16 Here Mectilde refers to St. Augustine's tripartite division of the powers of the rational soul in his treatise *De Trinitate*: memory, intellect, and will, to which he compares the Father, Son, and Holy Spirit.

The Son of God, Our Lord Jesus Christ, tells us in St. John, chapter twelve, that if the grain of wheat falling into the earth does not first die, it remains all alone, but if it dies it will bring forth much fruit. The one who loves his life will lose it, and the one who hates it in the world will keep it for eternal life.[17] Oh! These divine words contain such mysteries! Let us give ourselves to Jesus Christ in order to experience their effects and receive the grace which they must produce in us. It is Jesus Christ who speaks, and we must listen to Him with attention and reverence. (n. 3117)

17 Jn 12:24–25; cf. Lk 14:26.

Walking by Faith

IT IS THROUGH FAITH THAT WE KNOW GOD

My dearest daughter, I am answering your letter without saying anything more to you about the one that good Mother *N.* wrote to you. I must find it good that God humbles me in my nothingness as it pleases Him.

Concerning what you write to me, I see that you always work to see and to know. You have a secret curiosity which will cause you a great deal of trouble, because you must be deaf, blind, and mute, and I see that you are very far from this. In the interior life it is not the way it is with exterior things which we see, touch, taste, and understand. The life of the spirit is completely contrary to this: faith is its light and its security. Therefore, you must learn how to live in this life and ignore your senses more than you have done in the past.

You do not apply yourself enough to the practice of faith; you do not make progress in this because you want it to be perceptible and your mind cannot die to the attachment it has to seeing and knowing. When it does not have this expectation fulfilled, it supposes it has done nothing, it is discouraged and downcast.

You say that you do not understand what your soul is. You do not have the ability to understand this, any more than you do to understand God. You cannot know the one or the other except by faith and through their operations. You perceive that you have a soul because you experience the operations of its faculties. Do you not see that you have a memory, an understanding, and a will? You remember, you understand and know, and you love. See, then, that you have a soul, since its powers are working. Would you think to see your soul as some visible form? Don't you know that it is made in the likeness of God? That it is pure spirit, and therefore, that it is in no way sensible? Likewise, God is not sensible: He is neither seen nor felt.

You will ask me why it is sometimes said, "I saw God who did this thing." This is because of His operations, which are sometimes felt and seen in the soul. Therefore, the soul might say that it saw God who drew it, who supported it; and this is an effect of grace operating in us, sometimes sensibly, in order to strengthen and encourage the soul. At other times it works in secret.

You must understand that the soul's power of sight is through faith. It is the light of faith which causes it to see. And this sight is nothing but a simple belief which keeps it in the truth. The crude senses take no part in it. The interior senses sometimes participate in it, when they are very purified. In the same way you understand you have a soul because it operates and you frequently experience its various functions.

One thing troubles me in your mind: it is that, having the same inclination as our first mother who conceived us all in sin, you have retained and kept one part of her dispositions, without, however, wanting to be opposed to God. You think that the grace of prayer and all the holiness of the interior life are acquired by the power of the mind's labor, through reasoning, light, and learning. And you believe this so much that when the light or knowledge is lacking to you, you no longer appreciate anything that happens in you. This is your stumbling block and a great delay for you.

Did I not tell you many times in the past that you had only a mind and not a heart for Jesus Christ? You have a natural penchant and inclination to know—and this is what caused the disorder in our first parents. You want to know, you want to understand, and you do not want to submit blindly to the guidance of Jesus Christ, your divine Master. You say often with your mouth that you desire to do so, but your mind is not submissive. All its difficulties arise from the fact that you maintain it in its penchant to see and know. And when you do not understand your disposition, you labor to discern something about it or you long to see what someone will teach you about it.

The fondness you have had your whole life to be instructed has harmed you a great deal and will harm you even more if you are not on your guard, for your ability is totally focused on knowing and there is nothing for love. Your mind exhausts your heart. I am grieved by this flaw in you and won't allow it any longer. You must humble yourself in poverty of mind, since your spiritual path requires it of you. I must be pitiless to your self-love; and this knowledge that God gives me concerning your soul, my dearest daughter, is a very great mercy for you. I assure you on His behalf that herein lies your delay and that it is what is most opposed to the sanctity of His reign and His pure love. You are not poor in spirit because your interior ground is entirely filled with desires. When you have learned to remain in nothingness and to be content with that, you will see much more abundantly and in a much more purified manner.

> Since I put myself in nothing
> I have found that nothing is lacking to me.[1]

These are the words of a great saint who truly experienced it. You are mistaken, my dear daughter; the interior life does not consist in lights, but in pure abandonment to the guidance and Spirit of Jesus.

It is good to see what God shows us as our own misery, our nothingness, and our powerlessness, and to remain in humiliation, and to be convinced that we are nothing and can do nothing except by His grace. Such knowledge is good because it is given to us by God. But those who seek through the activity, power, and diligence of the human mind are very arid before God, because they do not have the anointing of His grace.

The only way to make great progress in the spiritual life is to recognize before God our nothingness, our indigence, and our powerlessness. With this perspective and this conviction, which we have many times experienced, one must abandon oneself to God, entrusting oneself to His mercy, to be led in the manner that pleases Him, whether in light or in darkness; and then simplify one's mind without allowing it to see and reason so much.

You must be content with what God gives you without seeking to have Him in some other fashion. It is not by force of arms that grace and divine love are acquired. Rather, it is by the power of humbling oneself before God, acknowledging your unworthiness and being

---

1 St. John of the Cross. Mother Mectilde freely adapts several of the lines of poetry in *The Ascent of Mount Carmel*, Book I, ch. 13, as well as lines inscribed on the sketch of the Mount of Perfection. See *The Collected Works of Saint John of the Cross*, rev. ed., trans. Kieran Kavanaugh, OCD, and Otilio Rodriguez, OCD (Washington, DC: ICS Publications, 1991), 110–11. This statement is reminiscent of: "Now that I no longer desire them, I have them all without desire."

content with poverty and lowliness.[2] You must be content to be nothing and

> you will be more, the more
> you want to be less.[3]

The life of grace is not like the life of the world. In the world, it is necessary to advance oneself and put oneself forward in order to make a show and be something in it according to vanity. However, in the interior life one advances by going backward. This means, you are a success there by wanting to be nothing and you appear greater in God's eyes the less renown and prominence you have in your own eyes and the eyes of creatures.

> In order to be something in all
> You must be nothing at all.[4]

The wealth of the life of grace is supreme poverty. You are far from possessing it, because instead of stripping yourself, you clothe yourself under the pretext of doing something much better. When the sun is too strong, it dazzles; when you have too much light, it blinds you. Your natural understanding is delighted when it does not remain fasting, but when it has neither light nor feeling, it begs for mercy, it disturbs you and pulls you away from peace. My dearest daughter, you must force it to do penance: we are at the right time for that; and you must not have pity on its wails. It is for the sake of its own interests that it shouts. You must close your ears to its complaints and be content in your ignorance, weakness, and poverty.

Up until now you have not sought God in a pure way; rather, you have pursued yourself. Your hidden (and often manifest) tendency was only to content and satisfy your mind, which has always been given the biggest share; and provided that it was peaceful, you thought you had accomplished much. Learn now a contrary lesson, which is to please God, abandoning yourself to His direction in faith and simplicity without scrutinizing it, resigning humbly to His holy will,

2 RB 7.

3 After St. John of the Cross.

4 Reminiscent of the statements in St. John of the Cross's sketch: "To go from the all to the all, you must deny yourself of all in all" and "To arrive at being all desire to be nothing."

awaiting in patience His grace and His light, without the natural activity of your mind anticipating it in order to devour it and satisfy itself.

This is an important lesson, which I have given you contrary to my original intention, since I was not thinking about saying anything of this to you. Nevertheless, I have told you the most urgent truth regarding your interior state. Moreover, I find myself so replete, so certain about the truth I have told you that I cannot doubt it at all. Think about this, my dearest daughter. These are your interior bonds, which are much more malicious than you suppose. Ask Our Lord to break them and to grant you the grace to be like a little child, entirely submissive and simple toward His holy guidance.

I have preached about these qualities to you for a long time; try to be occupied with them and renounce all desires to know, to understand, to feel, and so on.

Ut jumentum factus sum, says David,[5] "I have become like a beast of burden," and I remained with you. Remain with God like a poor beast incapable of anything except being what He pleases; ignorant of everything and knowing nothing except His holy will to which you will be abandoned and submissive without knowing it. And you will see that His grace, His love, and His spirit will reign in you. (n. 1391)

ON THE EFFECTS OF FAITH

My dearest daughter, I had a great desire to write to you this morning about the Gospel, but Providence gave us Holy Mass very early. This is what spoiled my plan, but which filled me with a very deep desire to see your soul established in the grace of the Transfiguration. And I found myself very focused on praying for your soul during Holy Communion. If you are faithful, you will understand something of the wonders which are in God and which He causes His chosen ones to experience.

I have always exhorted you to have a high esteem for God in your spirit, to prefer nothing to His love,[6] and to refer everything to Him. Weigh well the importance of what I am telling you and the obligation you have to become faithful to it. This, my very dear daughter, will be through the practice of faith.

---

5 Ps 72:23 (73:22). 6 RB 4:21; 72:9, 11.

Someday I must speak to you about its excellence and its effects, so that you may be convinced of the necessity you have to exercise it. By faith, your soul rises to God; by faith it knows Him. By faith, the soul submits to God's adorable and inscrutable designs for it. By faith, you have continual possession of God present. By faith, you depart from creatures to enter into Jesus. In short, it is by faith that you are united to and transformed into Jesus. O holy faith, what grace and power you have! And what holy and divine fruits you produce in a soul which acts and works by your light and by your power!

If you desire to be transfigured, you must go to the mountain of pure prayer. It is through prayer that the soul is truly transfigured, that it is wholly stripped of itself and clothed with God. One climbs to God on the mountain in order to find God there by the path of prayer and of mortification. When the soul arrives at the summit, it finds Jesus Christ there, transfigured and speaking of the excess of His love in His divine sufferings. The soul then hears that adorable voice: "This is My beloved Son, in whom I take delight. Listen to Him."[7]

On this mountain, the soul is most attentive to God, it hears the divine Word clothed in our flesh who speaks to its heart, and teaches it about His love and His mysteries. Oh! With what marvels, what prodigies, what graces, the soul is filled by this divine utterance! It is on the mountain that God makes His voice heard; on the mountain that He manifests Himself; on the mountain that He speaks of His cross.

Let us allow ourselves to be led to this blessed mountain! Let us leave the jumble of the senses and creatures and ascend by faith and hear the heavenly teaching of our adorable Master. He speaks to us of the violence of His Passion, to teach us that Jesus's glory and happiness were to suffer for us and prove His love for us.

Let us have a great reverence and love for Jesus's holy words. Let us desire that they be operative in the depths of our hearts, and that they imprint on us a mighty love for His cross, since the signs of the transfiguration of a soul are union with Jesus Christ on the cross, loving and speaking about the cross, and being consumed on it. Be transfigured in this manner and do not have any deeper satisfaction than to suffer for Jesus Christ and with Jesus Christ.

---

7 Lk 9:31–35.

Here are the little sallies of my mind, which the deep affection I have for you sends forth to your soul. (n. 884)

HOW ONE MUST WORK IN FAITH

My very dear daughter, I hoped to answer you as I had intended upon reading your letter, but Providence arranged things quite differently, binding me so strictly to silence that I found no capacity to say anything to you, except that you must learn to keep silent and suffer well. This is the response I found in myself, for you, after Holy Communion.

I must leave you a bit in poverty and silence, and your excessive desire to know harms you very much. I saw it very clearly. Therefore, I am resolved to leave you for a little while to bear your cross and see what your fidelity will be.

My dear daughter, I have not again imposed on you a yoke too harsh or difficult, rather you must find it good that I am helping in your destruction according to the grace God has given me. Do not take on too much labor at once. One lesson is enough for many days, and I would like you to train yourself in faith.

Here is how: believe that God is present by faith, without seeing or feeling Him; act for Him as much as you possibly can, that is, do and suffer everything in His holy presence and in His love, trying to purify your intentions and animate them with His sacred love. Perhaps you will say to me that you do not find this purity and detachment in yourself and that if you want to make some effort, it would be of your own making, which, not having the unction of grace, will not have its effect; and you will not experience its blessing. I answer you that your insensibility does not make your action less good; on the contrary, by this it is doubly purified, because you renounce your self-love, being without satisfaction.

Here is the lesson I give you: do all your actions with purity. For example, I drink, I eat, and nature wants to take some pleasure in it, but in spirit I turn away from this gratification and desire with all my heart to not cling to it, so that I may eat and drink for the love of God and out of obedience to His guidance which obliges us to do so, and my plan is to remain in that intention. If I leave this through weakness or infidelity, I go back to it by a simple remembrance or desire to be there, and in this way I do my work in the presence of God and for God, as much as I can.

God wants me to work with His grace in certain encounters; and in others He wants me to be completely passive and adhering completely to the powerlessness He causes me to experience. We must follow Him just as it pleases Him to lead us. You have an example of this in yourself, in the inspiration you were given to offer yourself as a victim for the *N.* families. You must bear this attraction[8] by leaving yourself at the divine disposal, that He may give it such an effect as it pleases Him, without your hurrying or resisting much, in this way leaving yourself to God to be His victim. He will apply you as He wishes. For, in attractions or inspirations about extraordinary things, we must beware of temptations; our own mind sometimes suggests certain things to us, which is why it has to be distrusted. Here is how you must behave in such a situation to avoid illusion: you must place such things back in God with abandonment and trust in His grace, remaining bound to His most holy will, and never separating yourself from it, and without paying too much attention to particulars, for fear that this would little by little lead you into aberrations and distractions.

Therefore, be entirely God's for everything that He pleases, because it is right that the victim be immolated to the glory of the one to whom it belongs. It is for Him to make use of you for whom and for what He pleases. Your motive must be only His pure glory, not turning away from it for a moment—that if He uses you for the salvation of souls, your zeal must be only for Him, to see Him reigning everywhere and honored by all. If you leave that simple insight, your natural and reasoning mind will lead you far afield into various thoughts, into fears, into creatures, and into its own musings. We must close the ear of our soul to everything it wants to say, and remain submissive, that is, patient in the attraction from God. Do the same also with other things which come to you, returning or leaving

8 The French, with a refined vocabulary for the life of man with God, speak of *les attraits spirituels*, that is, of certain spiritual attractions. God gives souls an attraction for the things He waits to give them. Saint Thérèse: "More than ever, I understand that the smallest events of our life are conducted by God; He is the One who makes us desire and who grants our desires" (Letter 201).

all things to the divine disposition. By this means you will remain in God, filled with God, because the will of God is God Himself. Doing this, you will not be mistaken in wasting time with what happens.

You wanted to know what obligation this state of victim, which you have a prompting to suffer for *N.*, will place upon you. It would make you responsible for all offenses and you would do as Jesus Christ did for you: die and suffer for them. You would be obliged to satisfy the divine justice for what they owe. In a word, this is to give yourself as a prey to every kind of suffering and to death, since sins deserve infinite punishment.

Give yourself to God for whatever pleases Him, and tell Him that you give yourself to Him as a victim for *N.* if He desires this of you. For if He does desire it, His grace will accomplish it in you. But do not put yourself forward on your own account. Look at your weakness and your lack of fidelity. Thus in view of your nothingness, misery, and poverty, remain abandoned to the divine will. That is enough on this point.

I return to the beginning of my letter and conclude it as I began, telling you that you must suffer and keep silent; namely, you must embrace your cross as it will please Our Lord to give it to you and remain alone with Him, without being dispersed among creatures. Be solitary in the midst of difficulties so that your spirit may be detached. Do nothing in haste, for show, with attachment, or with self-interest; and working for God and out of submission to His good pleasure, you will remain free and will act in His holy presence without being polluted in your actions. I pray Our Lord to grant you this grace.

(n. 1435)

THE SAME SUBJECT, CONTINUED (I): HOW TO WORK IN FAITH

Love God, my dearest daughter, love God for love of Himself. Those people in the Gospel today[9] liked Jesus and pursued Him to make Him king because He filled and satisfied them with bread and fish. Oh! How few souls there are who love God for love of Himself and make Him to reign in their hearts! As long as we feel the sweet effects of His graces, as long as we have the light and inclination, we

9 Jn 6:1–15.

follow Him and adore Him as our God and our King; but if He takes away His sweetness and turns us upside down, we no longer know Him.

Jesus is always God, full of grandeur, full of love and holiness. He is the same in privations and in the weaknesses you experience every day. Therefore it is necessary that you love Him and adore Him with the same heart, that faith raise you above your senses, and that you understand through faith how you must live detached from yourself, from the supports in yourself, and your self-love.

Raise yourself in simplicity to God who is continually and truly present to you. Strip yourself of all your lights and all your likings, all forms, all images and appearances. God is a pure spirit; He desires to be adored by you in spirit,[10] stripped of all sensible representations.

Faith teaches you that everything which meets the senses and comes into human comprehension is not God. No, no, my dearest daughter, everything you feel, everything you taste, and everything you see is not God. It may well be some effect of His grace, but it is not God, the source of grace.

And in order to find Him in His divine purity, you must raise yourself above all that you feel, and, through a simple ignorance of all things, you must dwell by faith in God; that is, believing in what He is, you will remain in an abyss of respect in His holy presence, without forming other reflections. You will yield to God's power so as to be the victim of His love. You will remain at rest in this attitude, not allowing your mind to reflect, ignoring yourself in order to be abandoned entirely to God and filled with Him. And if temptation assails you, you will ignore it the same way, as if insensible to your own interests, because you must lose yourself if you want to possess your God. "The one who loses his soul will keep it for eternal life."[11]

I write these things to you on my knees, prostrate before the adorable majesty of my God, who gave all of these to me, as well as many other things to tell you this morning after Holy Communion, when I was moved in a very particular way regarding you. Oh! How indebted you are to God's goodness! How many mercies He is preparing for you! Your vow will not be in any way harmful to you, because most

10 Jn 4:23.

11 Mt 11:39, Jn 12:24–25.

certainly it is accepted by God in the way that I explained to you. But be faithful and abandon yourself perfectly.

It is necessary that you become worthy, through the power of Jesus Christ, to receive the graces He desires to give you. Be determined to be wholly God's and be resolved to die at your post and in the manner that obedience will show you.

I am not your visible angel; I am a sinful fiend, but God desires me to teach you His ways, and you to bear the weight of this humiliation: that you are linked to a sinner by the divine command. But you must set aside the creature in order to give yourself entirely to God, through the creature. (n. 9)

THE SAME SUBJECT, CONTINUED (II): HOW TO WORK IN FAITH

I could not write to you yesterday. I am using an hour of my time after Matins to write you a few words concerning your letter from yesterday, in which you ask me about three things.

The first is that you desire to be instructed about how to act by faith and how to see everything within God's order, as He saw and knew everything from all eternity. You are asking about what you know already. The faith teaches us that God is God, that He sees everything, that He knows everything, that He can do everything, that He pervades everything, and that nothing can be hidden from His divine eyes; that He has disposed and ordered the ways of our sanctification from all eternity; that a hair does not fall from our heads without His order;[12] that good and ill, affliction and joy, repose, pain, and so on, are in His hand; that His most wise and most loveable Providence arranges everything in the most sweet and holy manner,[13] for the good of souls who abandon themselves to God and who live by faith.[14]

Now, what is the practice of faith? It is to believe in these truths, those which I just told you about, and all the others which are in God, although you are not aware of them. For example: someone opposes me. I accept this contradiction from God's hand without permitting my mind much reasoning and I resign myself to His most holy will in patience, believing that God sends this to me for His

12 Mt 10:30. 13 Wis 8:1. 14 Rom 8:28.

glory and my salvation. I believe that God sees me. I believe that He is full of love and mercy for my soul. I believe that He does nothing except what is just and holy. And in necessities, you can make some act, such as saying, "My God, I believe You love me with an infinite love since You died for me. I believe You will care for all my needs, and that Your grace will lead me to You. I believe in Your holy Providence and that not a hair falls from my head without Your command. And consequently, I believe You see the least of my thoughts and that with You there is nothing accidental, that all You send me is good, and that You never permit anything for me which is not for Your glory and the good of Your elect, even if I do not understand it. I believe, my God, I believe in You, and in Your holy mysteries, and in all the holy truths You revealed to Your Church." At other times, you may say, "My God, I work because You will it. Sin has reduced me to this punishment; I endure it for Your love in a spirit of penance." You can drink, eat, sleep, and the rest in this disposition, doing every day what God wants, avoiding sin because He desires this avoidance, and He hates sin.

The practice of faith means to believe in God and in His divine words, and to work in the power of this conviction. I do not know any other method for it. Many books describe beautiful practices, among others, Fr. Jean-Baptiste de Saint-Jure[15] in the book he wrote, *On the Knowledge of the Love of Our Lord*. I do not like too much multiplicity. But when the mind is in need, one can avail oneself of such things. These worthy authors have written on this subject, you can make use of them.

The second thing you ask about is how you should receive everything in a spirit of penitence. My dear daughter, this is because we are sinners, and in that capacity, as I pointed out to you a number of times, we are not worthy of any grace or happiness. Therefore, we must bear our troubles in a spirit of penitence. This means, I make it my penance since my sins deserve it and require God to leave me in

15 Fr. Jean-Baptiste de Saint-Jure, S. J., who was born in Metz in 1588 and died in Paris in 1657, devoted himself with great zeal to the apostolate of souls. His ascetic writings reveal a man well-versed in the ways of God and the science of the saints.

my abjection. For example, someone says something insulting to me. I bear it in a spirit of penitence, namely, with the thought or feeling that I have sinned, and that in the capacity of a sinner I deserve it; and thus I allow it to humble me. We have spoken and written these things to you: you can turn them over in your mind at your leisure.

The third thing is the consent of the superior part[16] in faults or imperfections one commits. Every time you have evil feelings, like anger, contempt, and so on, you do not consent to them. I do not see that there was consent, but sometimes there can be a little negligence, by which I mean that you do not separate yourself so promptly, as regards the superior part, from the imperfection; I do not say always, but sometimes.

I told you that God never impinges on our senses. You may indeed experience there the overflowing of His grace, but not Himself, because He is a pure spirit and His dwelling is in the highest point of our soul from which He does not descend. We will talk about this, and you will see ever more clearly the solidity of the path of death and *anéantissement* in pure faith, wherein the soul's union with God is not mediated. In states of rapture, revelations, and so on, there is more of the senses, and consequently more attachment and less purity. Nonetheless, one must also discern about what affects the senses: whether it is an effect brought about in the purity of the soul which overflows without the senses contributing anything to it, or whether the senses themselves are searching for such gratifications. We need to have a little conversation about these matters in order to understand them more easily. (n. 1147a, and the last paragraph n. 1660)

ON OUR NEED TO BE IN JESUS CHRIST, TO BE JESUS CHRIST'S, AND TO DO ALL OF OUR ACTIONS FOR JESUS CHRIST

I greatly desire speak to you about Jesus Christ, to make Jesus Christ known to you, and to see you completely full of love and esteem for Jesus Christ. Oh! How great He is, how holy, how loveable and adorable He is! Let us be all His, live only for Him, breathe only for Him, think only of Him, and desire only Him. I confess to

16 Mother Mectilde seems to be speaking about the will, a higher power in the soul than feelings, imagination, etc., which is free to consent to sin or not.

you that I take a singular pleasure in speaking to you of Jesus Christ, and in seeing your goodness in allowing unclean lips like mine to speak of Him.

The sacred name of Jesus Christ is so fragrant and sweet that there are delights in pronouncing it. O Jesus Christ, Jesus Christ, Jesus Christ, be in us and fill us completely with Yourself. A soul who has Jesus Christ has no need of any other thing. If you ask me who is able to have Jesus Christ, I will tell you that all Christians have received Him in baptism. You have Him in you, but He does not always show Himself. It is faith which reveals Him to you, and sometimes He communicates Himself so particularly to the soul that it experiences Him in a wondrous manner. Jesus Christ is the life of your life, He is the spirit of your spirit and the soul of your soul. If Jesus Christ were not in you, you would not be anything that you are.

Therefore, adore Jesus Christ as your life, your soul, and your spirit, that is, see in you Jesus Christ more than you see yourself. We must not see anything except with the eyes of Jesus Christ, desire nothing except through His desires, and love nothing except through His love. In short, we must be, as that worthy lover[17] of Jesus Christ, St. Paul, says, completely clothed with Jesus Christ.[18]

It is a great happiness for a soul to have a high esteem for God and to see that nothing is great except Him, to see that nothing else is worthy of our reverence, our worship, or our love except Him, so that in this truth we render Him what we owe to His greatness and holiness. From this point of view, you cannot do anything except for God, you cannot desire anything except God, you cannot love anything except God, and in everything you see God and tend toward God.

God, God, God alone, that is: may only God be in your thoughts, in your words, in your intentions, in your actions, in your desires, and in your affections. God uniquely everywhere: God in humiliation, God in life, God in death—in fine, God everywhere.

The Gospel tells us today briefly in what Christian holiness consists. It is a wonderful lesson, listen to this please. The law says, "You shall love the Lord your God with all your heart, with all your soul, with

---

17 Other manuscripts have "imitator" rather than "lover."

18 Rom 13:14, Gal 3:27.

all your strength, with all your mind."[19] Weigh these things well and you will see how much you are obliged to give God the very smallest of your actions. If you must love Him, by the requirement of His commandments, with all the capacities of your soul, judge if you do not owe Him all your thoughts, all your movements, and even every beat of your heart.

The Law says, "with *all* your soul, with *all* your strength."[20] If you will consider the importance of these words, by obligation of the commandment you owe yourself completely to God. In addition, St. Paul tells you, "You are not your own, you are redeemed at a great price."[21] You will find in an endless number of places in Holy Scripture your inability to dispose of yourself—indeed, of even one of your thoughts—if you do not want to steal it from Jesus Christ. For by right you cannot. You have been purchased: the one who buys the tree, buys the fruit; hence, you are not yours at all. Ponder this truth, and repeat these words often: I am not mine, I belong to Jesus Christ. He ransomed me through love, thus I am necessarily the slave of His love. O worthy slavery!

After you will have understood this truth and the Spirit of our Lord will have made an impression on your soul, you will know by an experience of grace that you belong wholly and without any reserve to Jesus Christ; that it is an absolute necessity for you to be completely His; that you cannot any longer deny this. Having been convinced of this truth, which you must believe as a dogma of faith, you see next how much you are obliged to give yourself to Him. That is, to consent to all the rights, powers, and authority He has concerning you, and to abide in Him. This means to never depart from His holy presence and to do all things by His spirit. As much as possible for you, to never have in your ideas any other object than Him. Briefly, in everything His pure glory must be the reason you act, even in your smallest actions. Do not think that there is anything small in regard to God: all is great, all is holy. His love sanctifies all things.

Therefore be very exact in the smallest things. All is done for a great God. You must do everything with understanding, that is to say,

---

19 Mt 22:34–46. This is the Gospel read on the Seventeenth Sunday after Pentecost.

20 Dt 6:5.

21 1 Cor 6:19–20.

with attention to God, and with a simple desire to glorify and please Him in all things. We must not listen to nature or the human mind which complains of its slavery. May that slavery make you free[22] one day, after which you will have subjected all to Jesus: your feelings, your reasoning, your reflections, your interests, your passions, and your self-love. For then you will have an inner freedom so holy that you will be amazed at how you have learned to make yourself captive for God, who is so full of goodness and love.

To the one who leaves what he has in order to follow Jesus Christ, He will give a hundredfold in this life and eternal life in the next.[23] Oh! What reward! He gives the hundredfold in this world. Yes, my dearest daughter, the freedom you love so much and which your pride fears to sacrifice will be given you doubly. That is to say, you will be freer and nothing will imprison you anymore. Creatures will have no more power over you, all things will be below you, and nothing will be able to trouble you.

Is it not, therefore, a great happiness to lose our liberty to Jesus, to make a voluntary sacrifice of it to Him, since He will make it entirely holy for us? Therefore take yourself captive for Jesus even in the smallest things. He wants you to have this fidelity, and then He will raise you to greater ones. He who does not pay any attention to little things will soon fall into great disorders.

Self-love pollutes great actions much more than it does little ones. Self-satisfaction and vanity secretly ruin everything. But in little things everything is little, you are humbled in them; they are not splendid, and you do not receive the vain praise of men. Self-love does not like little things. The wicked inclination toward our own importance which sin placed in us always makes us aspire to high things, and we see few souls who do not long for great things under the pretext of their Master's glory. Do not be deceived, my very dear daughter. Follow the true light and the lessons that Jesus Christ gives you in His own person. If you want to be great in grace and in God's gifts, be so little and so abject in yourself and in creatures that you can no longer be found. Make your dwelling in nothingness, be nothing in everything, and you will be all in Jesus Christ.

---

22 1 Cor 7:22.

23 Mt 19:29.

Do not consider little things with the perspective of your human mind. See them within the order which Jesus Christ set up over you, to which He subjects you by the compelling movements His grace impresses on you. You must have a prompt obedience, without considering the littleness of the action. It is enough that God commands you to do it. You must obey to the point of blindness, without going back and without reflecting on your action. And if He only wants little things from you, should you not be content with that? Is it for you to give laws to God? The slave has no right of choosing or refusing. She must be subject at every moment, without knowing why.

Therefore, love faithfulness in little things, and remain subject to it. You can glorify God more by picking up a straw out of submission to God, than by doing fifty lashes with the discipline or other greater austerities, following your own mind. If God is pleased with these little things, you must do them purely and with the same perfection, the same love, and the same fidelity as if you were converting the whole world. Your little action has God for its end and its object, just like the greatest. Hence, it must be done in a holy way because you must honor God and do everything for His love and through the direction of His Spirit.

1. In order to carry out your action well you must do it *for* God, namely, for His love and out of reverence and submission to His good pleasure, for Him alone, without considering yourself, without reflecting on your own satisfaction or interests.

2. You must do it *in* God, that is, in His presence, remaining united to Him in heart and mind.

3. You must do it *through* God's Spirit, that is, you must entrust yourself to God so that He may act in you, and that it may be His grace and power which make all things worthy of Him.

When our actions are carried out in this manner, they are glorious to God. How do you know your action is done in this way? When carrying out your actions, you will perceive that you will have no other motive than pleasing God. You will remain in His holy presence, if not experiencing it, then at least believing, that is, through faith; and you will entrust yourself to Him with a pure abandonment in order to carry out that intention in the way that will please Him.

But there is no need to have these three points distinctly in your thought in every action. The simple application of your mind to God, through a simple and loving desire, puts you in possession of these three; and your inner ground contains them in faith, and this suffices. Do everything, then, with the perfection you can, imitating Our Lord who did everything in a holy and perfect way; who did everything according to what He judged most for His glory.

Do all that you do:

1. With presence of mind.
2. Without haste.
3. Willingly and gladly for Jesus Christ.
4. Without listening to the complaints of nature.
5. With a loving satisfaction in the accomplishment of God's will for you. If you have to write, write having God present in faith and with tranquility, without hurry.

See only God and His good pleasure in what you do; and although they are human actions, you render them divine by the divine motive which animates you. In your other labors, do the same, and beware of being the owner of your work; do not be complacent about it or attached to it. Readily leave everything at the least sign or prompting of God's command. Do everything you do with great liberty. Become indifferent to every kind of work: as long as it is [for] God, it must be enough for you. But it will always be [for] God when you do not consider creatures and your own interests.

When you do any task, do it in God's sight and for God, with the perfection you can. Give glory to God by doing perfectly what He commands you. I have known souls who would have scruples about not having done a task as perfectly as they could, their thought being like a reproach that they did not act according to the full extent of the grace or perfection which God placed in them. There are souls so pure and so delicate that they notice even the littlest things, viewing nothing as little which could and should honor God. These souls make use of the whole capacity God placed in them to glorify Him; even the least things in life they do with some degree of perfection. In order to succeed in this, it is necessary to conceive a deep reverence for God in faith and to consider yourself blessed to be spent for His glory, even if He never rewarded you.

Here you are, then, regarding your actions and your obligations to be faithful in small things, and how you must do them with all the perfection you can; because it is for God and not for a creature that you are acting. What I said about one action, I say for all.

Let us say a little bit about services which are rendered to you and those you render to yourself.

First, you must not appropriate any service given to you: it is to Jesus Christ in you that it is given. And assuming that those who serve you do not have these opinions, you must not for that reason appropriate to yourself what is not yours; and you must make up for the lack of light and grace in your servants by referring to God all the services you receive from them. Be very faithful on this point, so that God may be in everything and that the creature may not be the idol of the creature. For, ordinarily, domestic servants only have human views about the services they give. You are Christian, which is why this fidelity is required of you; and in this disposition, humbly receive all services rendered to you, whether you are well or ill. This little exercise of fidelity makes the spirit very free and causes you to bear with humility all the services you receive; remember that it is not yours, or for you, but is Jesus Christ's in you.

As for the services which you render yourself, you must have the same attitude, that is, to render them to Jesus Christ in you; for Jesus Christ is more you than you are yourself. You can also perform them as to one of Jesus Christ's poor. For, although you do not beg for your bread like the beggars in the streets, are you not poor and truly poor since you have nothing of yourself? You are begging every day; thus, in truth, you are poor in every way: poor in virtue, poor in grace, poor in perfection, poor in good — in a word, poor in everything. Is it not God who gives you all, and do you not ask Him for bread every day? Yes, you are poor in the riches of heaven and of earth. Nothing belongs to you, not even a thought; and all the goods of fortune could be taken away from you in one moment, as with Job, and you brought down to a dung heap, covered with disease.[24] Oh! When God wants to cause a reversal, He finds extraordinary means for it!

---

24 Job 2:7–8.

Therefore, you are poor, and you must live poverty in complete detachment from everything; and in this spirit, serve yourself as you would a pauper. Apply to your body the charity that you would give to another, as if giving it to Jesus Christ in yourself, and so as to have a greater ability to serve Him. It is not necessary to deny the body everything, because it must serve your soul; that is why you must feed it, not out of love and fondness for nature, but to be more able to glorify God. Therefore assist the body out of charity, but do not please it by too much humanness. Without scruple, give it what is necessary and do this always with a divine motive, having God and His glory for your object.

When you are in good health, do as much for yourself as you can and as prudence allows, considering yourself unworthy that a member of Jesus Christ be employed in serving you. But when you are unwell, receive all necessary services in the manner described above.

I would still have many things to tell you, but I fear too much food would upset your stomach. Study this lesson attentively, not once, but several times, gently, without effort or strain. Receive what it will please Our Lord to bring about in you. Do not be troubled about anything, not even your imperfections; we have to write to you something about that when Our Lord pleases. You must not overburden your spirit. Remain peaceful in your miseries and allow God to defeat and humble you in the way that will please Him. (n. 674)

Continual Obedience to God

HOW WE MUST SERVE THE SICK

God be praised for the graces He gave you in stopping your hastiness in the activities where His holy Providence engaged you. Bind yourself to its effects and serve your dear spouse as you would the person of Jesus Christ, if you were to see Him on earth. In doing so, you will be acting as St. Paul advises you,[1] and in doing your duty to a creature according to your obligations, you will honor God through your intentions.

Beware of a little secret haste which rules you and causes you darkness and sometimes a little anxiety. See everything within the order of God, and receive everything from His holy hand. It is He who caused your husband's illness and it is He who requires you to serve him. Employ your time and ability for this work out of obedience to Our Lord, who desires it and who obliges you to it. Serve him with love and with respect; in a certain way he is your master, and he is also . . .[2]

At the sight of his sufferings, do not be so human. Do not sympathize according to nature. You are a Christian woman, you must really act according to Christian grace; to do otherwise is to fall away from the dignity we have received and to scorn God's orders which require it of us. Have compassion on the suffering he endures, but in a Christian way, seeing the hand of God who gives it to him. Consider God's designs upon his soul and body and offer him to God as a victim; for he is part of yourself through the sacrament which united you. You are obliged to ascribe to God all the rights you have in this, in the desire to see him belong entirely to Jesus Christ, and so that He may sanctify him through his sufferings.

We must not love with a love of flesh and blood; instead, we must love with a pure and detached love which has God alone for its first

1 Eph 5:21–24.

2 This phrase is not finished in the manuscript. Instead of an ellipsis, some more recent copies end with "your spouse."

motive. Creatures must never remove this, since you only serve the creature out of homage and obedience to God. Therefore, raise your mind to God who is present to you and who is more in you than you are in yourself, and do all that you have to do in His holy presence and through the motive of His pure love.

Give yourself freely to business and to servitude when God desires this of you. Be content with all the dispositions in which God places you, as much for the interior as for the exterior. Do not be busy out of your own understanding, but allow yourself to be employed by Providence, which will not fail to visit you through its happenings. Be faithful in this without either anxiety or haste. Be content with the divine will which you must accomplish in everything. You must not pay attention to yourself, but rather pay attention to God, and His Holy Spirit will give you excellent lessons.

Do not imprison yourself, be free in your exercises of piety, and when the command of God takes you away from them, be submissive, and beware of annoyance. You must be all things to all men[3] and always in a state to do what God desires, not having any attachment to any particular thing. Give God His freedom to employ you in whatever He pleases.

Never do anything you are not willing to leave at a moment's notice, if God and obedience order something else. God alone must control us, and not creatures; and yet, very often we willingly make ourselves their prisoners through unfaithfulness and blindness.

Providence is worthy of adoration, having arranged for the privation of two or three things that I wished to direct you to do. Bear it gladly, and let us begin to die to all the props and pursuits of our self-love.

I willingly desire to be deprived of your presence; it is enough that I find you in God, where I take pleasure in seeing you, and that creatures no longer possess you. Another time I will tell you how it is necessary to pray for your neighbor. Work with fidelity, following the Holy Spirit's movement. (n. 353)

---

3 1 Cor 9:22.

HOW WE MUST DO EVERYTHING OUT OF OBEDIENCE TO JESUS CHRIST

Since divine Providence permitted our conversation to be interrupted and it seems to me that your soul had nothing or very little to carry away from the conference[4] today, I believe that Our Lord desires that I tell you my little thoughts about your dispositions; however, this will only be a repetition of what we have told you many times.

The first thing which I notice in you, my dearest daughter, is that you do not have enough esteem for small things. You do not envision them within the order of divine Providence; that is why you have little attention and respect for them, and in this you lose a great deal of grace. If we must render an account to God at the judgment for one useless thought, for one action badly ordered, why will we not mend the many useless actions which could honor God if we gave them life by the pure love which must enliven them? Bad habits cause us great evils and I am not surprised that spiritual persons say that a habit is a vicious one—even though it is not something of mortal consequence—when it causes a dreadful delay to the soul.

God sometimes asks only for a small act of fidelity in order to make us great saints.[5] You must always be in a state of holy and loving attention toward God, to give yourself to Him in every way, as much in natural actions as in others, since you must not live one moment apart from God. And since everything must have life in Him, why do you want one part of your actions to be without this divine life which you draw from the pure love of God? Why, I ask, will it not be animated by His divine Spirit? If you could comprehend the waste you bring about when you act in a purely human way, you would be inconsolable. Is it not a great fault in a soul who is capable of giving glory to God and who nevertheless deprives Him of it, so as to yield to his own reasoning, which wants to convince him that life's small actions are mere nothings and do not need to be directed? O my child, if you had really understood how you are ransomed and how you belong to Jesus Christ, you would take much more care about honoring Him. If one beat of your heart is not yours, how

4 "Conference" is used in a fully and specifically religious sense, as a giving of instruction.

5 *Grandes saintes*: women saints.

much more does your smallest action, which always lasts longer than one heartbeat!

Have a high esteem for God and for all that He obliges us to believe over the course of our lives, never having any other goal than His pure love. That divine fire must purify us, and nothing is worthy of God if it has not passed through its flames. Therefore, do all things for God, and take care that all your actions are referred back to Him, doing them, as I told you, out of obedience to Jesus Christ. Eat by this spirit of obedience, sleep out of obedience, work out of obedience, relax out of obedience, in short, do everything you do out of obedience. Pray out of obedience, suffer out of obedience, mortify yourself out of obedience, accept all crosses and contradictions of soul out of obedience, practice the virtues out of obedience, love your neighbor out of obedience, visit the poor out of obedience.

Always keep before your eyes your divine exemplar Jesus Christ, who became obedient even to death on the cross.[6] May your whole life be a continual obedience to God; this is your path, at least it is the disposition in which grace has placed you and to which you owe an inviolable fidelity. When you pull yourself away from this submission, you put yourself in danger of a multitude of miseries. This is what supports you in your state of darkness and weakness.

In the Gospel, wanting to work His marvels, Our Lord asked only for faith on our part. "Do you believe that I can heal you?"[7] Likewise today, desiring to work in you the marvels of His grace and His love, He asks for the same thing. He desires that you have faith and that you entrust yourself to His goodness and power; otherwise, you make yourself unworthy of His action. Believe then, despite the impurity of your inner ground, believe in the power and goodness of Jesus Christ, which can purify you in one moment. And without doubt He will do it, after He has established you in the firm knowledge of your nothingness. This state is absolutely necessary for you and I beg you to be totally abandoned to the intentions of Jesus Christ.

Do not deliberate so much. Walk with trust. The one who supports you will not let you perish. Do not be troubled about anything,

6 Phil 2:8. 7 Mt 9:28.

provided that you are uniquely God's; He is enough. But for this to be as it should, you must live in a real dependence on His love and designs.

Beware of becoming possessive about your time and actions. You must always be in a state to willingly leave what you resolved to do, in order to do what God wills you to do in events. Provided that you do the will of God, you must be content. And when you find in yourself small annoyances, eagerness, and so on, this is a sign that there are hidden attachments to your action, that your pride is dominating and taking a part in it. From that moment you know, by this agitation, that you are not entirely abandoned to God's good pleasure, since you are attached to your inclination and you take life from yourself.

I indeed desire that you plan to do this or that thing; but you must carry out such a project only in the spirit of obedience which binds you to your duties, and with adherence to God's good pleasure, intending in this to do His holy will. However, when you see that His divine Providence overturns your projects and presents you with other things, abandon yourself, submit, and leave behind your plan in order to delight in God's command. In these encounters, be very faithful on this point. Otherwise you will always remain filled with yourself and your soul will not possess the true and holy liberty which makes it completely detached from itself. The soul becomes very polluted when it does the opposite of what I am telling you; for becoming attached to its own action, it prefers its choice to God's will; it casts itself gradually into darkness, losing the peace and the presence of God.

Now, to be delivered from this secret tyranny, you must remain detached from the activities of your mind, not doing what it wants; and when you perform an action, always be ready to leave it when Providence takes you away from it, in any manner whatsoever.

Never determine anything of yourself. You are no longer your own, you are Jesus Christ's. It is for Him to dispose and for you to acquiesce in His designs. Strive to be detached from everything, be tied or attached only to God's good pleasure. We must be very disinterested and allow God the freedom to do with us what will please Him.

Here are the few words which Providence gave me when thinking about writing to you. Try to practice them without always being troubled or anxious at seeing yourself so helpless. That is what must cause you to rejoice, because you understand from your experience that all your happiness comes from God, and that there is nothing in you except misery and sin. In this disposition, you abandon yourself without reserve to the power of grace and you see how continually dependent on it you are. The more you are gradually established in the profound knowledge of yourself and secretly enter into a holy abhorrence of yourself and everything of your own making, the further you will be from deriving glory and vanity from them.

I am answering you and your present state. It is good, but be very faithful in it. God wants you to be all His. Strive to give yourself to Him as much as possible, and His mercy and love will do the rest. *Adieu*, my dear daughter, pray for my miseries which are extreme.

(n. 2531)

IN ORDER TO HONOR GOD BY OUR OBEDIENCE

God and nothing more!

The light and grace necessary for you to perceive your state in depth will not be given to you through the efforts of your mind, but rather in your presenting yourself as continually as you can to Our Lord, with a profound humility and handing over of your whole self to Him, awaiting with trust, respect, and patience whatever it pleases Him to work in you for His glory, and waiting for Him to shed on your soul a ray of His light and some small spark of His pure love.

Beware of inner haste. Yes, this would be my desire, if it could be, that you be ignorant of many things about the interior life. All your labor has only been on the surface, curiosity, vanity; the pure love of God does not have any life in you. Realize that all your knowledge is nothing; because the one who knows everything and yet does not know Jesus Christ crucified knows nothing, says the Apostle.[8] The true science is to know and be acquainted with Jesus Christ, but through holy experience. Give yourself truly to the power of His Spirit in order to conquer your own and reduce it to the nothingness in which it must be.

You will honor Jesus Christ by your obedience in being subject to God and creatures, in view of and in union with His obedience

8 1 Cor 2:3.

to His eternal Father, to His holy Mother, and to His executioners. The obedience He gives to His Father teaches you the respect and submission which you owe to God's eternal commands concerning you; it teaches you to receive all the events and accidents of your life from His holy hand, accepting them with love and bearing them with resignation to the good pleasure of God, and (if you can) with consent and contentment to see God accomplishing His designs in you, as He did in His Son. The obedience He gave to His holy Mother teaches you the submission you must have to the direction that the Holy Spirit established in the Church. And that which He gave to His executioners teaches you how you must receive crosses, afflictions, privations, and the rest. Jesus Christ allowed Himself to be stripped, laid down, and fixed to the cross, not from pure submission to men, but through the sight and perfect knowledge He had of His Father's will with regard to His death. He submitted to the cruel treatment of men, in such a way that one can say that love for the good pleasure and glory of His Father put Him to death, creatures being only the instruments of His execution.

Do not burden your mind with multiplicity. It is only too full of its own lights and its inclination to know things which please it or which are uncommon to it.

Be a little child in the hand of God and allow yourself to be led. Follow grace; it is not for you to foresee it. Humble yourself and do not be discouraged. You must receive the lights God gives you, through Himself or through another, with great simplicity, allowing them to make on your soul the impression they must, through grace, and not through your efforts. (n. 1873)

Esteem Gives Rise to Love

ON OUR NEED TO KNOW JESUS CHRIST, AND THAT THE ATTRIBUTES OF GOD HELP A GREAT DEAL TO KNOW HIM IN PURE FAITH

My desires to see your soul completely united to Jesus Christ cause me to take the liberty to tell you my little thoughts and to instruct you again, through His light and His Spirit, about the need you have to know Jesus Christ and to live from His life. For a long time I have wished you to be all His and I pray that He draw you to this.

It seems to me that I perceive something, according to my poor capacity, of Jesus's adorable desires toward souls and the very great blessings He wants to bestow on yours if it makes itself faithful. Oh! How wretched is the creature to refuse so many mercies! How many of them have you rejected and even scorned! Oh! It is a great secret in the interior life to follow the line of Jesus Christ's holy design! May it please God that I can tell you what I have learned about this matter, and how we must dwell in Jesus Christ and live from Him. But alas! I pollute everything, I profane everything, and I am unworthy to speak. I beg Jesus Christ to speak for me and in me, and cause me to say what will please Him. I am loath to speak of something so noble and the angel of the Lord must do to me what He did to a prophet, which is to purify my lips and make me speak words of eternal life, since Jesus Christ contains in Himself the true and only life.[1] For outside of Him there is nothing but death. O holy and divine life, when will we live from your life?

My soul, being stirred with love and reverence for Jesus Christ, could not prevent itself from groaning under the wretched weight which continues to separate it from its All and removes that loving attention. And often my soul would cry out with St. Paul, "Who will deliver me from this body of death?"[2] Who will free me of my bonds and the turmoil of creatures? And who will give me a profound

---

1 Is 6:6–7; Jn 6:68; Jn 1:4.

2 Rom 7:24.

solitude which distances me from all things so as to unite myself to Jesus Christ and to be satiated with Jesus Christ? The blessed are filled and occupied with Him eternally, and that plenitude and perfect occupation constitutes their beatitude.

All the felicity of the saints consists in seeing Jesus Christ. O holy and adorable sight, I cannot see you without interruption! Alas! Who will give me the wings of a dove[3] to fly with one simple flight into Jesus Christ, and there make my dwelling, living separated from everything else? Oh! If we knew the happiness of a soul who is in Jesus Christ, could we live one moment without obtaining the same grace for ourselves? How long will we be immersed in its opposite, namely, impure creatures? O miserable creature, how much must I despise you, since you deprive me of the object of my heavenly beatitude! Is there no way to separate ourselves once and for all? With me, enter into pity for our extreme misery and our blindness, which make us so continually prefer the very unworthy creature to Jesus Christ.

Will we never see you in profound solitude in order to be filled with Jesus Christ, to no longer see anything except Jesus Christ, to no longer think of anything except Jesus Christ, and no longer love anything except Him? It seems to me that my soul would sigh for this unique happiness which would cause us to enjoy a foretaste of that divine life. But alas! I long for a grace of which I am unworthy. It is reserved for the pure and clean of heart and those who no longer defile themselves as I do constantly. But despite my impurities, Christian grace demands that I aspire to it through the most profound humility, and I am permitted to desire Jesus Christ as the life of my life. You have the same obligation—that is why we are joined together to desire Him, to seek Him, and to possess Him.

Let us begin with a high esteem for Jesus Christ. I do not intend to explain to you His grandeurs, I would demean and profane them in an extraordinary way. It is necessary for us to use faith to believe with humble reverence what we are not able to understand.

One of the most important points in the interior life is to regard God with an esteem worthy of Him, so that He may be above all things in our mind and heart. This esteem gives rise to love, and love

3 Ps 54:7 (Ps 55:6).

brings about the holy union. But however great love may be, never leave reverence, and always remember that He is All and you are nothing. And what kind of relation is there between the one and the other, between holiness and sin? Therefore, never forget your duty, whatever high grace you may receive from Our Lord. I like to see respect and love in a soul. These two must walk side by side. Never forget. This is a repetition, but it is necessary to make you better understand its importance.

This esteem and this respect for God keeps you at your duty and causes you to communicate with God in a way which honors His greatness; and in this disposition, you render homage to the divine incomprehensibility. You humble yourself and acknowledge your inadequacy. And this thought of the incomprehensible God limits all the mind's curiosities and subjects it to a simple and very respectful belief in what God is, without wanting to understand Him, since it is impossible. Only God can understand Himself; and this truth must give us joy. God is so holy, so divine, and so ineffable that He cannot be known essentially except by Himself. Oh! What consolation has a soul who loves God to see that He is incomprehensible! I know a soul who was for a long time occupied by this divine attribute, which caused in her a loving satisfaction to see her God to be incomprehensible. She was lost and engulfed in this divine incomprehensibility. And this saying, "God is incomprehensible," nourished her marvelously because in it her soul was fixed in a profound silence and reverence which folded down the wings of her mind, and she no longer desired to know anything except God as incomprehensible.

All the affirmative statements we use to ascend to the knowledge of the divine Essence distance us infinitely from the reality of what it is. Simple faith has much more efficacy, because making use of negations gives much more glory to God and produces more love and submission.

It is good for you to know something about the divine attributes and their operations in your soul, so that you may enter into them and not oppose them. The knowledge you should have of them does not come through speculation, but through a humble and loving attention to their effects in you.

The divine attributes serve to give us a greater knowledge of God; but faith, which raises the soul to a holy ignorance of all affirmatives, makes it enter into a simple and loving belief about what God is in Himself, surpassing all light and all knowledge. The soul believes in God in the truth of His essence, without giving to Him any form or image, unbounded as He is. This manner of knowing God is the most perfect. But while waiting for the soul to receive this grace, it must climb degree by degree, even until it finds the God of gods in Zion, says the Prophet.[4] Therefore, make use of the divine attributes and the understanding given to you, until that grace is infused in you.

In the pure and holy practice of the interior life, see how a soul is entirely clothed with divinity: it is by the intimate union and loving transformation the soul has with God, which, becoming entirely one with Him by the force of that divine love, is all filled with His holy and divine qualities. It is holy by a participation in the divine holiness; it is good by an emanation of the divine goodness; it is just by the divine justice; sweet by the divine sweetness; charitable by the divine charity; patient and gentle by the divine patience, and so on. All the graces and virtues which are manifest in it are effects caused by the divine attributes, so that a soul in this state sees itself adorned with the divine perfections. It feels strong by the strength of Jesus, unchangeable by His divine immutability, and thus with the rest. This causes the soul to not appropriate any of these gifts. It sees all in God and from God, and nothing in itself, or from itself, except sin; and this is what keeps it so perfectly united to God without leaving its nothingness. The soul sees its dependence, and how all graces and mercies are in Him.

This knowledge confirms our weakness and obliges us to live united to Jesus Christ for two reasons. The first, through the love we owe to Jesus Christ, knowing Him to be our unique principle and the goal of all things;[5] in brief, out of reverence for Him, since He alone is worthy of an eternal love. The second concerns our own interest, that is, our need for Jesus Christ, but a need so great that we could not do a single good action without His cooperation. At every moment, we must receive His mercies or perish. Our dependence on Him is

---

4 Ps 83:8 (Ps 84:6). 5 Rev 1:8.

so profound that we have life only in Him. He is the life of our life and the soul of our soul. Finally, He is everything to us, without Him we have nothing at all. Therefore, Jesus is our divine sufficiency, and we have nothing except in Him.[6] If this is a truth from Scripture, then let us remain submissive to it and admit that our own existence makes us experience our real need for Jesus.

With this insight and understanding, we must remain very closely united to Jesus Christ; we must do nothing except through Jesus Christ;[7] we must receive everything as His order, and be continually tending toward Jesus Christ.

Here is how: I feel my neediness, my weakness, and my poverty. I know by faith and even by my experience, and by the truth of the gospel, that I can do nothing without Jesus Christ. I am then pressed and required to give myself to Him in order to remain in Him, so that the adorable words He spoke may be effective in me. In St. John: "Whoever remains in Me and I in Him bears much fruit. Without Me you can do nothing."[8] It is Jesus Himself who speaks this truth. Thus, necessarily I must remain in Him, just as the branch remains in the vine, as He says Himself in St. John, because the one who does not remain in Him will be thrown out and put into the fire.[9]

O dreadful word! There is no salvation except in Jesus, neither fruit nor good works for eternal life, and the one who does not remain in Him will be rejected forever. Behold the double necessity I have of being and remaining in Jesus Christ. Since, if I withdraw from Him, not only do I do no good, but I necessarily perish. For the one who does not remain in Him will be cast out and put into the fire, that is, will be eternally rejected. This truth condemns me if do not give myself to Jesus. Hence, I am convinced by this that I must be His and work through Him, since I have no life except in Him.

The first thing I have to do is to come out of myself, that is, be renewed in my desire to go to Jesus. The eternal Father has given me to Jesus and Jesus has redeemed me. Therefore, I am His according to obligatory right. I am again His out of necessity. It remains for me to be so by choice on my part, and by love. This is the first step

6 2 Cor 3:5; Jn 1:3–4, 15:5.

7 Col 3:17.

8 Jn 15:5.

9 Jn 15:6.

I want to take, my first step in order to leave myself and enter into Jesus Christ. This is a return toward Jesus from the most intimate depth of my heart through an unreserved desire to give myself wholly to Him, to restore to Him the rights over my soul which I have usurped, like so many thefts. Respectfully, I must give an account of all the profane uses I have made of it, as much in my own regard as with regard to creatures.

In the third place,[10] I must present myself often to Jesus Christ so as to be bound very strictly to all His appurtenances, to all His rights and powers over me, desiring to leave myself completely so as to yield the place to Him, and that He may reign absolutely.

Fourth, I must give or leave myself to Jesus Christ in order to work through Him; and I must be so much hidden in Him that, as St. Paul says, only Jesus Christ can be seen in me.[11] Everything must be Jesus Christ, everything must manifest His fragrance and express His virtue, and my life must be nothing but a following of His life.

Now, in order to continue the life of Jesus, I must live like Him, love like Him, think like Him, speak like Him, I must act like Him, and have His way of looking at things. How? In all my works and actions I must envision Jesus Christ, I must view things as He did when He was on earth, how He spoke, and how He suffered. I must give myself to His Spirit to act by His power, in such a way that I put an end to myself and all my natural ability, so as to act through the Spirit and divine power of Jesus Christ. I leave myself in Him, in order to speak, act, and suffer through Him, and in this holy practice I remain, by desire and affection, reduced to nothing in Jesus, allowing Him to be in me all He must be, giving Him the honor and glory for everything, since all is done by Him. In this state, I guard myself from appropriating anything, from becoming vain about my actions, since it is Jesus Christ who does them in me. Faith teaches me this truth and my real dependence on the grace of Jesus Christ in everything confirms it. What a grace and mercy to be bound to Jesus Christ in this way!

---

10 It is not entirely clear what the second step is, since the text mentions a first and a third, but not a second. Perhaps it is the giving of an account of profane uses made of one's soul.

11 Col 3:3.

It is not enough, however, to know — by faith and by the splendor of the divine perfections — Jesus Christ in the bosom of the Father as His eternal Word,[12] through whom He made everything, and through whom He sanctifies us; rather, we must know Him in His life as a pilgrim on earth in order to conform ourselves to it. Our souls must be united to the soul of Jesus Christ, and all our actions must have a resemblance to His. That is why we must do what He says in the Gospel, "If a man would come after Me, he must renounce himself, carry his cross, and follow Me."[13] Hence, we cannot follow Jesus except in carrying our cross and renouncing ourselves. In another place He says, "The one who does not leave his father, his mother, his brothers, his sisters, his wife, her husband, and all that he possesses, is not worthy of Me."[14] He is not worthy to be His disciple.

One can follow Jesus only by the stripping away of all things. It is so necessary to lose everything that we must lose ourselves. A soul who keeps something back cannot perfectly find or experience Jesus Christ. He said to His apostle, "Follow Me," and that great miser left everything at this divine word.[15] Alas! How many times are we inwardly urged to leave all, to withdraw our affections from the earth in order to follow Jesus in His poor and suffering life — but our attachments are so strong that the divine Wisdom must send us catastrophes, losses, and accidents in various manners to take by force what we do not want to give up out of love.

It is not without reason that the more enlightened souls call earthly afflictions visits of Our Lord and effects of His holy love. If you were able to fathom the love that Jesus Christ has for souls and His infinite desire to sanctify them, you would take great delight in afflictions, in crosses, and in sufferings; since, within the truth of God Himself, these are inventions which His love uses to attract His elect and to require them, by the pressure of their sorrow, to return to Him and to separate themselves from creatures.

O cross, O affliction, O loss, O disaster, how beneficial you are! We must confess our blindness and acknowledge that we are very miserable and that sin corrupted us to have such horror of what

---

12 Jn 1:1–3.
13 Mt 16:24, Mk 8:34, Lk 9:23.
14 Cf. Lk 14:25–27, Mt 19:29.
15 Mt 4:19.

sanctifies us and makes us true disciples of Jesus Christ, and makes us worthy of Him. Let us begin to see our crosses with an eye more enlightened by the true light; let us no longer flee their approach, but instead go to meet them. Let us be united to Jesus Christ poor and suffering; and if we are not in affliction, let us humble ourselves as unworthy of it, and leave ourselves in Jesus's holy and adorable hand to be whatever pleases Him.

Therefore, we must know Jesus Christ in the life of suffering in which He merited for us the grace you have received in baptism and which you receive continually. It is through Jesus crucified that you are what you are. Be closely united to Him through desire, doing nothing without Him and doing everything through Him. When you must suffer something, desire that the grace of His sufferings make a use of yours which is worthy of Him. In humiliations, wish for His blessed humility to sanctify your abjection. Have a likeness to Jesus Christ in all that you do, say, and think; desire that all may be united to Jesus, and that it draw its power and perfection from Him.

Take up the devotion, which I saw practiced for a long time by a certain soul, of offering yourself often in spirit to Jesus, to receive into yourself His grace and virtue. I know how efficacious this virtue is, but it requires some patience and perseverance. I can say in fact that the soul who is faithful to this practice receives something which I cannot put into words, and I pray that you will experience it. I would like you to take a quarter of an hour in your day, at your leisure, in order to expose yourself to Jesus Christ according to your needs. Sometimes in order to invoke the power of Jesus Christ over your weaknesses. At other times, feeling your impurity and the sinful ground which is in you, expose yourself to His holiness, abandoning yourself to it in order to receive its effects interiorly, and likewise with the rest. In your ordinary practices, give yourself to His grace and His spirit; in your actions, desire that Jesus Christ perform them in you, and never do anything except by His direction and out of obedience to His guidance.

If you correctly understand what I mean and if you are faithful to it, you will see the good results it will produce in your soul, and, as if imperceptibly, you will find yourself filled with Jesus Christ. You will be always in His holy presence and always attentive to Him. You will see all things in Him and you will be bound to His command and good pleasure at every moment and in every event. You will give Jesus Christ a constant obedience; and by these means you will find yourself continually united to Him and all your words will have the fragrance of Jesus Christ[16] and your actions will be more purified. What must give you even more consolation is that your whole being, filled thus with Jesus Christ, will give glory to God in union with His Son. Your smallest action done in this spirit will be glorious to God and meritorious for your soul. You leave yourself, as if without thinking about it, and follow Jesus Christ.

Would to God that all Christian souls desired to experience what I am describing. I know it is a little trouble to gain these habits; but from the little that one labors at it, one gains marvelous profit. The souls who practice this can confirm the truths I am saying. (n. 2054)

SOME ATTRIBUTES OF GOD

God is through Himself
God is Spirit
God is simple
God is immortal
God is perfect
God is infinite
God is immense
God is immutable
God is eternal
God is one
God is invisible
God is ineffable
God is truth
God is faithful
God is good
God is beautiful
God is admirable
God is life

God is gentle
God is pure
God is holy
God is king
God is sublime
God is exalted
God is loveable
God is praiseworthy
God is incomparable
God is rich
God is lawgiver
God is blessed
God is creator
God is preserver
God is savior
God is glorifier
God is Trinity
God is wise

16 2 Cor 2:15.

God is sovereign
God is great
God is powerful
God is light
God is love
God is peaceful
God is merciful
God is just
God is judge
God is strong
God is generous
God is kind
God is beneficent
God is magnificent
God is patient
God is clement
God is sweet
God is independent
God is providence
God is happiness
God is righteous
God is meek
God is mild
God is vigilant
God is longsuffering
God is inaccessible
God is Father
God is understanding
God is Word
God is image[17]
God is will
God is gift
God is fruitful
God is all in all things

Here are some of the divine attributes. I pray Our Lord Jesus Christ that He will impress them on us; that is, that they may operate in us, each according to its holy and divine effect. A soul who is totally Jesus Christ's participates in them. The Holy Spirit is its divine Teacher. I pray that He will instruct us, and I confess before God my extreme ignorance. I beg Jesus Christ that He will supply for everything.

When He pleases, we will discuss these divine attributes. I would want to show you how our soul reveres and adores them through different dispositions and how they operate in the soul. This is a desire well beyond my ability, so I left myself to Our Lord Jesus Christ to speak of this through His light and His spirit.

If you knew the secret of the ways of God in souls, you would not complain of your darkness, nor of any other disposition. Oh, the great mystery of being abandoned completely to Jesus Christ, completely to His Spirit, and completely to His guidance! My God, how unable I am to express to you what my soul understands! But it is necessary that everything remain in silence. (n. 341)

17 The Son is the image of the Father. Col 1:15, 2 Cor 4:4.

Christian Perfection

THE WHOLE OF CHRISTIAN PERFECTION consists in real attention to Jesus Christ, and a constant adherence or submission to His good pleasure. These two points contain everything, and their faithful practice will lead you to the highest degree of perfection. Blessed is the soul that observes them.

The first point consists in seeing Jesus Christ in everything, in all events and in all our actions, in such way that this divine sight removes the sight of creatures, ourselves, and our interests from us, in order to see nothing except Jesus Christ. In a word, it is to be aware of God's continual presence.

The second consists in being really submissive to His holy will; in being so much subject to His good pleasure that we no longer have any return, at least voluntarily, by which we can withdraw from this respectful obedience.

If you dwell on these two points, you will know clearly that if you want to avail yourself of them, you will be completely surrounded by Jesus and completely filled with His love.

Have Jesus Christ printed and carved in the center of your soul. Have Him in all your soul's faculties. May your heart be able to think of and long for nothing except Jesus Christ. May your whole inclination be to please Him. Attach all your fortunes and your happiness to knowing and loving Jesus Christ.[1] May nothing earthly, however great it seems, prevail in you against the effective union you must have with Jesus Christ. May neither heaven, nor earth, nor hell, ever be able to separate you from Him.[2]

How long will we be insensible to Jesus Christ? Will we always have eyes and ears closed so as to neither see nor hear His loving reprimands? Will we never thirst for His pure love? Will we always be drinking from the impure waters of created things? Let us put enjoyment aside, my dearest daughter, let us go, that I may make

---

1 Jn 17:3. 2 Rom 8:35–39.

you my companion, let us go to Jesus Christ to drink the waters of His divine graces,[3] desiring to be intoxicated with them, and may we never be able to find any relish in creatures.

O Jesus, all powerful and all love, produce in us these two effects of mercy: attract us by Your omnipotence and transform us into Yourself through Your love.

O love, O love divine, will you not burn in us, will you not consume everything in us that is contrary to you and opposed to the holiness of your operations?

O life that is not animated by love, how can you be called life? You are a hideous and most terrible death.

O pure and holy love of Jesus Christ, do not allow a single moment of my life to be spent without love; make me die and cast me into hell a thousand times rather than not love Jesus Christ!

Oh what a frightful hell[4] a soul suffers who is deprived of divine love! Its pain is incomprehensible, I compare it to that of the damned. Alas! What should be my pain, then, seeing that I spent so many years without love! Alas! I should say: which I spent in the sins of my past life.

O abyss of mercy which sustains me, what return can I make to an infinite goodness like Yours? All that You desire of me is that I remain immersed in the center of my nothingness where, ceasing to be, I confess and proclaim in silence that You are, O my God, the One who is, and the only One worthy of being eternally. Amen. (n. 2826)

HOW ONE MUST OFFER ONESELF IN THE CAPACITY OF A VICTIM[5]

My dear daughter, tomorrow you will be in the state that Our Lord will find it good to place you. I am of the opinion that you have abandoned yourself most sincerely and completely to His mercies and to His heavenly Spirit's guidance, without making choice or election in your mind about any particular disposition, except for the one from which you ought never to depart, namely, to give yourself to

3 Jn 4:13–14, 7:37; Rev 22:17.

4 *Imitation of Christ*, II.8.2.

5 It seems that this letter was addressed to the Countess before she made her vows of obedience and of being a victim (as mentioned in other letters, such as n. 1435, p. 39).

God. Entrust yourself to His goodness. I assure you that He will do His work and be glorified in you after He will have destroyed and reduced to nothing all that is opposed to the holiness He wants to establish in you. If in this precious act you leave yourself in a state of death, be content that it strips you of the life you have always led in yourself and in your senses.

Tomorrow must be the day of your true and genuine sacrifice, the day that you are made, with Jesus, the victim of His Father; the day that you allow yourself to be bound by the holy vows and promises of your baptism; the day that you let yourself be led and guided by the holy Spirit of Jesus into the path of pure mortification and renunciation of yourself, the "narrow path" which the Gospel tells us "leads to life."[6]

You must let yourself be slaughtered: this means you must give your consent to die to everything in you which is contrary to God, and allow the means of the most wise and adorable Providence, through its secret workings, to make you die to yourself, to your supports, and to the hidden pursuits of your pride. You must be consumed by the fire of Jesus's pure and divine love. However, the fire burns the victim only after these other effects have preceded it, to show us that the sacred fire of divine charity is lit in the heart only after all the impurities of ourselves, which are in us, are slaughtered and destroyed. Picture yourself as this victim condemned to death in order to receive a new life in Jesus.

Give your own dispositions few backward glances, but give yourself very much to Jesus to be clothed with His Spirit and with His holy dispositions. Ask Him humbly and fervently to perform this action in you Himself; that He may be your virtue, your strength, and your grace to accomplish it as He desires; that he may grant you the grace of taking up a new kingship and sovereignty over you; that from this moment you surrender yourself entirely to Him, with regret at having spent your past years with so much ignorance and impurity.

The most important disposition you must have, and which God does not deny you, is nothingness. Withdraw into your nothingness in the presence of the Holy Trinity, and, in the deepest humility you can enter into, abandon yourself to the Trinity's holy operations in

---

6 Mt 7:14.

your soul, and believe that He will bring about a renewal in you, even though you do not perceive it; and it is good that your senses have no part in this, at least voluntarily.

Live in a spirit of death since you are a victim. Beware of looking for life in your senses and yourself. You must be reduced to nothing in yourself in order to live in Jesus. Remain in peace and tranquility of mind. Do not forget the reverence you must have for His divine presence, for the movements of His grace, for His orders, and the submission of mind to submit to them and fulfill them, although it costs you. Do not part company with discretion, you know what I told you about this. (n. 3146)

INTERIOR INSPIRATIONS TO OFFER ONESELF AS THE SLAVE OF JESUS CHRIST

I received your letter yesterday, my dearest daughter, with a very great consolation, and I observe how Our Lord takes up a new authority in your soul and seems to keep it more intimately united to Himself. Oh! What grace! I entreat you, my daughter, to esteem it as you must, and truly cherish this holy captivity which Our Lord causes you to enter. Oh! Blessed slavery! Do not retreat from it; allow yourself to be bound and tied down with the chains of pure love, and listen to the divine lessons of our adorable Master.

Do not be troubled about your actions. The reproaches given to you interiorly are loving reproaches. God is jealous for your soul; He wants it to be all His, but all pure and without any voluntary blemish. Allow Him, then, to act in you to purify it and to make it worthy of Him.

I have many things to tell you about your letter, it would take too long to write them to you. I will only say that when Our Lord grants you any mercy, I have a thousand times more joy in it than if it were given to me. And I feel that in truth I love you for your salvation: first, that God may be glorified in you, and then, for your sanctification. Your soul is dearer to me than my own.

Let us be God's, my dear daughter, so that you help me to be converted, and so that we can both glorify God eternally. I am in Him all yours. (n. 1374)

ABOUT THE QUALITIES OF A SLAVE AND THE DISPOSITIONS WE MUST HAVE TO BE ONE FOR JESUS CHRIST

My very dear daughter, may Jesus alone be everything for you.

I was a little vexed that I could not write a response to you. I had the inclination and the will, but Providence did not give me the time for it. I am taking the opportunity to write you a word about the blessed slavery that you have had the honor to bear.

Oh! How holy this is and how noble this title in the sight of God! Jesus Christ had it first. Holy Scripture teaches us that He made Himself a slave for His people.[7] The holy Virgin was one out of love and reverence for God's commands concerning her.[8] And we have a great number of stories which show us how many saints, both of the Old and the New Testament, bore that title with reverence.

As for you, my daughter, you bear it, or should bear it, in a particular way, not with constraint but from love, inasmuch as it is not fear or the sight of divine justice which holds you captive; rather a stroke of pure mercy and love, which forces you, with a sweet and loving violence, to be captive beneath the yoke of God's holy law, which is all holy and all love; and where only those who allow themselves to be led by pure love have entry into this loveable slavery and servitude.

It is in this holy captivity that the soul enjoys in reality a complete freedom, but so sweet and so pleasant that at every moment it reveres and adores the bonds which have placed it in that blessed captivity. The soul cannot esteem its good fortune highly enough.

Alas! If one regards oneself as honored to be the servant of the great ones of the earth, what an honor and privilege to serve Jesus Christ! There is no greatness on earth which compares to it. Scripture says that the servants of God are kings[9] and this is most certain. "To serve God is to reign." And in fact the one who is entirely subject to God is above all things. He reigns above creatures, himself, and his passions. In short, he possesses a supreme happiness.

But first, before telling you about the slave's qualities, you must know that there is a great difference between the slave of Jesus and the slave of creatures. The first is glorious, holy, and free. The second is shameful, imprisoning, and grievous, plunging the soul into

---

7 Phil 2:7; cf. Mt 12:18, Is 42:1. 8 Lk 1:38. 9 Rev 5:10.

an endless number of very great imperfections. Let us leave behind that miserable slavery to creatures so as to lovingly make ourselves slaves of Jesus Christ.

The first quality is loving fear and respect.

The second is an obedience and submission so complete that it finds no objection which can dispense from it.[10]

The third is that the slave is so ready to do the will of her Master that at every hour, at every moment, she is ready and willing to carry out His orders in any way He pleases.

The fourth is that the slave considers herself as so humble and so subject that she does not pay attention to herself in any way. She can have no other interests than those of her Master.

The fifth is that she lives only to belong to her Lord and Master. And Jesus's slave regards herself as so honored to be necessarily in this subjugation that she desires that every moment of her life be sacrificed in this blessed slavery. The slave no longer thinks about her life, she is not her own, but belongs to the one to whom she is subject in the state of slavery.

The slave has no will of her own, at every hour she sacrifices herself and obeys.

The slave is continually bound to the orders of her Master.

The slave has nothing at all which is hers, everything that she is belongs to her Lord.

The slave works and rests as it pleases her Master to ordain for her. She can no longer desire anything but pleasing Him in everything and she lives only to glorify Him.

The slave can never have a place in the esteem of men or in their affections. She wills and desires that her Master reign everywhere, that He be glorious and loved by all and in all. The slave does not have a word, a thought, or a movement in her power. The slave must not have any inclination, preference, choice, or election about anything.

Here, my dearest daughter, is one part of the qualities and dispositions of a slave. It remains to tell you that fidelity is the most

10 In religious life, to seek a dispensation is to seek permission to not do something which is required by the rule of the order; e.g., to be dispensed from fasting. Mother Mectilde speaks of an obedience so absolute that there can be no exceptions to it.

important one; but a fidelity so constant that it does not cease for a moment: a fidelity not from mercenary fear, but from a loving respect which keeps her in continual attention, always ready to obey God.

I pray Jesus Christ to give you some share in His holy dispositions and those of His most holy Mother. Say often with the intention of participating in it, "*Ecce Ancilla Domini.*" Behold the very humble slave of the Lord. May it be done unto me according to His holy and divine word, that is, according to His good pleasure. (n. 692)

YES, *M.N.*, LET US BEGIN WITH THE SIGN OF THE CROSS, since it is through it that we have the strength and virtue to die to ourselves; and Our Lord says that if we want to follow Him, we must take up our cross.

Now in order to follow Jesus Christ, we must leave earth and the abode of ourselves. We must leave the region of the senses. But you must remove the shoes of earthly affections, because the ground on which you walk is holy.[11] Be barefoot and bareheaded, like our divine Master—you understand what this means—and let us walk generously, cross in hand, with an invincible patience.

And do not be disturbed at seeing the attacks of your mind. All the battles in which it will engage you will be useful to your soul and glorious to God. Right now, you cannot take it completely captive, but Our Lord will do so one day. For this, you must await that blessed day which will deliver you from the tyranny of yourself, which is the most cruel and unfortunate imprisonment you can ever experience. (n. 2435)

YES, MY DEAREST DAUGHTER, SINCE OUR LORD HONORS you with the office of Mary, moderate that of Martha a little, so that you may be attentive to Jesus Christ. That is your primary concern, it is the "one thing needful"[12] which Our Lord praises so highly in His faithful lover, and which He wants to establish in you. Do not be so miserable as to refuse Him. (n. 2443)

---

11 Ex 3:5. 12 Lk 10:41–42.

Pure Love

THE NATURE OF PURE LOVE AND ITS EFFECTS

I find myself in a frame of mind to answer you very fully about this phrase "pure love," what it is and how it operates. This is an enterprise which surpasses my ability. But I do not intend to speak to you about it like those great souls, but only as I am able, according to my stupidity and my little light, not being worthy to speak to you about this pure love, for it needs the ability of the seraphim and their intelligence. I confess my extreme ignorance and I acknowledge that it is necessary to have experienced the effects of pure love to speak about it effectively. I can indeed say with the prophet, "I am only a child; I cannot speak."[1] The Holy Spirit must be the one who teaches you this divine lesson. It is only He who can really teach you. All that I can say to you about it will diminish its excellence.

But since I must speak without artifice, I will tell you then that the pure love of God is Himself. "*Deus caritas est.*" God is charity and the one who remains in charity remains in God.[2] Yes, these are the words of St. John, which you cannot doubt.

A soul in charity, this is a soul dwelling in love. This is a soul completely filled with God, completely occupied with God, completely zealous for the interests of God's glory; who can no longer do or suffer anything except for Him alone; who no longer considers itself or creatures; and in its operations, no longer has any inclination or desire except to please God. Such a soul is not concerned about receiving any reward, not concerned if it will be more perfect, if its work is meritorious, if it will have more grace or peace of mind. Its sole and unique motive is to please God, without thinking about the interests of self-love. The soul works so much out of reverence and love for God alone that it cannot consider anything but His good pleasure. She does not consider whether she is pleased, because she

---

1 Jer 1:6. 2 1 Jn 4:16.

does not act for herself, but only for her uniquely adorable Jesus Christ. Every sort of suffering and trouble is agreeable to her, provided that her divine Master is content. In sum, God, God entirely alone, without any admixture of our interests or of creatures.

Pure love does know what it is to be selfish, or to regard one's self. It cannot bear the slightest taint of vanity or creatures. It does everything for God. It gives everything to God without ever appropriating anything to itself. Its tendency is to advance the reign of God, to glorify Him in everything, without troubling about itself.

Oh! How powerful is the pure love of God and how great are the fruits it produces in the soul which it controls and in which it finds no resistance to its operation! What did it do in St. Mary Magdalene? What did it do in the seraphic Catherine of Genoa? And what did it do in all the saints? Oh! How admirable it is! And what will it not do in us if it has the freedom to operate? Let us give ourselves often to its power so that it destroys our resistance.

Oh! If you understood the life of souls penetrated and animated by pure love, you would be in great wonder. But we are not yet in a state where we have the ability to comprehend it. Do you not know that our present condition is to know and taste our nothingness and the depths of our misery in order to establish us in a profound humility? Let us revere those loving souls, but let us wait for the moment when divine mercy will draw us out of our impurities, after we have known well and experienced the stench and bitterness.

Pure love is beautiful and entirely filled with delights, but we are still too impure to possess it; it could not remain one moment in us. It makes its refuge in souls who are completely reduced to nothing, and until you are, patiently endure seeing yourself in this hard and cruel privation. You must understand that you are not worthy to possess it; and to become worthy of it, you must be in the abyss of humiliation. For as long as pride reigns in you, pure love cannot dwell in you.

Let yourself be destroyed, humbled, and consumed in the center of your nothingness, and after that you will see pure love take up its rest in you as on its bed of repose. But know that pure love cannot permit the slightest impurity, the least self-interest, vanity, and self-satisfaction. It is kind in its possession [of the soul]; it is very rigorous in its operation. It is a monarch so powerful that it subdues everything under its power, and does not leave a soul at rest unless it has effected a complete overthrow. It is without pity and without mercy: it shatters everything, it destroys everything. It goes even further, for it consumes everything. It cannot bear the slightest resistance. It has the most powerful weapons, and it comes to make martyrs. In sum, it is a great conqueror. It desires to subject souls to Jesus Christ, wresting them from the tyranny in which sin has held them so long.

The souls who hope for the reign of pure love, hope at the same time (without knowing it) for a terrible war which must reduce them to nothing. There are many who desire pure love, but there are almost none who desire to endure its assaults, its blows, its destruction, and its upheavals. Whoever speaks about pure love without understanding its effects believes that it is nothing but delight and sweetness. But a soul which possesses it knows very well, by experience, that there is no making a truce with pure love. Everything must be surrendered to it and it slays everything which has life in us in order to give us life in itself.

Pure love is never without suffering: the cross, sorrow, and contempt are its food. With these it is fed in souls. And if you want to keep it with you, you must have something with which to feed it. Lay in a store of crosses and sufferings, otherwise you will not keep it long. The cross maintains pure love, and pure love sustains the cross. They seem inseparable, and when the soul does not feel its cross, it suffers from not suffering.

Oh! How far we still are from having pure love in us! Nevertheless, we have some reason for consolation, because it has already sent its quartermasters[3] to prepare its dwelling. I am certain it desires to be billeted there. But it must clean it and put it in order. And that is what it is doing with you right now. Therefore, allow yourself to be purified. And if you tell me that you cannot see this, I answer that your eyes are too impure to see it and that God does not desire feelings from you but pure faith. This is why you must exercise it. I have

---

3 Quartermaster: a low-ranking officer sent in advance to see to lodgings and food for an important personage on campaign. A symbol for graces already given to prepare the soul as a dwelling for Jesus Christ.

been preaching this lesson to you for a long time, but so accustomed is your mind to reasoning, seeing, and feeling, that this word "faith" is so new to it that it cannot be subjected to it. Nevertheless, this is your path, and if you do not walk in it, you will not taste God and you will never adore Him in spirit and in truth.[4]

Enter, then, into the practice of faith. Possibly, however, you will ask me, "What is faith?," so that you can exercise it better and your mind can hold to its practices. Faith is a gift of God, which you have received in baptism, not to allow it to disappear, as you and almost all Christians do, but rather to make use of it. Faith is a firm and sincere belief in God and in the truths He has revealed to His Church.

One calls faith a dark light. Why? Because it is not sight, but belief. Thus it is a simple belief which assures the mind and makes it live in the truths that it is made to understand, without seeing or feeling, and without any other support than this simple faith which strips you of all images, and all reasonings, and which keeps you in the truth essentially. (n. 1014)

CONTINUATION OF THE SAME SUBJECT, AND THAT THERE ARE THREE KINDS OF DEATHS DUE TO LOVE

I say many things to you in my deep silence, and my soul cries very loudly in the ears of yours: Love, love, love!

Oh! The one who could live solely from pure love and make a nothing of all the rest, I would consider happy! My God, must it be that our lives are spent on something other than Jesus Christ's divine love? Will the fire that He came to bring to earth never burn?[5] Oh, if it could make us die, that would be a most glorious death for us. But alas! Such a death is for the righteous and for the Lord's favorites. My death must be the death of a sinner who is buried and engulfed in the nothingness to which sin has reduced her. I greatly desire to die such a death in homage to the divine holiness. It is just that I should die with a sense of sin, since all my life I have been a sinner. Let us die in the way it will please Jesus Christ, but if possible let us die of love. It is commonly said that as one lives, so one dies. Therefore, if we live from love, we will die from love.

---

4 Jn 4:23. 5 Lk 12:49.

There are three kinds of death from love, according to the stages of the soul. The first death is to die for love, the second to die in love, and the third is to die of love for love.

All Christian souls try to die for love, raising their intentions at least to spending their life for love of Our Lord. One can indeed die *for* love, without dying *of* love. You can die for love just as you carry out an action for love. This intention is very good, but it is still better to die in love and of love.

To die in love, this is to die in the practice of pure love; and to die of love is that adorable love which caused the death of Jesus and His most holy Mother, but in a way which is beyond words and beyond our minds' comprehension. This is the love which carried away the life of many saints about whose lives we read. Will it be this same love which grants us the death that will make us enter into life?

"I adjure you, O daughters of Jerusalem, if you find the beloved of our hearts,"[6] that you tell Him that we languish with love, that we are dying of not dying, or rather, that we mourn that this pure and heavenly love of Jesus does not consume us. Weep for my soul's hardness and the infidelities that it commits every day against the Saint of saints[7] and the uniquely adorable one. Sigh, do penance for my sins, beg mercy from Jesus Christ, and pray Him that His blood may not be profaned in me; but that His grace and love repair them, consuming me with that same love.

We are created for love. Therefore, let us love Our Lord Jesus Christ without ceasing. Let us love always, living and breathing only in the purity of divine love. All that you do, do it in love. May your tendency be toward love, so that by love you may be perfectly united to and transformed into Jesus. Thus you must begin to live from pure love, that is, purely for God, without any return to your own interests. Lose yourself, forget yourself, in order to be filled with God alone.

If only once you could truly abandon yourself to God, you would know truly what it is to act in the spirit of prayer. Oh! How wise you will be! But until you have received that grace from our divine Master, I will tell you, according to the light He gives me, what it is to be in continual prayer.

---

6 Cant 5:8.

7 *Saint de saints*, the Holy [One] of the holy ones.

A soul who remains in constant attention to God present is in a state of prayer; and to act in this spirit is to be more in God than in the action. You lend yourself to the action, but you do not give yourself to it.

Three things converge to perform your act in a spirit of prayer. The first is attention to God. The second is love and respect for Him, doing it only for Him and out of submission to His holy will. The third is detachment of spirit, not becoming the owner of your action, having no attachment to it, ready at any moment to be separated from it and leave it if God's order and obedience indicate something else to you.

After your action is done, you must not think about it. If you have committed some infidelity in it, you must humble yourself, knowing that you are not capable of anything else. You must bear your miseries in patience, and always do what you are obliged to do according to your grace and your condition. When you have a moment of free time, you must use it to recollect your spirit; for in that holy solitude it draws the strength from grace to be faithful in important circumstances.

(n. 1712)

TO ALLOW PURE LOVE TO REIGN, WE MUST BE ABANDONED IN EVERY KIND OF STATE AND DISPOSITION

My dear daughter, you are good; endure all that God sends you: shadows, ignorance, and your weaknesses. Everything is good since God gives it: He Himself will bring about in you the practices He expects from you. When I say that you must abandon yourself, I mean to say to you: remain in your misery and weakness, and wait in confidence till Our Lord delivers you from it. You must indeed suffer in another way: you have only begun.

Do not be disheartened. I assure you that Our Lord will be your strength and that He will not forsake you. And when you no longer know what you must do, say, "My God, I am a beast.[8] I have neither grace nor understanding. Do for me and in me all that will please You." Say this in your heart or with your mouth (it is not important), and then leave yourself in helplessness and in the cross, enduring the reproaches of your conscience concerning the impurity

8 Ps 72:23 (73:22).

of your actions, both for the past and for the present; and wait for the time that you will be clothed with power from on high[9] to act more purely and with more sanctity. Our Lord ordered His disciples after His ascension to withdraw, to rest, and to wait till they were clothed with His Holy Spirit. Do the same, I pray you, and leave yourself entirely to Our Lord, and trust in His goodness.

Your present state will not be of long duration; after sorrow comes joy. Desire nothing, seek nothing, love nothing except God's good pleasure in all things, being content with every condition, with every disposition, in short, with everything that divine Providence will cause you to experience. Be the victim devoured and consumed, and rejoice at being in shadows, helplessness, captivity, and so on: all of that is good and produces good results if you continue to be abandoned. You do not see what God is doing in you; you feel your pain and your nature's groaning, but you do not see that God purifies it in destroying its satisfactions. Oh! If your soul had enough courage to leave itself as the prey of pure love, what glorious results there would be! But because we must suffer and it overthrows our self-love in order to establish His divine empire, this pulls us from our abandonment and deprives us of such a holy possession.

The soul's entire felicity and happiness is to love God and this is the occupation of the blessed in glory. Why do we not begin as early as this world, since we can love God and He commands it? Let us love as God desires and as He wants to be loved by us. But to love as is necessary is to love Him in every way, and to find good everything that He does; it is to approve and consent to all His hidden and manifest designs concerning us, to submit our whole will to His, to prefer nothing to His love,[10] to consider Him in all things, to receive everything immediately from His holy hand. It is to agree to our losses, our humiliations, and our crosses. In a word, it is to be made, by means of this same love, entirely one with Him, through the complete loss of ourselves.

My God, how happy is a soul who can be plunged irrevocably in the love of God's good pleasure! Oh! How abominable is the corruption we have contracted through sin, since it renders us so malignant

---

9 Lk 24:49. 10 RB 4:72.

that everything grace desires to produce, we destroy. Truly, it is good that we are permitted to lament with St. Paul and say those same words, "Who will deliver me from this body of sin?"[11] How sorrowful life is for a soul pierced by this truth, for one who feels its weight! But what? It is necessary to live and die, all together. We must endure our impurities in view of the divine and adorable sanctity of Jesus. It is necessary to die to death itself and to live in submission to God's good pleasure.

We don't have to be anything to ourselves, and as long as God is pleased it is enough. You please Him when you abide in His holy presence, having the spirit of a victim which accepts life and death without any other choice than the divine will. It is there that you are commanded to remain. Do not think much about your present condition; have patience, God will do His work; and when He has irretrievably brought you to nothingness, He will be pleased with that. If your suffering causes you too much depression, you are allowed to have a little diversion, but do not throw yourself too much into creatures.

I ask you to observe one thing and to write us about it if you can: what is the tendency of your soul at present? Can it take some pleasure in creatures? Can it withdraw from its sorrow? Does this sorrow cause secret anxiety, does it trouble the mind? Does this suffering cause scruples about enjoying yourself and doing the duties required of you? Where do you have trouble doing them? Is your mind dull or does it reproach you? (n. 3057)

YOU LEFT ME YESTERDAY WITH YOUR MIND OCCUPIED by your sorrow, my dearest daughter, and I presented myself to Our Lord in order to offer it to Him and ask for light about your condition. I have, it seems to me, always more faith in the grace He desires to grant you of making you all His, and, for this reason, of causing you to leave yourself and creatures totally. There is no longer a way to resist this. It is necessary, at this time, that the pure love of Jesus Christ prevail. It is necessary to surrender to His sweet violence and give up altogether what hinders you from being His.

---

11 Rom 7:24. St. Paul says "body of death," but his argument includes Mother Mectilde's meaning.

What mercy you receive, and what have you done to God, to be chosen, attracted, pierced, and illumined with divine truths, to the exclusion of an endless number of others who remain in darkness and ignorance for their whole lives? Oh! How deep are the judgments of God and how incomprehensible are His ways![12] You have an infinite obligation to be God's. Begin, then, to be faithful to Him. May today be the day that you will to die to everything in order to have life in God alone. Blessed is the soul that gives itself, or to put it better, surrenders itself, totally to God!

Love God, adore God, be God's, glorify God: you can do all this through the loss of yourself. A soul who lives only for God and from God lives a heavenly life. It has no pleasure in or attachment to the things of earth. Creatures are displeasing to it, for its only delight is in the one it loves. Leave all things for love of Jesus Christ. Lay aside all desires, while awaiting the time that you can leave them in fact. Free yourself from everything that can pollute you. Do not possess things except out of pure submission to God's command which has tied you to your state in life. But beware of appropriating them: you must give an account of them. All goods belong to God like everything else and you should not keep them except as something borrowed, always ready to return them to your divine Master, who loaned them to you to make some use of them worthy of His glory, and to give you the means to merit something for eternity.

Therefore, be poor in the midst of your wealth. Imitate the great emperor Theodosius who, under the royal purple and the diadem, was poorer than the hermits of the deserts. Poverty does not consist in possessing nothing outwardly, but in being detached inwardly. The one and the other are excellent. But the exterior poverty which one vows in monasteries is only one means of arriving at the poverty of spirit which is so highly esteemed by Our Lord in the Gospel,[13] and at complete detachment of heart so as to put into practice those divine words which He still utters: "If we do not renounce all that we possess and ourselves, we cannot be His disciples."[14]

Alas! If we are not the disciples of Jesus, whose will we be? There is no middle point, we must belong to God or to the devil. Our Lord

---

12 Rom 11:33.   13 Mt 5:3.   14 Cf. Mt 10:34–40.

says, "No one can serve two masters."[15] Is it not right that we serve Jesus, that we are all His, since we are redeemed at the price of His blood and His life, and He goes before us with so many blessings? It would require a frightfully ungrateful heart to deny this; do not be this way. Make yourself worthy of the graces that God prepares for you by abandoning yourself, humbling yourself, and detaching yourself from everything, so that your heart is always in a state to be raised to God above all things.

Let nothing keep your soul or affection captive on the earth, for fear of being deprived of the many mercies God makes you experience. Always be at liberty to hear God in the depth of your interior and to follow Him. Do not be like those in the Gospel who refused to go to the banquet because of concerns about mud and earth.[16] Our fortune is in eternity: that is where all our crosses will be destroyed and covered with glory. But in this world it is necessary to suffer.

Our Lord says, "If someone wants to come after Me, let him renounce himself, take up his cross and follow Me."[17] Here is what we have to do on earth: renounce ourselves and be on the cross. Souls who are truly illumined by the light of grace fix all their happiness on the cross and regard it as a kind of punishment when they are not immersed in sufferings. This is because pure love transforms them into the beloved and makes them similar, by conformity of state and disposition, to Jesus's holy soul on earth, which always loved poverty, sorrow, and contempt. Jesus's holy and adorable life on earth was never for a moment separated from these three virtues. And this is what truly Christian souls must love and they must have as much likeness to Him as possible. This is what we promised in our baptism; and if we made profession of Jesus Christ, did we not make profession of His holy life? Yes, it is our obligation to live the life of Jesus, to suffer with Jesus, to be poor with Jesus, and to be despised and rejected with Jesus. In short, to die on the cross with Jesus and live from His resurrected life, which means, to be detached and separated from the earth.

Let us give ourselves to His grace to have a share in the holiness of His life, and abandon ourselves to the power of His love to yield

---

15 Lk 16:13, Mt 6:1–4.

16 Mt 22:2–10, Lk 14:15–24.

17 Mt 16:24, Mk 8:24, Lk 9:23.

its effects. What things I would have to say to you about so holy and so ineffable a subject! But I must conclude by leaving you entirely to Jesus Christ, for I fear it would take too long. Ask God, I entreat you, if He will permit you, for me to have the grace to be what He desires me to be. We must ask only for this.

Everything we desire without perfect indifference and which we undertake from our own will is a pursuit of self and self-love.

Jesus Christ died on the cross to draw man to Himself[18] and to lose him, by continual and loving plunging, in the infinite abyss of His love.

Unfortunate is the one who, having the ability to love God with all his powers and with an ever-perfectible love, only loves Him with the love common to all creatures.

He who has a perfect love of God never asks Him for anything but what will be for His greatest glory and in perfect conformity to the divine will.

The highest and worst of human miseries is not to know God, not to feel Him, not to desire Him, and not to taste Him.

One knows the love of God and its consequences when the soul which is moved by it is deeply humble and truly despised.

The place, the habit, the profession, the vows, the rules, and the statutes do not sanctify the monk, but outstanding charity, love, and profound humility. All the rest are only excellent means ordered to this.

Reasoning in order to love God is to sin against pure love.

(n. 3098)

---

18 Jn 12:32.

Persevering in Prayer

SCHEDULE IN THE FORM OF A JOURNAL ABOUT THE DAY'S MOST IMPORTANT ACTIVITIES

I have a very great desire to satisfy the request you made to us to write for you a little schedule for your day. But the more I wait for the grace and light, the less I find it in my depths. In such a way that seeing myself pressed by your need, I abandon myself into the abyss of darkness that surrounds me, begging our divine Master to guide my pen according to His good pleasure and by His Holy Spirit to impress on my soul what He desires me to tell you for His glory.

Previously we gave you little daily schedules arranged by a very holy soul: I hope that you can someday make a good and holy use of them. While waiting for grace to purify and simplify your soul in order to make it capable of a rule more holy, we will prescribe only the most important actions of your day, leaving to the Holy Spirit the order that should be observed within it.

Get up every day at 6 AM, go to bed at 11 PM; if you retire later, get up at 6:30 AM.

As soon as you are awake, you will raise your mind to God, not only as one who is present in you, but as the immensity in which you come to rest.

If your mind is found to be distracted or dulled by illness or sleep, you will make an act of faith in the reality of God, and an act of adoration and complete abandonment of your being, surrendering yourself entirely to God, and continue what you have to do in this spirit.

If on waking you God goes before you by some inner attraction or feeling, you will follow it, allowing yourself to be carried sweetly and gently by the great mercy of Our Lord who has gone before you.

When going to your prayers, enter into your oratory as into the sanctuary where you should be in communication with God; or if you want, as into the place where your sacrifice must be accomplished. In this spirit, kneel in order to immolate and completely abandon yourself to the pure and holy Spirit of Jesus Christ.

After you have turned your hourglass, do not leave [prayer]; keep your body and senses captive; the first half-hour (at least) you will spend in the deepest and most reverent silence you can, becoming very attentive to God present, and leaving yourself entirely to the power of His grace and His love to act in you according to His most holy will.

Do not cling to the curiosity and activity of your senses. Do not move your clock, if it has not stopped. Do not be occupied with your mind's lack of mortification, which would like the hour to pass in order to leave its captivity. Bear in mind that you are there to be a victim, and a crucified victim. In a word, you are not there to enjoy some consolation, but to bring about your destruction.

You will surrender to all the states and various dispositions that Our Lord wills you to endure there, without ever complaining about His actions concerning you or permitting your self-love to oppose them.

The first thing you must do in your prayer is to make an act of faith, which requires you to believe in God. The second [act], which obliges you to adore Him. The third, to sink into your nothingness, regarding yourself as most unworthy to converse with God and to be in His holy presence for one moment. Remain in lowness, not raising yourself up with presumption.

Allow yourself to be led in the manner that will please Our Lord. Be very pliant to the touches of His Spirit and always yield to His cause against yourself. And when activity assails you, resist it by ignoring its attacks and by letting yourself die rather than be unfaithful.

You find many hours and time for creatures; it is most just that you find some for God, and that during the employment of the hour to be given to Him you be inaccessible except out of obedience to your *N*. . . . ,[1] or to business which cannot be put off. Be very faithful on this point.

In the second half-hour, if you are too tired, you may sit; but always in a posture of attention and respect, so that laxity does not rob you of the grace of your prayer.

After your hour of prayer, you will dress. But take care not to leave your prayer; you must preserve its spirit and act in everything

1 Probably, *husband*.

with an attitude of prayer. Thus, leaving your oratory, you will not leave your recollection. Since truth teaches you that you never leave God, why would you leave the attention, reverence, and submission you must have to the particular movements of His grace and to the designs which His holy Providence desires to fulfill regarding you?

Therefore, do all that you have to do or suffer in this spirit of recollection, taking care not to pour yourself too much into created things. Always distrust your mind which will not miss an opportunity to make endless assaults by its constant activity.

Be composed in all your actions. Do not be hasty, do not be eager or anxious about what may happen to you.

Mortify the natural inclinations of your mind, which may still have some preference and attachment to something. Do not excuse it for not having surrendered its weapons to you; enter into a holy renunciation of everything which can still give it some vain satisfaction.

Have no pity for the laments of your self-love. Be inexorable toward nature's complaints; there is no longer any mercy for it: it must die.

When you undertake any affair, see it always within the divine ordering of things, and see that He subjects you to these labors for His glory. Do them in conformity with His designs, and always in a spirit detached from all your contentments, interests, and satisfactions. If the action is repugnant to you, do it with great attention, patience, and submission, seeing in it more clearly the divine arrangement and His will.

Every day you will hear the holy Mass with love and reverence, and with great attention to this holy mystery and surrendering yourself to be sacrificed with Jesus in the host so as to be offered with Him solely for the Father's glory. I will not expand on this worthy subject. I think I have said something to you elsewhere and you are not ignorant about it.

When taking your meals, mortify yourself in something, at least in quality; and eat out of obedience to God who subjects you to this need to sustain the life which you must spend in His love. Eat a sufficient amount and indifferently, if you are not sick. And if your mind lowers itself toward sensible objects, you must raise it again gently to give it a little practice in abiding in God. In Him must it rest; and with respect to creatures, it must not touch or taste them except in passing and from sheer necessity.

In conversation with your neighbor, be free with a holy liberty, without being anxious. Speak when Christian charity obliges you to do so, but be sober in your words and actions. Love silence and its practice, as much as possible for you. Never say anything that you would not say before Our Lord. Let your words be gentle, humble, and charitable, manifesting the good fragrance of Jesus Christ.[2]

Sometime after dinner, you will take half an hour of your free time, if Providence gives you liberty, to renew yourself in attention and in love to God who is present. And entering into your oratory, you will prostrate yourself on the ground in a spirit of abandonment and the renewal of all the sacrifices you owe to the divine Majesty.

(n. 844)

INSTRUCTION SHOWING THE DIFFERENCE BETWEEN MEDITATION AND PRAYER

What is prayer? It is a raising of the mind to God and a tending toward divine union, or even a possession of this divine union for those more advanced. And we must not have any other goal than this, generally speaking. But souls have various personal dispositions. You must have three, which, however, you will not multiply. The first is the faith by which you believe and adore God in the truth of Himself, and this faith keeps you in reverence before His greatness. The second is an offering of yourself to the divine power, being stripped of all your concerns, and all the productions and pursuits of self-love. The third is a humble submission to all God's action concerning your soul, an abandonment to His good pleasure, and a loving acquiescence to His designs. With these three dispositions, you will make a quite excellent prayer.

Why do we go to prayer? Doubtless it is to fulfill our duties toward God: adoration, sacrifice, and love. In short, it is with the intention of giving ourselves absolutely to Jesus Christ. It is from our desire to be clothed with His Spirit, and to become one with Him. Now, in order to arrive at the goal of prayer, the soul must suffer very great

---

2 2 Cor 2:25.

and difficult sacrifices. It must be stripped of its habits and renounce many supports. In a word, it must be destroyed and entirely renewed. And this is the reason why many souls suffer in prayer — sometimes dryness, at other times repugnance, darkness, and a thousand other pains that we experience in it and which show us that in these sufferings God tears down our pride and establishes His reign secretly. But the soul must abandon itself to the suffering and resign itself humbly into Our Lord's hands to be the victim of His good pleasure.

I have told you in the past that we should do on earth what the blessed do in heaven. They behold God in pure contemplation and are consumed in His love. Through faith, we must have a continual gaze toward God and always tend toward His love. Now, perfect love does not consist in being moved in the senses; instead, it consists in a total conformity. Being perfected, this is what makes the continual union of love with God, like that of the blessed, a union we can preserve even in actions and in the bustle of our obligations, by doing all things out of love and submission to God.

There is a great difference between meditation and prayer. Meditation is a holy study in which one learns the Christian mysteries and truths; and prayer is savoring them, tasting them, and being filled with the grace they contain. The first sees and considers God's beauty or His greatness; the second adores Him, loves Him, and unites us to Him. The first is multiplied through many considerations, subjects, and reasoning; the other is purer, simpler, and more unifying with God. In the first, the human mind has something to be occupied with: the light, tastes, and reasonings feed the understanding — and often our self-love. In the other, we are immolated, and our operations are reduced to nothing, or at least purified and simplified. In the former, we depend on our labor; in the other, we receive the divine operations, being very simply exposed in a spirit of abandonment and loving acquiescence. In the first, it is the understanding that acts. In the second, it is God who leads. And if a soul has a tiny bit of courage to persevere in prayer, although full of every kind of misery, I am certain that Our Lord will help her and lead her into holy union. But it demands constancy, because the devil and nature are the enemies of prayer and do everything possible to lead the soul astray from it.

Be persevering, my daughter, you will not always suffer such difficult battles there. Take heart: it is for the interests of your divine Master Jesus Christ, and for the establishment of His reign in you. I pray Him to support you and to unite us perfectly to Himself for ever.

(n. 2613)

CONCERNING THE PRAYER OF PURE FAITH AND *ANÉANTISSEMENT*

In your prayer, I think it good that in the second half-hour of your prayer, you were allowing your mind to be occupied with truths you have learned. But be on guard against your mind's constant activity, which, being so prolific, will be occupied much more with itself than with the pure light of God. That is why you must distrust it and very peacefully observe if it is rushing in its thoughts, in its views and considerations. The Spirit of God is peaceful, and it is the sign of His Spirit when He causes us to perform our actions in peace. Visiting His disciples, Our Lord said to them, "*Pax vobis.*" This is the first effect of God's veritable presence in the soul: peace is established, and calm makes itself felt even in this ground of spirit.

There is a clear difference between our productions and those of grace. Those which come from us are always impure and cannot rise to God, since they have only our own interests as their object. That is why they are lights and operations produced from ourselves. Such things have neither power nor vigor to remain raised to God; and if the soul makes some small effort, it soon returns to itself, and consequently, is neither filled with God nor empty of itself. The operations of grace are of another kind: they come from God and return to God. They elevate the soul, detach it from itself and earthly things, making it capable of receiving God, that is, His reign; and the soul, being faithful to the workings of grace, makes wonderful progress in a short time, becoming fit for the mercies of God.

When you find yourself in helplessness and darkness, do not think that your time is wasted. God causes you to bear these dispositions in order to teach you little by little how to die. The human mind, being accustomed to act, suffers agonies when it finds itself in dryness and privation. And the blindness with which we consider holy things makes us think that we are not in God's favor. And imperceptibly, the soul hastens to pull itself from its pain and captivity, in order to procure the satisfaction of feeling something else.

It is a great infidelity for a soul in this state to try to leave it; we must let ourselves be reduced to nothing. This disposition [of dryness] happens for two reasons. First, it can come from God who tests us, in order to strip the soul of its own supports. Second, as a chastisement for our faults. And both of these are useful for our souls. That is why the soul must make a holy use of them. The first of these uses is by a consent to God's action concerning it, finding good that He makes use of it as He pleases. "*Bene omnia fecit.*"[3] The second, out of submission to His justice. And in both of these, the soul must always remain reduced to nothing, waiting in patience for God's good pleasure.

What is a soul that is dead or reduced to nothing? It is a soul without desire, without affection, without election, without choice, without wishes, without inclinations, without will,[4] without passions. In this state of *anéantissement*, the soul has become a pure capacity for God. What does that soul do, thus reduced to nothingness? It is clothed with Jesus Christ,[5] it is filled with Jesus Christ. It is Jesus Christ who animates it, acts in it, who thinks for it, who loves and desires for it, who chooses and wishes for it. The great apostle knew this from experience when he said, "*Vivo ego, jam non ego, vivit in me Christus.*"[6]

If you had tasted for one moment the blessed state of *anéantissement*, you would find that the interior life is very easy; all the trouble we experience in it comes solely from our resistance to the death of ourselves. I want you to have this spirit to rule your actions and to give God the glory that you owe Him. You know what I told you about this a few days ago in conversation and in writing.

Your difficulty at present is to know when you must carry out actions or when you must eliminate them. You must perform them

---

3 Mk 7:37. He hath done all things well.

4 RB 33: "Monks are allowed to have neither their bodies nor their wills in their own power."

5 Rom 13:14.

6 Gal 2:20. I live, now not I, it is Christ who lives in me.

when God's Spirit gives you the inspiration for them. As for those from your own mind, you must reduce them to nothing. You will know those that the Holy Spirit produces in you by the fruits they will produce, and they will always be effective in the ground of your soul: they will bring about the effects of detachment from self, union with God, dependence on Him, peace, and tranquility. "*Dum medium silentium*,"[7] in the midst of a profound silence, that is, a profound calm; God's Spirit speaks in silence. O adorable mystery!

Therefore, make acts of sacrifice, of abandonment, of patience and humility, but see to it that you do them according to the direction of God's Spirit. They should be brief and gentle and fill you with God, leaving yourself to the power of His grace to form them in you.

No matter how many acts you may do of yourself, I do not think they will cause you to make much progress. If all of our own actions are like a filthy rag before God, following what the Holy Spirit teaches us in Scripture,[8] judge what kind of glory they give to God and what happiness we can attain from them! Of all the operations which are in our soul's power, there is not one of them more useful or less opposed to God than holy humility, which the soul must never leave, however elevated it may be. We must never forget our nothingness.

During the day, you can make some acts when you have the prompting.[9] But when you find yourself recollected with God in love and adoration, do not leave this in order to make your acts. Do not leave God in order to look for the God you already have. Converse with God as long as His mercy is pleased to keep you occupied. In that pure and simple occupation, never leave God if He does not directly permit it by His particular order, or indirectly by the tasks of your state.

The acts which God's Spirit causes us to produce fill us with God; and those which we do by our spirit fill us with ourselves. It is not

---

7 Wisdom 18:14–15. *Dum medium silentium tenerent omnia, et nox in suo cursu medium iter haberet, omnipotens sermo tuus, Domine, de caelis a regalibus sedibus venit.* While all things were in quiet silence, and the night was in the midst of her course, Thy almighty Word, O Lord, came down from heaven from Thy royal throne (traditional Introit of the Mass for the Sunday in the Octave of Christmas).

8 Is 64:6.

9 "Acts" here would refer to formal vocal prayers such as acts of faith, hope, charity, contrition, adoration, self-offering, conformity to God's will, and the like.

necessary to make an act in order to consider your actions; all that is needed is a simple view of God, which will soon make you see and even feel the impurity that you commit in doing them.

The actions connected with your obligations—you have known for a long while that you must not neglect them. Those which belong to Christian propriety can be performed as needed; as for those which are useless, you must cut them back or regulate them. I do not even mention those which are bad, knowing quite well that you would not wish to do them.

It does not require a great deal of investigation to understand your obligations; the conscience in your soul teaches this and will not allow you to be mistaken if you are attentive and faithful to its movements. There is no need to make acts in order to discern these things, but simply [a need] to look at God and His pure love, which must cause your actions and order them. Yes, our whole life takes place in outward actions; but our soul remains inwardly and mystically reduced to nothing, allowing itself to be governed by God's Spirit; so that it is no longer active in its operations, but patient in what God works in it. The soul allows God to do in it what He pleases, what is His good pleasure and for His glory, not living for itself, but uniquely for Jesus Christ. (n. 312)

ON PRAYER MADE IN SIMPLICITY OF SPIRIT, ACCORDING TO THE OPINIONS OF A GENTLEMAN OF GENEVA[10]

My dearest sister in Jesus Christ: the more I progress, the more I understand clearly that Our Lord guides souls to the prayer of a very simple unity and unique simplicity in the presence of God, by a complete abandonment of themselves to His most holy will and by the care of His divine Providence. The blessed gentleman of Geneva[11] called prayer a simple giving of our whole selves to God, which he said was entirely holy and salutary, and that this comprises everything which could be desired for serving God.

---

10 This letter reproduces a text from St. Jane Frances de Chantal, with some variations. The text is found in *Réponses de notre très honorée et digne Mère, Jeanne Françoise Frémiot*, Paris, 1665, p. 508.

11 St. Francis de Sales.

Now, I know nevertheless this is a difficult battle for those whom God leads by the way of discourse and reasoning. And many souls have been troubled by this, saying they are idle and wasting time. However, without lacking in the respect I owe to such persons, I assure you, my dearest sister, that you must not lay aside your attraction [to God] for the sake of such reasoning. For the blessed bishop of Geneva, who brilliantly understood every kind of prayer, as you can see from his writings, always approved this one, and said, "While others eat diverse fare at the Savior's table, let us rest our souls and all our affections, through an utterly simple confidence, on His loving breast."

With such solid advice, we must remain steadfast and faithfully follow this way from the time we are drawn to it. For what is required is not bringing ourselves to it, but awaiting, with humility and patience, the hour that our divine Savior has ordained to introduce us to this happiness. For after all, to go to God and to arrive at Him, we must let ourselves be led by His Spirit. What He chooses is [always][12] the best for us.

Now there are various degrees in this manner of prayer, as in all the others. Some have this unique simplicity of repose in a more eminent degree than others and they receive various lights therein; but finally, all end up there, almost without knowing that they arrived; and it seems that God makes use of this single procedure to make them arrive at the end of the journey, [namely, perfection,] and there we find and receive all the light and strength we need for everything. This attraction becomes so proper to us that the souls which are pulled away from it seem to leave their center, losing freedom of spirit and entering into a certain constraint and knotting, which take away their peace and impede them considerably on their way. I have only too much experience of this insight [truth].

Walk, then, in this heavenly path henceforth with a very humble assurance and do not bring to it any method or activity except to follow very simply and faithfully the attraction of God, being content with the lot that is given you, without desiring anything further. Those who are led by this path are obliged to a great purity of heart, lowliness, submission, and total dependence on God. They must greatly simplify their mind in everything, cutting off all reflections

12 Brackets indicate Mother Mectilde's additions.

about the past, the present, and the future; and in place of considering what they are doing and will do, they must regard God, forgetting themselves in everything as much as possible for them, by a continual remembrance of God, uniting their spirit to His goodness in everything that happens to them moment by moment; and this [must be done] simply [without any strain].

It often happens that souls who are on this path are plagued with many distractions and they remain without any sensible support, Our Lord withdrawing the feelings of His sweet presence and every kind of aid and inner light; so much so that they remain in complete helplessness and feeling nothing, although it is sometimes less so. This surprises souls who have not yet experienced it. But they must remain steadfast and rest in God above all thoughts and feelings, and enduring, receiving, and cherishing equally all the ways and workings that it will please God to effect in them; being sacrificed and surrendered to the discretion of His love and most holy will, without any recourse, without seeing or wanting to see what they are doing or ought to do. With the highest part of their soul, they must join themselves to God and lose themselves entirely in Him, by this means finding peace in the midst of war and rest in the midst of labor. In short, it is necessary to remain in the condition where God places us; patient in troubles, and enduring in suffering.

Also, the sure marks of a good prayer are when it produces the fruits of true virtues in a correct and faithful observance of our Christian obligations, and the soul is constantly faithful in all good works, in the midst of desolations and bitterness, or in the enjoyment of divine consolations and favors.

Blessed is the soul who becomes devoted to and perseveres in this holy practice, despite the difficulties which it meets there. For it is by these that the soul will be enriched and will receive the bread of grace, which will nourish it in eternal life.

Now, among all the gifts, that of holy prayer is obtained principally from God. That is why we must ask it of Him continually with a deep humility and without ever growing weary.

I find it helpful to speak about the benefits that come to us in prayer: it enlivens and makes us more devoted.

Prayer is the true life of the soul and from it we draw strength for the practice of solid [true] virtues.

Prayer and mortification are the two principal works of the Christian life.

A soul that desires to be reduced to nothing in itself and lost in God no longer worries what it becomes as to the body, the mind, perfection, and glory. The pure, pure, pure divine disposition pleases it, in itself, and in others. For this reason we must abandon ourselves completely into the adorable hands of God who desires that we live in Him, dying to ourselves.

"Quickly, quickly, take me from my being and put me into the attainment of my end."[13]

Quis liberabit me de corpore mortis?[14] (n. 2471)

THE THREE WAYS ONE CAN PRAY FOR ONE'S NEIGHBOR

I pray Our Lord to make me worthy to tell you about how we can pray for our neighbor:

1. Vocally.
2. Mentally.
3. In pure spirit.

The first way is to say some prayers such as the Rosary, the *Veni Creator*, and so on, for their intention.

The second is to pray in thought and with interior words, such as by offerings, sacrifices, and aspirational prayers,[15] made to God's majesty for their intention.

The third is made in pure spirit, completely given to and absorbed in God; sometimes by a loving glance or a simple elevation toward Jesus Christ; or by a simple remembrance of the troubles that have been commended to us; or in simple faith, content that God's good

---

13 The quotation is from the *Life of St. Catherine of Genoa*, ch. 32. To explain how man is reduced to nothing in God, St. Catherine uses the image of a piece of bread being consumed. She imagines the bread protesting because its being is destroyed in being eaten. But when it is explained that the end, the *telos*, of the bread is to be consumed, then the bread asks to be eaten quickly. See also Dominique Tronc, *Les amitiés mystiques de Mère Mectilde du Saint-Sacrement* (Paris: Parole et Silence, 2017), 133.

14 Rom 7:24.

15 *jaculations*, that is, prayers launched like arrows.

pleasure be accomplished in everyone and in particular concerning the one for whom you pray.

When and how must we pray? Two motives oblige us to pray: God and our neighbor.

Why does God require us to pray? Because He takes pleasure in giving to us, in order that "our joy may be full," as it says in the Gospel.[16] He Himself commanded His disciples to ask Him.

What is it necessary to ask of God? The sanctification of His holy Name, the coming or establishment of His reign, and the accomplishment of His most holy will.[17] You can ask for everything which concerns His glory. For a neighbor, you can pray for his conversion, his sanctification, and ask for the graces and virtues necessary for his sanctification, but always in relation to the pure glory of God.

When is it necessary to pray? When God's Spirit urges us, when obedience commands us, or our neighbor and our obligations bring us to it. Sometimes the soul feels itself urged to make particular prayers for God's interests, at other times for a neighbor. The soul must pray as it is made to pray, simplifying itself and praying out of obedience and love for the glory of God; sometimes out of charity and compassion for another's afflictions.

How must one pray? It is necessary to pray with love and confidence, but also with a profound submission and with reverence for God's action concerning all things, and especially concerning souls, taking a special delight that the divine will is accomplished in every way in heaven and on earth, in the netherworld, and everywhere.

If you ask me what is the best type of prayer among the three I propose to you, I will answer that all three are good. But the third is the most pure; it distracts the soul least and keeps it most deeply in its union [with God]. The one which is most free of images, representations, and phantasms is the one most fitting for a prayerful soul.

But in the end it is necessary to pray as God causes us to pray. And it is necessary that your soul be so detached from its operations and its actions that it is indifferent to all the ways in which God will wish to employ them. So that when God or obedience requires that you pray vocally, you will pray with freedom of spirit. For provided that you

16 Jn 15:11.

17 Mt 6:9–10.

are doing what God wants, you must be content. I say this to you in passing to show that we must not be attached to our interior practices, and that we must always be ready for everything that God desires.

If, however, you ask me how you must pray ordinarily in the state that you are in so as not to do violence to your [spiritual] attraction or even leave it, [I say] you must pray in the third way which I just explained to you. Firstly, your soul must be detached from all human concerns, and the same with respect to all created things. Your only desire and inclination is that God be glorified in all creatures, that He reign in them, and that He accomplish all His designs in them. Those are the three motives which oblige you to pray and which you must uniquely regard above all other views, concerns, natural compassion, and so forth.

Learn, therefore, to pray in faith, without reasoning in your mind. What does it mean to pray in faith? It is to pray in silence, content to present your needs to Our Lord, or those of our neighbor, and to abide in a firm trust in His goodness that He will give the necessary remedies: in a word, that His eternal charity will provide for it, in this way lovingly putting all things into God's hands. He will take unfailing care of things and will give us and our neighbor what is necessary for us.

A soul who is walking in the path to which God has granted you the honor of calling you, must no longer have choice or will for herself, or for her neighbor, and all her delight must be to see God's good pleasure accomplished. But sometimes you pray and it is only self-love that causes you to pray. Therefore, do not pray for anything except for God's interests in yourself and in your neighbor. And when some accident happens on earth, you must not be surprised or troubled about it. Instead, you must immediately adore God's hidden judgments in these distressing events, as much in your own regard as in regard to others, and the proceedings of His wisdom and eternal knowledge, which you cannot understand. And without being troubled or anxious, you must endure God doing what He pleases, in you and in your neighbor, and not be anything except content with His works, although it may be contrary to your feelings. And if God wished to overturn the whole universe, you must be steadfast and constant, esteeming nothing as worthy of existence except God; and in consequence, regarding all the rest as nothing; we should not be distressed if God annihilated it.

Now, you can still pray inwardly and without any worry or strain on your part. Sometimes you are even imperceptibly led to pray for some business or person in particular, or for something else. At such a time, one must not resist, but pray as the attraction urges you to. This kind of prayer is good, since it is God's Spirit who causes you to pray. Thus, when you find yourself pressed to pray for something, pray without scruples, but always with the interests of God in view or in your intention. But ordinarily pray in silence, as I just told you, and be certain that this silence calls very loudly, that it pierces the heavens[18] and comes even to the heart of Jesus Christ. Pray, then, in this way.

How is it that you will fulfill your obligations to pray for the Church, for the dead, for sinners, in short, for all the many things that are continually recommended to you?

I told you previously that as a Christian you are a member of Jesus Christ and that you form a part of His Mystical Body which is the Church. You can be separated from it only by renouncing Jesus Christ and your baptism. Therefore you are eternally linked to the Church; and in this union you necessarily enter into all her intentions, even though you are not continually focused on these, and it is impossible for it to be otherwise. Thus, my daughter, you pray with the Church, for the Church, and for her intentions. You have only to renew this once a month or once a year, telling Our Lord that you renew in yourself all the interests and intentions of your holy mother the Church, for time and for eternity, according to His designs and the obligations to which holy baptism subjects you, and that you desire to have a perpetual intention to this effect. This is enough once for your whole life, if you do not depart from the society of the faithful. Therefore, do not be scrupulous. If you do not pray for distinct things, you pray as God desires, and this is enough for you.

Still, you will be glad to know how it is necessary to pray when your neighbor urges you to promise to pray for him or for some affair. You must inwardly give yourself to God or leave yourself to Him to cause you to pray as He will please, without being eager sometimes out of kindness or natural compassion. And if you must answer such

18 *Imitation of Christ*, III.21.4.

persons, say that you will give yourself to Our Lord to pray for this or that. Do not ever promise to pray for anyone, but say that you will do what you can, always leaving God the freedom to make you do what He pleases.

Remember that you are not your own[19] and that you are powerless to dispose of yourself in any manner or for anything whatever. However, have the will to do what God wants you to do, even without knowing it. Your union with God's most holy will causes you to do many things in God which are pleasing to Him and which you do not see.

When God causes the soul to pray, its prayer is always efficacious; but when the soul prays through its own understanding, it is normally useless.

Always be simple before God, with the intention of being and praying according to His designs. This is a good and holy disposition for prayer.

As for vocal prayers, those which are required must be said with a simplified intention or a simple attention to God. It is good to say the *Pater Noster* every day out of pure obedience to Jesus Christ our divine Teacher who taught it to us. You must recite it according to His intentions, with great reverence and with the desire that it have all the efficacy that Our Lord intended to give it when He taught it to us.

You must say the *Credo* to be renewed in the faith and in the Church. Say it with reverence and complete belief in the mysteries in contains.

You must say the *Confiteor* to humble yourself before God's greatness and majesty, as a criminal and a sinner; and through this prayer you make a public confession of it before God and His angels. Consequently, you must recite it with a profound humility.

You must say the *Ave Maria* to honor the mystery of the Incarnation and reverence the maternity of the most holy Virgin and also to honor her as your good Mother and Mistress, and with the desire to give yourself to her, in order to be given by her to Jesus Christ her Son.

You can say still other prayers when you have the devotion, but do not neglect to say those I have specified to you, every day. (n. 1324)

---

19 1 Cor 6:19–20.

Confession

INSTRUCTION CONCERNING CONFESSION

The best disposition you can have is a profound humility which makes you see that you are a sinner and brings you low before God's majesty, confessing yourself a sinner and worthy of eternal rejection by God.

2. You will cast your eyes on Our Lord Jesus Christ in the Garden of Olives where He prayed and exhibited the most perfect contrition that could ever be shown before His Father's divine Majesty and the only one worthy of satisfying God's justice.

3. See how Our Lord was in this posture of humiliation in the capacity of a criminal. He had no sin in His person, He could not sin; but He was charged with our crimes and appeared before His judge as a criminal. With this insight, enter into the abyss of your nothingness.

When you go to Confession, see yourself as a sinner through the actual commission of a great number of sins. See that you are in truth a sinner, but that Our Lord Jesus Christ took only the quality and appearance of it to present Himself before His Father who is incensed against sinners and sin. And in this sight He rejected Him and condemned Him as if He had committed all the sins of mankind.[1] For Jesus Christ received the rejection and punishments we deserved, and bore them for us, in such a way that Scripture says that He was rejected by God as the object of His anger and justice.[2] And the eternal Father discharged all His anger on Him, as if He had actually committed all the sins with which He was charged through the great love He bore for men, or rather, the great zeal He had for the glory of His divine Father, knowing that no one except Himself could make reparation for them.

And one can say, following holy Scripture, that God took vengeance on His Son for all sins, and He was not only rejected as a sinner, but

1 Rom 5:8. 2 Gal 3:13, Mt 27:46.

condemned as a criminal for divine high treason.[3] He condemns Him and in a certain way could not endure Him; not in His capacity as His Word, but in the capacity of a sinner, because He was covered in our sins. And the eternal Father, hating sin with an eternal hatred, treated Jesus Christ as if He had been sin itself.[4] And Our Lord Jesus Christ suffered such an extreme pain from the rebukes which God gave Him as sinner that He proved His sorrow with these divine words: "My Father, if this chalice cannot pass without My drinking it, Thy will be done."[5] He desired that God might be satisfied with His extreme agony; but the sentence of death was pronounced: He must die, because He was made the ransom for sinners and, as Scripture tells us, "as soon as you sin, you are subject to death."[6]

Now in this capacity as a criminal which Jesus Christ carried before the majesty of His Father, He was also afflicted by the rejection of all creatures. For each one according to its ability conspired in His death to avenge the dishonor which sin had done to God. The result was that our divine Savior suffered from humiliations on the part of His Father who condemned Him and on the part of creatures who rejected Him. O incomprehensible humiliation! Oh! What an utterance is St. Paul's, speaking of Jesus: "*exinanivit*,"[7] He reduced Himself to nothing. Yes, through His love, He became the disgrace and the outcast of God and of men. A God covered with the form of a sinner, charged with all the crimes of the world! Oh! What an unfathomable mystery, who will be able to comprehend it?

It is for you that Jesus Christ, your divine Master, bears this title; it is for you that He is rejected and condemned; that is what you and I must be, and nevertheless, we do not think about it. Let us wake from the sleep of ignorance and begin to employ a most holy contrition, which Jesus Christ exercised and practiced for us. Yes, it is for you that He is contrite and humbled. He bears the rebuffs of God which you deserve. He does the penance you are incapable of doing, all your sufficiency not having the power to achieve it.

---

3 This harsh phrase was removed or softened in all but one manuscript. Analogous ideas are found in Bérulle and St. Marguerite-Marie Blanchard.

4 Is 53:6–8, 2 Cor 5:21. 5 Lk 22:42. 6 Rom 5:12.

7 Phil 2:7. He emptied Himself.

Behold Jesus Christ who is your ransom. He suffers for you, He makes satisfaction for you. You must enter into His holy dispositions and do not render useless what He did for you, or vain the grace He merited for you. When going to Confession, you must have whatever disposition makes you have a likeness to those Jesus had and clothes you in His contrition, in His most holy and perfect horror of sin, and His profound humiliation to which He was reduced before the greatness of God His Father—a contrition and humiliation so profound that through it He remains prostrate and as if utterly reduced to nothing.

This is how you should be at the feet of the priest who represents Jesus Christ for you. You should bring to Confession a humbled and contrite spirit and a heart broken with horror and regret for your sins.[8] Not that I intend to command you to have sensible feelings; but I want you to focus on the holy dispositions of Jesus, so that, remaining at His feet, with a mind raised to what He did and suffered for you in the Garden of Olives, you may abandon yourself to His grace and love to receive some fruit from them, offering to the eternal Father His Son's contrition. For it is for you that He was contrite, it is for your sins.[9] Therefore you must expose yourself to Him, so that your soul may be filled with the grace of His holy contrition; or if you prefer, remain in silence and reverence, in a humbled disposition which gives you completely to God. See Jesus Christ contrite in you, who makes satisfaction for you; and thus, Jesus Christ hates and detests the sin in you, and through Him you are separated from it.

Do not confuse your mind about these dispositions: what you cannot comprehend right now, God's light will make you understand when He pleases. Only have the desire to bear in your soul a small participation in Jesus's holy dispositions and desire that everything you do and say have a resemblance to Jesus. Act as much as you can like Jesus, detached like Him from all human interests in order to have in view only the pure glory of God His Father.

Let us suffer and die in that pure desire to please God and glorify Him. Let creatures tear us to pieces—very good—provided that God be pleased. Let us allow God to destroy our pride in the way

8 Ps 50:19 (51:17). 9 Is 53:5.

He pleases. Yes, my God, I desire it, and I leave myself to the power and adorable inventions of Your love for this. I am Your victim — for so long a time now — so make me worthy to be consumed, make me worthy of Your cross, Your death, and Your eternity.

Here are a few words we have told you in order to refresh your memory and give you easy means to enter into the holy truths which the Church teaches you every day. I am very humbled to see that Our Lord subjects you to receiving them from one of the most horrible sinners who was ever on the earth. Make use of this humiliation which shames me by humiliating you also. I would greatly prefer that it pleased Our Lord to manifest His divine will to you through another, since in truth, I am unworthy of such a mission. Nothingness and hell are my portion, and so much so that I cannot find bad those who censure me or speak ill of me. Everyone has the right to insult me, despise me, and trample me underfoot; and even more, to punish me. I have committed enough sins for that. Alas! If one single sin merits hell, think what punishment I deserve! Oh, how full of mercy and love God is! I love with a deep love those who humble me, I have a very great obligation to them:

1. Because they render homage to the truth, saying that I am proud and entirely full of ambition: it is true and my vanity conceals it. But what good is it to hide our vices? Does not Jesus see into the depths of our hearts? I have a little hope that since He has detected the poison, it will not kill me. He will have pity on my soul by humiliating me. I adore Him and submit to His divine laws in every way.

2. The people who try our patience and afflict us do the work of God in us. They are the instruments in the divine hand by which He cuts us, fashions us, destroys us, and perfects us in the way He pleases. Oh, blessed is the soul who sees and receives everything in the light of God! It can never be disturbed. Events do not surprise it; it is, in some way, immovable.

Let us love God and abandon ourselves into His hands without any reservation, and then let Him do what He will. Let us no longer do anything but regard Him with a look of love and satisfaction, without ever finding fault with His arrangement of things or the orders of His good pleasure.

Let us keep silence on such occasions and beware of justifying ourselves too much. Jesus was accused and He was innocent, and nevertheless, the Gospel notes that He said not a word: "Jesus was silent."[10] We must keep silent in humiliations and contradictions. Let us rejoice that God does His work in destroying our pride through these.

Do not be troubled about your inner weaknesses, make them matter for humiliation and beware of destroying your activity by violence: that would be to lose everything. You must have great patience to bear yourself in your miseries. Your spirit will finish the job. Do not go so fast; always have humility at the ready in all events, whether interior or exterior, which would like to trouble or disturb you concerning your lack of virtue and fidelity. Humble yourself and realize your unworthiness. I acknowledge that it is your fault; if it is your fault, you truly deserve this punishment. If grace did not prevent you, you are not worthy.[11] Do you have any cause for complaint? Does God owe you grace and the rest of His mercies? In fact, He gives them, but He does not owe them to you. It is out of love that He goes before you and when He leaves you, it is to make you aware of the depth of your misery. Never complain, so that God does not chastise you according to your merits. Bear this truth in your heart: in strict justice God owes me nothing except hell, and if He does not destroy me at every moment, it is due to the excess of His divine mercy which upholds me. Engrave that statement on the depths of your heart; and when it is truly imprinted there, you will taste by experience that all God's arrangements are loving, even though they sometimes seem very harsh to nature.

If your [mind] is very active, bear your impatience, and after you have made a diligent effort to keep yourself in God's presence, if you cannot arrive at the goal, you must make a virtue of necessity and endure being your own executioner in your own crucifixion.

When your activity outstrips your intention, it is enough that you awaken your natural promptness to raise your thought to God, in

---

10 Mt 26:63.

11 "Prevent" should be taken here in the older, more literal sense in which one speaks of the prevenient grace that "comes before" our action and equips us to do good.

order to disavow in silence, that is, from the depth of your will, the natural outbursts of your mind. Do not make two evils from one by becoming anxious. Such a natural attack may be from pure weakness, which is not greatly sinful before God, and the anxiety which follows it is pride and self-love.

When you see your [mind's] activity on campaign, and you cannot pull it back, make an act disavowing all the productions that it will make, and humbly await the return of your calm, which God will doubtless restore to you soon after that little tempest. When there is a great deal of inner commotion, do not make so much effort to stop it, for you then commit a double imperfection. You need only endure in patience and from time to time raise your thoughts to God to invite silently the power and strength of His grace to stop it; and then continue what you have to do without being troubled.

It seems to me that I had yet another point on which to answer you, which you asked me about this morning. Our Lord permits me to forget it in order to mortify you by this privation and to give you room to resort to His goodness in your needs. I pray Him to quicken you with His holy love, to grant you a great heart to suffer well and an unshakeable fortitude to allow yourself to be crucified. (n. 1879)

CONTINUATION OF INSTRUCTION ON CONFESSION

I have a word to speak to you about your past Confessions. Beware of scruples and hidden anxiety. God is good and merciful as well as most just. Do not be disturbed about your past life; be humiliated and mortified, but not troubled. You must see the source of your sorrow. And why do you want to confess these things which you already minutely examined? You must bring your soul into repose, without taking it away from the sorrow it must have for its infidelities and the bad use it made of the Blood of Jesus.

Take heart! Do today as the poor prodigal son did: he is the figure of the sinful soul, which is far from God through sin. Like him, go back to your Father, saying to Him, "My father, I have sinned against heaven and against you. I am not worthy to be called your son, make me one of your hired servants."[12]

---

12 Lk 15:18–19, 21.

Oh! How powerful is humility for attracting heaven's mercies! You know how it drew the Word from the Father's bosom to clothe Him in our flesh in the virginal womb of Mary. Humility has a power that the other virtues do not have; it charms God and makes Him forget His greatness and even His justice, in order to fill with grace the sinner who brings into His presence a humbled and contrite heart. It is impossible for Him to stop Himself from going to meet this prodigal soul. Just like the father of that son in the Gospel, He receives him with mercy, He gives him the best robe, and He embraces him, and gives him the kiss of peace, of reconciliation. He puts a ring on his hand and sandals on his feet; in fine, he has the fatted calf killed as sign of jubilation; and all of Paradise rejoices over one converted sinner.[13]

My child, let us be converted, let us return to our heavenly Father. Let us ask Him to be the slaves and servants of His servants. Not being worthy of the title of children, let us take humiliation for our own, and never depart from it; whatever grace and whatever elevation we may have, let us abide in nothingness. The soul I told you about, whom Our Lord commanded to enter into nothingness—from that moment, she did not leave it; the nothingness of being and of sin, these are her noble origins; God's ire and eternal damnation, these are her birthright.[14] Form an opinion about our extraction, our dignity, and our excellence. What is there to build your eminence on? We would be ridiculous and out of our mind not to be perpetually ashamed, since we have nothing in us except reasons for horror and humiliation. I like to see you humbled, but beware of anxiety and eagerness. Remain peaceful in the spirit of compunction.[15]

---

13 Lk 15:7.

14 Probably Marie des Vallées, a mystic from Normandy, supported by Jean de Bernières and St. John Eudes, among others.

15 Another manuscript includes this text borrowed from Condren (letter 134 in *Lettres du Père Charles du Condren*, Auvray et Jouffrey, 1943), which fittingly completes the thought of Mother Mectilde:

"Confess without showing your confessor the pain you feel in this, or as little as you can; give yourself to God in order to confess simply and confidently, in a spirit of humility and contrition, whatever you will have in mind about your faults; and if your mind is confused and you find yourself unable to continue, then finish without waiting any more, by saying something about your usual

Regarding your Confessions, it is not at all necessary to feel ill at ease. Go simply and confidently. You will accuse yourself very briefly of all the things that you have the prompting to say, but most especially: the secret esteem you have had of yourself, the products of your pride, your self-love, the vanity and self-seeking in the whole or the majority of your actions; not having rendered to God the honor you owe Him, not trusting in Him and not seeking His pure glory in all your actions, your words, and intentions; your often putting yourself forward among creatures; your having sought their approbation and their approval in your actions. In short, not having lived in the spirit and grace which you were given at baptism; having profaned it countless times, not making any effort in this, not examining the obligations by which you are bound; having been attached to creatures; having

---

faults, into which you have fallen through weakness, such as wasting time on useless things ([e.g.] 'I accuse myself of the foolishness of my past life, of the distractions and idleness of my mind, of all my failings in humility') and if you find yourself hindered from the start before you have said anything, begin in this way: 'I accuse myself of the many times in my life I have wasted time, and the many failures in resignation to God, of failing in strength and courage to follow His ways, and of my unknown faults,' and if the hindrance continues you will bring it to a close, unless you say what comes to your mind.

"As for the difficulties that you endure in your spirit, do not allow this to trouble you. This is a persecution you suffer in which you must trust in God and be faithful to Him, and although it may seem to you that your will is overcome by it, this is not true, and you, who are in difficulty, do not know how to judge. That is why you should follow the rule given to you, which is, that when you are not sufficiently sure of being able to judge if you have consented to an evil idea for the space of a quarter of an hour, with full freedom, you need not confess this; rather only renounce it before Our Lord, with your heart and with your lips or by some exterior act such as kissing the ground or making the sign of the cross; and do not refrain from Communion, rather, you ought to remain at peace in the resolution that is given, for then you are exonerated of it [i.e., sin] before God.

"Receive the penance that God imposes for your infidelities with a deep humility, respect, and submission to His justice and put yourself in a condition to receive absolution, which is nothing other than the power of the Blood of Jesus Christ which is applied to us, and which repairs the disorders of sin in our souls and reunites us to God, making us worthy of His graces. Jesus Christ has atoned for us in full, but He desires that we do some little thing on our part, as a little tribute we pay to His justice, recognizing that we are indebted to His mercy, and our penance should always be united to what Jesus Christ did for us whether in His life or in His death, but especially in the Garden of Olives."

been more occupied with them than with God; having worked at the means to please them; having spent a great deal of time on vanities, on useless trifles, and on superfluous conversations.

Finally, you will say what the Holy Spirit will imprint on your thoughts, and all this to render homage to God's justice and holiness, not for your personal interest. See yourself as a criminal at the feet of the divine Majesty, and remember that your ignorance hides the greater part of your sins from you; that is why you must confess them and believe yourself guilty of many more sins than you can understand,[16] in virtue of the ground of your impurity which produces only darkness, and which justifies itself by a cursed inclination which sin introduced into us.

I told you this morning briefly that you must receive the penance God imposes on you for your infidelities with a deep humility, respect, and submission to His justice. When you have fallen into some fault, you must beware of going to Confession merely in order to pull yourself from the pain and humiliation.

In Confession, be sincere and very exact. Do not go on about useless things or about matters which do not concern this sacrament. The devil does his best to cast you into distractions and to make you lose the grace given to you in it. You should be focused on your sins, and confess them succinctly in the pure sight of God.

Confess simply, as you have light and ability for it, without troubling yourself about being able to say what you suffer in your soul. You must suffer in humility and patience, without being able to remedy it yourself. Do not examine yourself much, because you cannot find anything in yourself except what is impure. All purity and sanctity is in Jesus Christ. Return to your Father along with the prodigal son and be content with your poverty and abjection, and when it pleases Our Lord, He will grant you some new grace. (n. 841)

16 RB 7:49–54, 64–66.

Holy Communion

ABOUT HOLY COMMUNION AND THE INTENTIONS ONE MUST HAVE FOR IT IN ONE'S SOUL[1]

My dear daughter, a long time ago I had proposed to write you something about what our intentions for Holy Communion were supposed to be. It is not that I intend to require you to have all of them distinctly in your mind, but rather to carry them in the depth of your heart, having the intention to give yourself to Jesus Christ for these purposes.

We must go to Holy Communion:

1. So that Jesus Christ may be in us all that He must be, and so that we cease to be what we are in ourselves, for the purpose of losing ourselves in Him, and being dispossessed of ourselves.

2. So that He may come into us to do away with all that is opposed to God, such as the generation from Adam and his rebellion, the reign of sin, the devil's empire and the dominion over ourselves which we usurped out of self-love; that He may bring about in us a perfect justice, crucifying the old man and establishing the reign of God. And thus our imperfections must make us desire Holy Communion, because of our zeal to destroy them.

3. The gifts and graces that it pleases Our Lord to communicate to us must induce us to receive Communion, in order that it may please Our Lord to come into us and take possession of His gifts and His graces, and that by our wickedness we do not set about usurping the domain and make its use our own.

We must go to Holy Communion out of obedience to the desire that Jesus Christ has to receive us into Himself, into His being and His life, putting an end to our present being and life, and making us what He is, namely: life, love, and virtue for God. Also, out of obedience to His will to have us as His members in whom He may live for His Father, and through whom He may work in time, as He did in His mortal life.

---

1 This letter was inspired by Condren's letter 18 (see the Auvray edition).

We owe obedience in the first place to Jesus Christ's desires to receive us and possess us; for Communion not only gives Jesus Christ to us, but also gives us to Jesus Christ, since He Himself says that the one who receives Him abides in Him.[2] Now this desire to receive us is as great as His charity, and as great as all His merits which give Him rights over us and love for us. It is a great infidelity to fail to respond to these desires of Jesus Christ if we do not have some proof of obstacles which in no way depend on us. (n. 636)

THE SPIRIT IN WHICH WE MUST RECEIVE COMMUNION

My dearest daughter, it is necessary to forget your past years, and to make mention only of the days from when you began to serve God. Let all the rest be wiped out in His divine presence, since all your conduct [now] is opposed to it. It is *now* that you must be completely God's and, consequently, entirely separated from created things. It is from this moment that you must begin a new life: a life that honors God, a life that reduces you to nothingness in God, a life that extricates you from your past habits in order to clothe you with the dispositions of Jesus Christ.

I want this new year into which you are about to enter to be a year of death and of life: of death in your senses and in your mind; and life in grace and in Jesus. May you have life in you only in order to lose it and consume it in God, keeping in your soul the Apostle's words: "You are dead and your life is hidden in Jesus Christ in God."[3]

Oh! What happiness to live in God, to no longer live in the corruption of our senses or among the contagion of creatures! Oh! What a grace to be continually in God, to live with His life, and become one with Him through the intimate union into which He draws us! To have God in oneself and to be in God Himself; to rest in Him and to work through Him. In a word, to be by grace and love what He is by nature. Must it be that the world, creatures, and your own self deprive you of such supreme happiness—indeed, of an infinite good the excellence of which is beyond understanding? What greater good fortune do you desire? It is to be everything that you can be, and is there anything great compared with God? Where are there

2 Jn 6:56. 3 Col 3:3.

earthly monarchs who raise their subjects to the crown? They do not so favor even their most intimate friends. Oh! How differently ordered is the court of our divine Master than those of earthly kings! In God, each is great, there each is loveable, there each is magnificent, and there each is precious. Finally, each in God is God with Him. His servants are kings, His followers are united to His grandeurs and participate not only in His crown, but in His divine perfections, and become utterly one with Him.

"To serve God is to reign." Blessed are the souls who have the honor to stand in His court and blessed forever are those found worthy to be His servants.

"Where I am My servant will also be," said Jesus.[4] Be the faithful servant of so good a Master, have no regret about abandoning yourself wholly to Him. Renew yourself in His service, but in a far different manner than in the past. Alas! You gave yourself to Him often, but your sacrifice and oblation were not complete. You were too involved in yourself, in creatures, and in your own concerns. You were not free to offer the victim to God alone; you were sacrificing it with one hand and withdrawing it with the other. When you were condemning it to death in one way, in another way you were giving it life, in an infinite number of ways. Behold how you mocked God.

It is true that in the past you were in darkness. But now that God illumines you with His light, will you be unfaithful as in the past? Will you always have before your eyes your own interests, human fears, and the satisfaction of your senses and of your own mind? No, with Jesus Christ I condemn all of that to death; it is necessary to begin a new life.

And if you ask me from what life you must live henceforth, I answer you that it is neither the life of good souls, nor of angels, nor even the life of the saints, but the pure and holy life of Jesus. Your years must be a continuation of Jesus's years, and in consequence, your life a continuation of His life. As St. Paul teaches you, you must fulfill in yourself what is lacking in the Passion of Jesus.[5] What does this mean except that, as a member of His body, you be reduced to nothing, crucified, dead, and resurrected with Him; that all your

4 Jn 14:3, 17:24.

5 Col 1:24.

actions be, in consequence, the actions of Jesus in you, that you do them through His Spirit, through His dispositions, and for His same intentions? There must be nothing except Jesus to see in you: may your thoughts be the thoughts of Jesus, your words the words of Jesus, your works the works of Jesus; and with Jesus, enter in spirit and by desire into His holy dispositions in order to act like Him. It is according to His spirit that you must receive Communion.

Since we have hit upon this subject, I will tell you what you must do in your present state. Now, in the past you have always been full of designs for yourself, so from now on you must enter into other dispositions. You must not receive Communion for yourself, neither for this nor for that, but only for Jesus Christ. You can indeed pray for everyone's needs and even for your own; but you must learn to communicate as God and His grace require you to do now. And your preparation will be to be nothing, to have nothing, to desire nothing, to be capable of nothing, but only to bring to Communion a disposition of total abandonment of yourself, leaving yourself to Jesus's power in the Most Holy Sacrament to be clothed with His mercies and Himself, as He intends it and not according to your own lights or the appetite of your senses.

Begin to enter into detachment and into the void of yourself. Do not see anything except Jesus Christ and His interests; put an end to all of yours. Let your most usual disposition be that of death to everything which can give you life in yourself. You are nothing in yourself or for yourself—at least, you must not be any longer. You are Jesus's, therefore leave yourself to Him completely. If the tree belongs to Him, do not rob Him of the fruits. Surrender everything to Him, faithfully, and consent that He may bring you to nothingness.

May your principal motive in Holy Communion be to give yourself to Jesus, to give Him the freedom to do in you everything that will be according to His good pleasure, without your considering yourself or your interests about your own perfection. In your past life you lived so much for yourself and received Communion so often for yourself; henceforth live and receive Communion only for Jesus, for His joy, for His designs, and for His intentions.

Receive Communion for the sake of adhering to His intention and the desire He has to see you be all His, to see the reign of His love in you, to unite you to Himself and to cause you to be completely one with Him. In Communion your soul is fed with God Himself, to show you that your soul must no longer subsist on earthly things—that, since it is fed with heavenly food, it is necessary that it live with a heavenly life, without lowering itself to creatures or the senses any longer. You must live as Jesus Christ lived for His Father; and Jesus's intention is that you live from Him and for Him.[6]

There is no need for you to form all these thoughts and intentions before Communion; it is enough if you have them in the ground of your soul. Without taking up or multiplying such thoughts, simply receive Communion for Jesus. Note: I say *for Jesus*, and not for yourself, not for your perfection; but so that Jesus may be living and reigning in you, so that through Him you may enter into Him, and so that His designs may be accomplished in you, in this way leaving yourself abandoned very simply to His good pleasure.

May He shape you as He pleases; whether He raises you or lowers you; whether He gives to you or takes from you; whether He caresses you or rebukes you; whether He places you in the light or keeps you in darkness; whether He gives you sweetness or gives you bitterness; whether He welcomes you or forsakes you; whether you feel joy or sadness; whether you are responsive or unmoved, whether in abundance or in scarcity, each must be indifferent to you. All these things do not cause the perfect union and God does not pay attention to these little arrangements. He does not descend to them. All of that is seen and received in the senses, that is why these things are very often the effects of ourselves in us; and if you think about them too much, you will withdraw from the purity of grace into which you must enter.

God performs His works in the soul above the senses; most often the ground of the soul (as the spirit's highest part is called) is not aware of them. We must remain reduced to nothing, and very simply abandoned to God's operation. Even though you do not recognize it, you owe it reverence and acquiescence, finding it good that God does

6 Jn 6:57.

His work in you above you. The impurity of our ground requires that God act this way, otherwise His work would be constantly polluted. We must even desire that everything God does in us, through His mercy, remain in Him, in order that we do not destroy His work.

Oh! There is such impurity in the creature! If God allowed you the power to lay a hand on His work, you would ruin everything. Your wickedness would make strange profanations of it. You are blind. Allow yourself to be led by the Spirit of Jesus. Desire nothing, ask nothing, seek nothing, love nothing, be empty, and God will fill you with Himself.

He wants you to be faithful to the lesson He is giving you. He opens the way of life[7] before you and gives you a little help to guide you there. Make use of the times and the means; the one and the other will run out for you. Do not neglect them if you do not want to be in danger of perishing in yourself.

After Holy Communion, remain in silence and faith, in reverence and love, above your senses. Do not be surprised to feel nothing, to be able to say nothing, or to be unable to think many lovely things. You do not go to Communion in order to find life in yourself, but in order to find death. Therefore, leave yourself in death, so that God can give you life through Himself. Remain in a loving acquiescence toward all God does in you and all that He desires of you, and continuing in this holy abandonment and in your sacrifice, you will be doing what God wants and you will not be opposing His operation. Do not listen to the complaints of your senses or the reasonings of your own mind: all must die, all are impure and sinful. Leave them then without listening to them and remain immolated to the good pleasure and the love of Jesus Christ.

It is not enough to bring this disposition to Holy Communion, but have it the same afterwards; and it must continue in you always, that you may always be in a state of abandonment.

It is not enough to know that you must go to Holy Communion. You must endeavor to have the favor of frequent Communion. Supposing that you persevere in your present condition, your temptation would be to refrain from it, under the pretext of seeing yourself little

---

7 RB, Prologue.

disposed to receive it. Go to God with trust and love, do not deprive yourself of Him from fear. Alas, what presumption in us to think that we are able to prepare for Communion! God alone can prepare us for it by His graces and mercies. Thus, you have nothing and you can do nothing if God does not give it to you. Present yourself to Him in order to receive what He wants to give you and ask Jesus to receive Himself and to glorify Himself in you, since you are incapable of doing this well. Let His love make up for everything and with this simple attitude, receive Communion often.

I observed in your writings that in your past life many motives kept you from Communion; sometimes you were not prepared, at other times it was under the pretext of business, and very often, through a liberty in yourself, for the sake of not wanting to be captive. There are very few souls who receive Communion purely for God's interests alone. I think you never received Communion as God desires you to do; you were always your own goal, or creatures occupied you.

(n. 530)

MY DEAREST IN JESUS CHRIST, YOU WILL RECEIVE COMmunion today, please, in the dispositions in which holy and loving Providence will place you; not reflecting as much on your dark frame of mind, as on the desire you have to give yourself to Jesus Christ, to put an end to the use you have made of yourself in your past life and your usurpation of His rights over you. Give yourself back to Him entirely and to His divine management, being content that God is content in Himself and that He is contented in you in the way that will please Him, without your senses having a share in it.

Remain in the state of victim which Jesus has in the Most Holy Sacrament, desiring to be sacrificed to His love. We will never be worthy of Communion, not having any disposition in ourselves; but Jesus Christ by His Communion sanctified ours[8] and merited for us the grace to communicate. Do not allow this privilege, which Jesus Christ has granted you, to be useless in you. Do not be surprised to feel nothing in your prayer; carry on without clinging to the anxiety which proceeds from your pride.

8 See St. Thomas Aquinas, *Summa theologiae* III, qu. 81, art. 1.

Receive Communion, in spite of your miseries, on the supposition that you have no other reason which might have obliged you to be deprived of it. Our Lord is testing you: this is a fog and a cloud[9] which will dissipate and give you the light of your divine sun. Courage, be faithful. I give you entirely to Jesus Christ by the power which you gave me in Him over your soul. (n. 3022)

FOR THE FEAST OF CORPUS CHRISTI[10]

This holy day contains so many depths, mysteries, so much grace and holiness, that I find that I am quite unworthy to speak about it. Please, let us be lost in our nothingness and adore in silence what we are not worthy to comprehend.

I want us to adore together the adorable Communion that Jesus made of Himself, when He instituted this divine Sacrament. Through that Communion He sanctified ours. Let us also adore and give ourselves to His intentions in this sacred institution. He considered you in it and in it He gave you a share in His grace and love. It is there that He joins you to Himself. Consent to everything He desires of you, and allow yourself to be engulfed in His love without feeling or knowing it. And pray to God for us: today is the true feast of the Holy Eucharist.

I beg you, my dear, to be all Jesus Christ's just as Jesus Christ is all yours in the host. Let us be in truth what we have promised Him to be and what we renewed yesterday in His holy presence. Oh! How dull and insipid are creatures to a soul who has tasted God. Separate yourself from everything that can distract you from His pure love in the slightest; and remain in this spirit of victimhood since, in reality, you are a victim with Jesus Christ. You form part of Himself. Lose yourself totally in Him and be very faithful to see, to receive, everything within the order of His love. Be content with His holy will and pray that He will look upon me with mercy and bring about my conversion. In Him I am, as you know, all yours.

Let us be wholly new in Jesus with a new love and a new faithfulness; for we are His in a manner which is in a certain way new. That is why we must be completely renewed in Him and through Him

---

9 Sir 2:2.

10 This text is composed of three letters united here but separated in other manuscripts.

in the Most Holy Sacrament, and begin to lead a new life which has some resemblance to His divine life, hidden and reduced to nothing in the Most Holy Sacrament.

Your miseries and your antipathies do not repel me at all. God does not do His work by halves. But let us begin truly to be reduced to nothing, walking in the secret paths of faith where the human intellect loses the way. May it please God that I might be worthy to serve you in them.

This spirit of faith and death is the true spirit of St. Benedict,[11] and if Our Lord grants me the grace to express what His light reveals to me about it, you will see that it is not without mystery that He chose the nuns of St. Benedict to be His victims in His Most Holy Sacrament, since the grace of this order has so much affinity with it. But the great misfortune is that this is not known and even the souls who have professed it do not understand it.[12]

---

11 One of the "instruments of good works" in RB 4 is "To keep death daily before one's eyes"; the third step of humility in RB 7 mentions the imitation of Christ who was "made obedient even unto death."

12 St. Gregory the Great narrates the death of St. Benedict in his *Dialogues*, Book II, chapter 37: "Six days before he died, he gave orders for his tomb to be opened. Almost immediately he was seized with a violent fever that rapidly wasted his remaining energy. Each day his condition grew worse until finally, on the sixth day, he had his disciples carry him into the chapel where he received the Body and Blood of our Lord to gain strength for his approaching end. Then, supporting his weakened body on the arms of his brethren, he stood with his hands raised to heaven and, as he prayed, breathed his last." Mother Mectilde places a great deal of weight on this scene, as we can see in a conference she gave on the feast of the Patriarch's *transitus*: "My Sisters, I will not tell you with what fervor we should celebrate the feast of our great Patriarch. It is enough to arouse us to honor him to know that he is our Father and Legislator, and that the adorable mystery of the Eucharist, to which we have the honor to be dedicated, was the whole love of his holy heart on earth; so much so that it is Jesus the Host who carried him away to Himself to raise him to heaven. St. Benedict, expiring before the altar, as a victim immolated to the Most Holy Sacrament, at the foot of the altar, bequeathed his soul to it and at the same time dedicated his entire Order to it. Can we not say that it is through the grace of this consecration that his disciples have the duty to battle bravely the enemies of this sacred mystery and be the heralds of the Most Holy Sacrament's glory? But it was not enough for that holy Patriarch that his Sons should loudly proclaim the marvels of the adorable Sacrament of the Eucharist; it was also necessary that his Daughters should be consecrated to it, in a spirit of homage and reparation, and that the

Let us ask Our Lord to stir up this grace and spirit in us. I include you in our number, since we cannot be separated in spirit, and it is possible we will not always be [separated] in body. God knows the time; let us remain in peace.

I greatly desire that you may be my Isaac, and that I may sacrifice you to the Most Holy Sacrament. But you must be clothed in the disposition of that dear Isaac. I hope that Our Lord will clothe you in it. In the meantime, keep the desires He is giving you; someday they will have their effect. (n. 167)

ON THE GOOD EFFECTS THE SOUL RECEIVES FROM FREQUENT COMMUNION

My good sister in Jesus Christ, I want you to be completely attentive to His holy love and completely consumed in Him. My desire would be to see you receiving Communion often, and if your confessor allows you to receive this blessing tomorrow, I would advise you to take advantage of it. You cannot give yourself too much to Jesus Christ, and you cannot surrender yourself too much to His designs to possess you through this adorable Sacrament. You need to sink your weakness in His divine strength and in the desire to be wholly filled with Him.

"As I live for my Father," said Jesus Christ, "so also all those who receive Me will live for Me."[13] O blessed life, to live for Jesus Christ and from Jesus Christ, to be fed and sustained with Him! It is for this purpose that He is in the host and that He will be in the host until the end of the world. And His desire would be to be frequently received, so that He might continually realize the effects of His love and mercy: so that He may live in us and we may live in Him. In short, so that we may be transformed in His love, being completely immersed in the divinity and made entirely one with Jesus Christ. It seems to me that a soul who receives Communion frequently receives much more strength, grace, and blessing than those who refrain.

---

devotion of this great saint be perpetuated in his Order until the end of time. Let us preserve with love and gratitude the inheritance and blessing that he deigned to leave us at his death" (document n. 1234, translated from *Catherine de Bar: A l'écoute de Saint Benoît* [Paris: Téqui, 1988]).

13 Jn 6:57.

Let us go to God with humility and trust. He is good with an infinite goodness. He knows our helplessness and our incapacity; by His divine sufficiency, He will make up for them. Oh! When will we be all Jesus's, so that our hearts will beat only for His love, so that we will live from His life and we will be imprinted with His sentiments? Let us give ourselves to His eternal desire to possess us for that. How sorrowful and unbearable is this life without Jesus and without being on the cross for Him! It seems to me that a Christian soul can take delight only in the hope of suffering something for the one who makes her live and die. Let us suffer then, since this is the only satisfaction for a soul who belongs to Jesus Christ, and who does not have and cannot have an interest in the world, or in all the satisfactions it can give, "*per quem mihi mundus crucifixus est, et ego mundo.*"[14]

(n. 1697)

MY DEAREST, I DID NOT YET RESPOND TO YOU, BELIEVing, as I had just received Communion, that you would prefer me to be attentive to the one who honored me with His presence rather than with the creature; since the moments closest to Communion, both before and after, are the most precious in our life, and the ones to which we owe a wholly special attention, fidelity, and reverence. Oh! What grace and holiness they contain! I believe you know this from experience.

My daughter, I invite you to celebrate with me the feast of the victories of Jesus, our divine Master. He triumphed for us over the devil, the world, and our very selves, which are our most cruel enemies. Let us be united to His divine power and give ourselves to Him, so that He triumphs in us, so that He vanquishes our enemies, and above all the pride of life, as the most evil. We have cause for rejoicing to see Jesus victorious over the devil; but let us also desire that He may be so over everything He finds in us which opposes the holiness of His reign. Let us withdraw into the desert with Him, there to be tempted, forsaken, and hungry; there to be in darkness, in penitence, and in supreme poverty; in a word, to suffer every kind of misery, privation, and sorrow, and to have nowhere to lay one's head.[15]

14 Gal 6:14. Through whom the world is crucified to me, and I to the world.
15 Mt 8:20.

Let us love privations and everything that makes us share in Jesus Christ's pure and holy states. We must be entirely clothed in them. St Paul exhorts us to do this.[16]

Love only Jesus Christ, desire only Jesus Christ, esteem only Jesus Christ, possess only Jesus Christ, taste only Jesus Christ, be filled only with Jesus Christ, hope only for Jesus Christ, will only Jesus Christ, seek only Jesus Christ, claim only Jesus Christ, delight only in Jesus Christ, rest only in Him, and be satisfied by being completely filled with Him and spent for Him.

This is the disposition I wish you to have, my daughter, as the richest treasure with which your soul can be favored. O Jesus Christ, Jesus Christ, Jesus Christ, how good it is to possess You! What are creatures compared to You? Alas! In truth I cannot say that they are anything but corruption, misery and sin, bitterness, and affliction of spirit. Let us not delay there, let us waste neither our grace, nor our time, with them. (n. 1225)

CONCERNING THE DEDICATION OF A TEMPLE

My very dear daughter, I desire you to be entirely filled with the fullness of Jesus Christ and wish that the work He did in the soul of Zaccheus, through His divine gaze,[17] may have the same effect today in you. This is the subject of the Gospel and the Office which we read today for the Dedication.[18] Your soul is the temple consecrated by the three Persons of the Most Holy Trinity. It is the house of Jesus Christ. But remember what He said, speaking about it: "My house will be called the house of prayer."[19] At Holy Communion, renew the dedication of your soul. Desire to be all Jesus's, and that henceforth your soul not be polluted by the disorder of creatures and of your senses.

If Our Lord permits you to come and see us, we will talk about the rest. (n. 1698)

---

16 Phil 2:5; Rom 13:14. 17 Lk 19:5.
18 Namely, for the feast or commemoration of the Dedication of a Church.
19 Mt 21:13.

Dedicated and Immolated

THE INTENTIONS OF THE SUPERIORS FOR THE ESTABLISHMENT OF THE NUNS[1]

Since the religious souls of this holy house are entirely dedicated and immolated to the glory of the Most Holy Sacrament, they must make an effort to be very punctual in paying their respect and adoration to it ceaselessly, taking care to fulfill all their duties worthily toward this august Majesty reduced-to-nothing, without omitting or neglecting any of them. This foundation obligates them to this in a very particular manner; they must ask Our Lord for the grace to exert themselves generously there to the full extent of His designs.

1. The first thing that must be done is to acknowledge before God the grace of this occupation of being in continual adoration, to which holy Providence has destined them; and that all our being and all our work are to be referred to the honor of this divine Sacrament. The religious of this house cannot be dispensed from being the victims of Jesus in the host; therefore, they must necessarily do their utmost to give Him all that He expects from them, and above all to live with His hidden and completely reduced-to-nothing life, since He granted them this favor of choosing them, to the exclusion of an endless number of others who would accomplish this more worthily.

2. After having weighed this favor and obligation, we must give ourselves to Jesus, reduced to nothing in His divine Sacrament, for the sake of working toward the holiness of this state, through Him, with an irrevocable determination never to draw back from this, whatever pain, temptation, and loathing may come upon us; whether from the world, from ourselves, or from the devil. And we must not imagine that we can succeed without struggle and suffering. This perfection is nothing other than the *anéantissement* of ourselves, and we cannot attain this without suffering. Thus, each one of us is immolated by God's hidden action regarding her soul, in order to lead it to its destruction.

1 This text is also found in *Documents Historiques*, with some variations.

3. The religious of this house must be resolved to be most abject, and to pass in the mind of the world as the same. They must have a great love for being unknown to anyone, except God alone; and in order to remain more hidden, in imitation of Our Lord Jesus Christ in His most adorable Sacrament, they must remain, as much as is possible for them, in a profound solitude, which they interrupt only out of need or through obedience.

4. They will take delight in being, as much as possible, poor in body and spirit, that is, being in exterior poverty as well interior poverty, in homage to Jesus Christ who is most poor in the Holy Eucharist. And when it pleases Our Lord to cause them to endure some consequences of this poverty, they will give thanks to Him for it, as for a very special favor.

5. Their most common occupation must be holy prayer. One must live in this house only from that heavenly nourishment. But each religious will be fed according to her grace and her state; thus, we must receive this daily bread from the adorable hand of Our Lord, who gives according to the soul's needs—to some more abundantly, to others less (according to appearances), but each one must be content with her portion, since it is our heavenly Father who is allotting it to us. We must entrust ourselves to His management, being certain that He gives everything to us out of an infinite love for our sanctification. And we must not consider whether it is great or small, but continue always to leave ourselves to the divine disposition, content with everything, and even have joy at being very poor interiorly, since we cannot bear a greater cross, out of homage to the one Our Lord bore and, in a different fashion, bears for us in the Most Holy Sacrament.

6. The principal focus during our prayer must be to remain before God's supreme majesty in the Most Holy Eucharist, with a most profound reverence, with complete trust and abandonment, with a submission and a simple consent to all the arrangements of divine Providence, each one according to the degree of her grace, whether by making some act or in another manner. With these three dispositions, we can always make a prayer which is very excellent and very pleasing to Our Lord, and when it seems that they fail us, faith makes up for everything, in a simple surrender to the affliction and to every privation.

7. The whole tendency of our hearts and minds must be to adore this divine Sacrament, to render Him homage for all the creatures who do not adore, and for all those who dishonor Him by so many sins and impieties. Further, if we rightly understand our obligation, we will see that we must be sacrificed to the eternal Father's justice on behalf of all the sinners who offend Jesus Christ in the Most Holy Eucharist, and that there ought to fall upon us all the contempt and humiliations which He suffers there still today and will suffer there until the end of the ages. This should be upon us so that justice may be done, out of our love and our desire to make reparation to His glory, by making to Him (as much as is possible for us) fitting atonement for all sinners and most especially for those who dishonor Him most wickedly in this most august Sacrament.

8. The reparation of honor made to the Most Holy Sacrament, with the candle in hand,[2] is an act of humiliation, confessing ourselves to be criminals, but it can be received by the Father only through Jesus Christ His Son. Therefore, in this holy action we unite ourselves most especially to Jesus Christ Our Lord, for the sake of making reparation to the glory of His Father and Himself in this divine Sacrament, through Him. This done, He leaves us[3] in faith in that true belief that He will offer reparation in us and make us worthy, through Himself, to glorify Him. It is necessary to remain in a simplified way in this union of faith[4] with Jesus.

9. Since our life is focused on and entirely consecrated to such a majestic, adorable, and noble mystery, it is necessary that our entire being correspond to it.

I. We must not profane it by affection for anything created.

---

2 The *amende honorable* (or *réparation d'honneur*) was a civil punishment that required an offender, divested of most of his garments, to be led into a church or square, where, with torch in hand and a rope around his neck, he would beg pardon on his knees for some crime. For her monasteries Mother Mectilde established a spiritual version of the *amende honorable* or act of reparation: the designated reparator of the day says the prayer in front of the Blessed Sacrament exposed, kneeling in the middle of the choir, with a lighted candle in hand and having, about the neck, the rope that signifies a humble and penitent solidarity with all poor sinners.

3 Another manuscript, "we must leave ourselves."

4 Another manuscript reads "union of self."

II. We must not have any inclination toward esteem and elevation[5] from creatures.

III. We must love and tend with all our hearts toward nothingness.

And when holy Providence will furnish us with occasions of humiliation, we must receive them with great respect as the most precious treasures which God reserves to bestow upon His elect. If the world despises us, we must believe that we are in the true condition that God desires for this house, for it would be neither just nor reasonable that — a God reduced to nothing in the Most Holy Sacrament being the unique object of our adoration and the model of our life — we should have public praise, while He dwells totally hidden in an abyss of *anéantissement* which is beyond the understanding of the angels, and as they cannot adore and marvel enough in their astonishment, the victims [of the Holy Eucharist] must be reduced to nothing.[6] And if they are permitted to take the title of brides of Jesus Christ, must they not be conformed to their divine Bridegroom in every way? Accordingly, we will not be surprised when we are rejected, condemned, humiliated, censured, and entirely reduced to nothing by the human mind; this must be our earthly paradise, our happiness, and our only joy and consolation, whereas esteem and honors must be for us endless suffering and the most painful crucifixion. (n. 2543)

---

5 Here, "elevation" means a sense of moral superiority.

6 By their religious profession of *anéantissement*, the perpetual adorers enter into the state of Jesus's victimhood in a way that the angels, in spite of their superior metaphysical status, are unable to do, and even unable to understand.

Constancy in One's Path

THE PATH OF *ANÉANTISSEMENT* IS THE ONE WHICH GIVES THE MOST GLORY TO GOD

My dearest daughter, I do not know if Our Lord will agree to give me the grace to say a few words to you about the constancy you must have in your path, without your being either occupied with or full of pride regarding the path of others. Daniel was told to remain in his degree[1] in order to show you that each soul must remain in its own path and stay within its degree, without wanting to enter into those that appear to us fine and pleasing in other people.

It is a great fault in the interior life and particularly in the way of *anéantissement* to enter by affection or desire into an arrangement to which God does not call you, to want to do good works in which God does not employ you. And under the pretext that you see the external acts of piety to be good and holy, your pride wants to include everything, without discerning if God desires this of you or not. Most often, with this way of acting, you do good deeds through the choice and inclination of your mind, without the order or prompting of grace, and thus it happens that after very long practice of these works of piety, you are not any more dead to self or more perfect. Therefore, it is necessary to do them through the direction of God's Spirit.

Second, you must beware of being occupied with all the good things you see done; because what God asks of one soul He does not ask of all. Some He appoints to charity and the service of their neighbor; others, to the consolation of the afflicted; others to humility; others to poverty; others to penance and austerity, and so on. It does not follow that all should do the same thing. Sometimes there is a similarity in the exterior works but a very great difference in the ground of the soul, because of the difference of the [spiritual] paths. In this what appears, in an entirely marvelous manner, is the power

1 Dan 8:17–18. Literally, "made me stand upon my standing," a late Hebrew idiom for "in my place, where I had stood."

and wisdom of God who has given to each one according to His good pleasure, for the sanctification of His chosen ones, without any of the paths being alike.

O, the depth of the wisdom and knowledge of God, who will be able to understand the sublimity and sanctity of Your ways?[2] Within the variety of paths from God, we find those who are dedicated to honoring the hidden and reduced-to-nothing life of Jesus Christ; and these, having a powerful attraction which draws them away from all that has renown, retreat into the abyss of their nothingness, in order to have no life among creatures. It seems to me, according to the insight it pleased Our Lord to give me about your soul, that you are among the number of these and that you owe it an inviolable fidelity.

Now it is not a small grace to know your path: for, knowing it, you can no longer go wrong except through an infidelity which can never be excused. You must give yourself to God in the manner in which He calls you. Therefore, if in your path you owe Him honor through the imitation of the hidden and reduced-to-nothing life of God's Son, you must lead a life withdrawn from creatures, a life of silence, of humble obedience, in short, a life of death, a life which no longer looks like your life, but a life hidden in Jesus Christ, as the Apostle teaches you.[3]

You must take delight in the path in which God placed you. It is not you who chose it, but eternal Wisdom chose it for you and requires you to give yourself to it without being anxious that you are doing nothing great or excellent for the glory of Our Lord. Faith teaches you that the greatest and most noble glory you can give Him is to be perfectly submissive to His good pleasure, to be the prisoner of His love, to be without choice, without life, and without any will; because when you are of this kind He is glorified in you perfectly. In that state, you glorify Him more perfectly than if you were to build a thousand hospitals and if you were to do many other good works from which your self-love took life on account of your good action. Whereas, in the path where God's goodness leads you, everything tends toward nothingness and the destruction of yourself. Your way is guaranteed; do not doubt that Our Lord calls you by this route: you

2 Cf. Rom 11:33–34. 3 Col 3:3.

receive too much grace and understanding in it to doubt. I confess that this way is more crucifying than the other; but it is more certain because there is less of ourselves and it gives us to God in a purer way.

Therefore, from now on be at peace when you see your neighbor who does the good works you do not do. Do not leave your path in order to enter into a foreign one and one that is not your own. And what must console you and give you peace is the union you have as a Christian with the Church. And as you form one body with all Christians who are members of Jesus Christ, all the good works that one good Christian does, you share in and contribute to in a certain fashion; because you are united to that member as forming the same body. Through this sacred tie, you are charitable, humble, and patient along with your neighbor. You, in your path, should not want to do what they do. You must not say, "I would like this or that," because the divine will must operate so powerfully in you that it is omnipotent in your soul, without allowing your self-love to wish [to do], or to be anxious about not doing, as much good as many others. If God does not want those works from you, then why do you want to do them? It is a vestige of the wickedness we received from Adam to always want to be and to do something that to us makes a show, it order to take a secret satisfaction in it. We cannot take hold of *anéantissement*; the thought of this tortures us and nevertheless it is our salvation. God desires you to be in this state; is it for you to desire another? Is not God's will more holy than all the rest? What God has chosen for you, is it not more salutary for you than all the good and good works you could do? Oh, my daughter, would we be so presumptuous as to give laws to God? For myself, I confess to you that I have so much respect for His good pleasure that I would prefer to pick up straws from the ground, by His order, than to convert the whole universe by the ardor of my own will.

Let us love this divine good pleasure; let us take our delight in being attached to it. The blessed do not have any other happiness, and the satisfaction they have in the accomplishment of the divine will comprises their beatitude. You also see certain souls on earth who, being completely dead to themselves, enjoy an anticipated happiness. For having lost their own will in the divine will, they are always completely content, seeing nothing on earth outside of God's good pleasure. O my daughter, when shall we be in that blessed death, which will give life to the good pleasure of God in us? It is indeed necessary to work toward the renunciation of ourselves. We must destroy our own satisfactions.

I do not know if you truly understood what I want to tell you regarding the good actions which are done by others. I am telling you that just as you pray with all Christians because of the union [in the Mystical Body], you act with them too. All the first Christians had only one will, just as they had only one faith, one law, and one baptism, as you observe in the Acts of the Apostles; all Christians have only one will in Jesus Christ, and all have one desire to glorify Him.[4] (At least, they could not have any other intention in their actions, or they would not act in a Christian way.) Remaining, therefore, within the intention of your good mother, the Church, you honor God in all the good works which are done by her children, because, as I already told you, you form only one body.[5]

Here is the disposition you must have in your heart to share in these: first, consent to all the good works performed in the whole Church; second, be glad that God is glorified in many ways according to His good pleasure. And when you see a good work done, offer it to God by a simple elevation, rejoicing inwardly to see souls who do God's work which you are not worthy to do. Do not regard your own path as better and more elevated than the paths of others. Be very reserved on this point; especially since you do not see each person's degree of grace and it does not belong to you to judge of it.

Remember that each soul has its way: the one that belongs to another is not yours. God gave to each one what is proper. If you were to enter into someone else's path, you would perish in it; and if another entered yours, it would not bring about his salvation. Therefore, let all souls do what they do and if they go astray, you will not answer for it. Be faithful in yours, and beware of focusing on this one or that one. Remain detached from creatures. Do not condemn what you cannot understand. And especially since sometimes you will find souls whose ways and modes of acting are offensive to your

---

4 Acts 4:32, Eph 4:46.

5 Eph 4:7–17, Rom 12.

feelings and even often to your reason, keep yourself from judging or blaming them. God does not give you any order or authority to condemn them; leave them to His judgment and do not be polluted by rash judgments. If there were souls under your direction, there would be something more to tell you; but since this is only in passing and in encounters with certain devout people, you must restrain your mind, which goes a little too fast on this subject.

Be very circumspect, then, for fear that you might reject what God accepts and disapprove of what He approves. And although the path of death and true *anéantissement* may be the most genuine, the most holy, and the most secure in the Church, you must respect the grace of Jesus Christ in souls and the differences of each. For it is in the sight of Our Lord as it is in the sight of a king who has all his officers: his court is comprised of different persons where each has a different function, and the ones that the king intends to be continually in his chamber and enjoy his presence must not dawdle in the kitchen. Each one must fulfill his responsibility and his office; otherwise there would be nothing but confusion.

Remain in your degree, and since the king, Jesus Christ, your all, does you the honor of keeping you in His holy presence and desires this fidelity from you, do not lower your arrow[6] in order to be occupied with creatures, not even with angels. When God keeps you busy with Himself, leave all creatures in God to be what God desires them to be. And you, my daughter, hide yourself in God Himself, in His divine essence which surrounds you; do not leave Him, if possible, at least voluntarily. Simplify your mind in all things, especially with regard to what you have neither order nor obligation to examine or know; in this way your soul will remain free and detached.

Learn a truth which surprises you so often: this is when I tell you that *N.* is in the lowest and smallest path in the Church. Meanwhile, we are assured, and Holy Scripture teaches it by the mouth of Jesus Christ Himself,[7] that the path of *anéantissement* is the holiest in the Church. And God's servants say that it is the most elevated, most

6 Mother Mectilde uses this image in several places. The arrow symbolizes the Countess's desire for God. If she were occupied with creatures, she would be lowering her aim.

7 Mt 10:39, Jn 12:24–25.

pure, and most sanctifying. As for me, by God's mercy, I see it in its excellence, according to my ability; but with all its holiness, I find it disparaged beneath all the paths in a certain way.

1. It is without renown.

2. It is almost unknown, and few persons make it their state.

3. A soul who follows this path understands herself to be so small and so much lower than everything that she cannot see in herself anything but nothingness.

4. She does not compare herself even to devils.

5. She sees herself as unworthy of all rejection, insult, and shame; so that she is infinitely beneath everything.

6. She has nothing of lights or gifts from God; she has no share in anything except nothingness.[8]

Now is there anything less than nothing? There, she is the lowest in herself and in creatures: she sees herself as nothing in everything. See, then, how low this path is. The soul who is brought here, can she raise herself for anything? If she were to do miracles and convert the whole world, she would never leave her nothingness. It is her life, her happiness, and her delight to be immersed in it and to be so low that she can no longer be found. O blessed loss! O holy and sacred *anéantissement*, what happiness and benediction you produce in the soul that has you!

See, then, that it is not without reason that I tell you that this path is low. It is the narrow and hidden path which Our Lord tells us leads to the true life,[9] since it leads you into God Himself, where you will receive a new life; but a life of grace, a life of love, divine life, life which cannot be understood except by those who experience it, a life so holy, a life so noble that all one says to expound its excellence demeans it infinitely below what it is. Oh how good it is to live with this life! How happy and a thousand times happy is the soul who allows herself to be led into it!

I want to keep silent, then, about the sanctity of this path and about its privileges and excellence, which it takes from Jesus. It does not belong to me to speak about such noble matters, poor and

8 This entire passage is very close to the thought of Saint Catherine of Genoa; see *Dialogue*, Book 1, chapter 10.

9 Mt 7:13–14.

worthless runt that I am. Alas! It is not at all the affair of sinners like me to speak about the favors and graces which the divine Spouse grants to faithful souls. I retreat into my nothingness and into the silence which I must eternally observe.

I think I am obliged to leave you some time to ruminate on what Our Lord wanted me to show you, although I am very unworthy. You will make use of it as will please Him, and you will learn to detach yourself entirely from everything and to purify and simplify your mind so greatly that the virtues of others will not be vices to you.

Our Lord says to you, "Let the dead bury the dead."[10] Leave creatures among creatures, and you, my daughter, retreat into God, in whom you must make your continual dwelling. Do not voluntarily leave Him to waste time among creatures. Do not leave the All for the nothing.

Farewell, my daughter, I think I will be unable to write to you for some time. I withdraw into my center to leave you with God. He is your divine Teacher, and I pray Him that He will instruct you, and pardon me all the infidelities I commit in not receiving with the purity that I owe them the truths which He makes me understand so as to express them to you; I diminish their grace and this is what makes me wish that you received [them] from God without any mediation. This will be when it will please Him. (n. 1191)

EACH SOUL HAS A DIFFERENT PATH FOR GIVING GLORY TO GOD

Oh, the ingratitude of the human heart! Oh, the blindness of our mind which, being so full of its own interests, cannot be separated from them to make room for those of Jesus Christ!

I confess that it is a blessing to be innocent: but who can assure you that you have this? And if you do have it, are you sure you will persevere in it? Oh! How uncertain is the salvation of a soul when it relies upon its life or dispositions, or on I-know-not-what inner habit which produces neither good nor evil! Compare these souls to the happiness of a soul who tends toward God, seeks Him, and loves Him. The difference is almost infinite. The soul who lives in a slack

10 Mt 8:22, Lk 9:60.

way never receives divine communications, it does not taste God, it does not know Him, it does not glorify Him, it is like one dead, or to put it better: in a sickness which tends toward death; and little is needed for these souls to fall into mortal sin.

Let us leave the proofs of this truth until our meeting (it would take too long now), in order for me to tell you that I feel inwardly urged to reprove you for your meanness and sloth with respect to God. See from your attitude — at least based on what you tell me in your letter — how full you are of your own interests, and the impurity of your depths in reflecting on yourself and telling you that you ask no more than to be assured of your salvation. Oh! How unfaithful you are after the promises you made to Jesus Christ, and which you renewed with so much ardor! Where are the resolutions to be purely God's out of reverence for God Himself? Where is that profession of Jesus Christ that you made in baptism, to live from His life and to be animated by His Spirit? See how well you are imitating your Head, and if you are, like Him, clothed with the interests of His Father's glory. The Son of God never acted for Himself as a man. His heavenly Father's glory was His perpetual and constant motive, in all His dispositions, and in all His actions. But you are satisfied with the certainty of being saved, wanting to abandon the rest without working anymore! This is a thought from temptation, which comes from your impure ground, and from your pride's secret fear of one day being stripped of yourself and clothed in Jesus Christ. You fear losing yourself and being given as prey to the spirit and grace of Jesus. "The one who loves his life will lose it and the one who hates it in this world will preserve it for eternal life."[11] It is Jesus Christ who speaks this truth to you, in St. John. Do you want to be assured of your salvation? Be stripped of your own interests, even about your salvation, and abandoning yourself to the guidance of God, go forward in poverty, seeking no other interest than to please God.

Are you not very miserable to esteem so little God's gifts and mercies? You noticed how He desires you to be entirely His — and you are so unfaithful that you do not want to give yourself to His love which wants to permeate you, or to His holiness which wants to

11 Jn 12:25.

sanctify you? You want only to be assured of your salvation, without caring about the operations or the other particular effects of grace? I cannot understand such ingratitude or rather, such blindness — to esteem God so little that you do not want to consider the interests of His glory!

"The one to whom much is given, of him will much be required," says Our Lord.[12] One soul will be saved with a small grace and another will perish in having an equal one. The matter of our salvation is in God's control and within His view and eternal designs. If He wants you in a perfect state even in this life, necessarily you must enter it and give yourself to His grace. For this reason, do not waste time considering the path of others, but consider and weigh your own correctly. Another person will be saved through a very ordinary life, and you, you would be shipwrecked there. We must give ourselves to God's designs and enter into the purity of the paths by which He calls us if we do not want to perish eternally. It is a great secret of the interior life to know one's path and to walk faithfully in it. Another's path is not your path, which is why you do not control the work of your sanctification: each one must follow what God desires of him. Understand this matter rightly and you will live in more peace and be more faithful.

In support of your position, you say that God, being essentially glorious in Himself, has no need of accidental glory. It is true that God was as glorious in Himself as He is now, before the creation of the world. However, He was pleased in His wisdom to create the universe and to fashion creatures in order to manifest His greatness and His divine perfections, and at the same time to oblige us to adore them. He delights in His works, He is glorified in them, and He requires us to glorify Him according to what is possible for us.

1. Because He is our creator: He drew us out of nothingness, we owe Him our being, and that being must glorify Him; it was created for this reason. But there are many ways to glorify Him, and each soul has an obligation and an inner path through which God desires to be glorified in it. And the soul must show here submission and reverence.

2. A king's glory increases by having many servants and persons subject to his greatness, and who render homage to his crown. Likewise

12 Lk 12:48.

(but without any comparison), God desires to have subjects who extol His supreme authority, who are obliged to render Him homage and are sacrificed to His greatness in order to teach us that He is King and that He must be revered; that He is God and must be adored; that He is our Master who must be respected; that He is our Judge who must be feared; that He is our Spouse who must be loved, and that He is our Father and our all, who must be obeyed and honored. In brief, He has obliged us to give Him glory, and it is His delight. There is nothing to say about this: it is for this He created us and it is for this He keeps us in being, and gives us His graces and so on.

O presumption of the human heart which says, "Why should we give ourselves so much trouble when we think we are in [a state of] grace, and Jesus Christ having completely atoned for our sins, we have only rest left, without [the need of] bothering ourselves further?" "God created you without you, but He will not save you without you," said a Church Father.[13] Jesus Christ repaired all the glory that sin took away from His Father, and merited for you the grace to cooperate in your salvation. You have nothing which has not cost His Blood, but He desires that you labor with Him to reduce yourself to nothing, to submit yourself, and to give yourself to His cause; you owe this to Him through a thousand kinds of rights and obligations. (n. 2404)

13 St. Augustine of Hippo.

Reduced to Nothing

THAT IT IS NECESSARY TO HAVE GREAT COURAGE TO SUFFER IN THE PATH OF *ANÉANTISSEMENT*

Having considered your letter of this morning, the content of which moved me, I have some compassion for you, my dearest daughter, but the graces Our Lord presents to you by bringing you into the state you know do not allow the tenderness of my heart for yours—although it is very great—to hold back for a moment the mighty hand of God who is working to reduce you to nothing. And on this occasion I believe I have as much courage as that good and generous mother who held the limbs of her child when the tyrants cut them to try to make him renounce faith in Jesus Christ.[1]

I acknowledge that the martyrdom one used to suffer in ancient times was cruel; but it was not of long duration. The sight of the reward would quicken them. But the martyrdom of the inner life is without respite: it ends only when life does. And we must have an invincible constancy to not become discouraged and lose heart with the attacks of so many violent temptations which come to assail us, whether from the devil, from ourselves, or from God Himself testing the soul. This requires fortitude, this requires patience; and to better win the victory, we must be reduced to nothing. It is a war in which we must lose ourselves to win. Your trophies will be shown by the magnitude of your privation. It is necessary to be generous amid discouragement, strong in your weakness. Not by making acts of resistance, but by abandoning yourself to the fires and tortures.

I greatly desire, in your miseries, that you separate yourself from sin, namely, hate in yourself your weaknesses, malignancies, and that which dishonors God. But you are not allowed to be separated from the pain and humiliation. Here is what you must do: I fall into some infidelity. At the same time nature would like to be saddened and I experience in myself some small bitterness in the heart which would

1 Probably an allusion to the mother of Meliton, a martyr in Sebaste in Armenia in the fourth century.

pull me toward seeing myself delivered from this wickedness. In such encounters, we can be affected by God and by ourselves. For myself, I discovered by experience that the majority of our soul's wailings are nothing but products from the spring of our self-love; and we have an insatiable tendency to deliver ourselves from the cross and from humiliation. This is what we must think about a little. For there is nothing that humiliates a soul more than its frequent falls, because, of necessity, it acknowledges its weaknesses and that it has need of a help more powerful than that which our pride and our sufficiency think to find in us. In consequence, we must perforce experience how small we are in ourselves, a distrust of self, and a tendency to be constantly detached from ourselves.

Understand, then, the blessing contained in your weaknesses. See if, in a certain manner, your miseries are not likeable. They are so useful to you that without the sentiments you have on account of them, you would never firmly possess a holy knowledge of yourself.

Therefore, you must hate your infidelities, because they dishonor God, but not be disturbed or anxious about them. Hate the sin, but love the pain dearly. Be grieved about opposing God, but be glad that this embarrasses you and shows you your wicked ground. I want you to groan, with St. Paul, under the weight of this body of sin,[2] but I desire that you enter into his profound humility. For the miseries that he felt cast him into such an extreme abasement that he called himself a little miscarriage[3] and unworthy of the name of apostle. Did he not say that he would glory in his infirmities? What were the infirmities of St. Paul? They were the stings of sin which he endured and continually felt in himself. And when he asked to be delivered from them, he learned that by all these miseries his soul was being perfected.[4]

My dearest daughter, do not be upset, your state is good; but do not think about things too much. Be more abandoned and have more trust in God. Your perfection is the work of Jesus Christ. Be

---

2 Rom 7:24.

3 1 Cor 15:8. The Greek is *ektroma,* which literally means abortion or miscarriage, with the secondary definition most commonly used in English translations: "one born at the wrong time/out of season."

4 2 Cor 12:7–11.

certain that He will crown it with His blessings. However, you must remain steadfast, enduring the destruction that He brings about of everything in you which is opposed to His rule. I pity your soul which is tormented in its darkness and its ignorance; and because it does not understand the path by which Our Lord draws it to give itself entirely to Him, it is needlessly tormented and troubled.

Become a little child, more submissive than ever and more simplified in your thoughts. Be assured that your own path is good and holy, and go forward in trust. (n. 57)

WHAT IT IS NECESSARY TO DO TO ENTER INTO THE WAY OF *ANÉANTISSEMENT* (I)

My dearest daughter, I remained this whole day in a very particular solicitude about your person in the midst of all my little affairs. I had you present in my mind, in the fear that your soul might be in some disposition which would crucify you and cast you into temptation. Nevertheless, I am entirely at peace in the goodness of Our Lord who will not allow you to be tempted above your strength.[5]

Entrust yourself to His mercy above your aversions and the malignity of your ground which pulls you as much as it can away from your precious abandonment. Do not leave it, do not give up, so that you may sink into a profound nothingness. This is your refuge; but you have not yet really perceived it. You are still very inexperienced in the ways of grace. You still cannot understand that you can live in dying and die in living.

Oh! How few there are to whom Jesus was speaking in Holy Scripture: "You desire to be perfect? Give your goods to the poor, renounce yourself, take up your cross and follow Me."[6] We still find many who give their goods to the poor, but we find almost none who follow Jesus Christ. Blessed is the soul who recognizes His call and follows it faithfully.

What are you afraid of? To lose yourself, or creatures? Alas, do not fear this, because such a loss is the beginning of your eternal happiness. It is in leaving ourselves that we find God and receive the grace to follow Him. Do not regret losing everything since this is the

5 1 Cor 10:13.

6 Mk 8:34 and 10:21.

only way to possess Jesus. Take care, my daughter, that creatures do not carry you off and rob you of yourself. Never be too eager for anything human and beware of preferring anything to Jesus Christ.[7]

There are two or three steps which will cost you dearly, but will also give you an immense happiness. The first is contempt for creatures, for their praise, and for the esteem that they can have for you; become insensible to their opinions and judgments. The second is to take your intellect captive to the continual presence of God. Before you acquire this habit, you will suffer in your mind, especially since it is very scattered in the senses and in attention to self. The third is abandonment above your feelings and human reasoning; the mind always wants to see and understand everything in order to draw from it support and its own satisfaction.

Oh! It is a very great secret to know how to be entirely abandoned in profound silence before Our Lord! Remain there peacefully, in the highest part of your soul; find it good that He will purify you as He pleases. Beware of wanting to give God laws about how to lead you. The humiliating states are the most holy and the most useful. If we were illumined by faith's pure light, we would never wish to leave the state of weakness and abandonment.

Oh! How good it is that you be reduced to your nothingness, without perceiving it, as the prophet says.[8] The soul which is reduced to nothing becomes a pure capacity for Jesus Christ,[9] it no longer opposes Him. Oh, my daughter, when will I see you in this *anéantissement*? Alas, for then you will see everything in a different light, because your senses will no longer deceive you. Let yourself be led there, in secret and as if by stealth, in order to avoid the obstacles that you may bring to it. The hand of God has an infinite power to lead you into it, only do not resist Him. Consent to every impoverishment which eternal Wisdom will bring about in you, whether it be regarding your soul's operations, or the created things that you still possess, to which you can still have hidden attachments. Present yourself to the power of divine love completely stripped, and you will

7 RB 4 and 72.
8 Ps 72(73):22. I am brought to nothing and I knew not.
9 Bérulle also wrote: "Man is a nothing capable of God."

experience its power. Our Lord looks for empty souls in order to fill them with Himself, and He does not find any. We are so stingy with respect to God. When you give Him one little moment of your life or suffer a quarter of an hour of pain, it seems to you that He owes you a great deal in return. You do not have enough gratitude for what Our Lord did for you, or for the love He bears for you.

You still have the fault of being too human, and of wanting to reconcile grace too much with fleshly prudence. You lower the trajectory of your arrow and sometimes you destroy it by examination or on account of human fears. You do not simplify your mind sufficiently and you do not surrender yourself enough to the divine action. You lose yourself in creatures. You are not faithful at seeing events within the divine ordering and within the divine dispensation. That is the point to which you must be most strongly fixed, and you must break, with the grace of Jesus Christ, the bad habit of always considering creatures, which you have had until now. This is the practice you must work at constantly, and gently keep your mind bridled, for fear that, like an untamed horse, it may escape.

Therefore, humble yourself once and for all. Consent in a spirit of humility to all the poverties and miseries that Providence makes you experience: the privations, the darkness, and the helplessness; all are good, since it is God, eternal Wisdom, who gives them to you. Only remain continually abandoned, and do not trouble about the rest. God will provide for all your needs: your sanctification is His work.

My daughter, I am writing to you the lesson I would have given you this morning, if Providence had permitted me the consolation of seeing you. I do not know if it will be useful to you. I still have many things to say to you, but you cannot take them in right now.[10] They must wait until your soul is a little stronger. In the meantime, work faithfully and without listening to the complaints of nature. I pray Our Lord to strengthen you with His graces and to grant me the light and gifts of His Holy Spirit to assist you in this, according to the affection He gave me for your soul and the obligation I have to work for His glory. (n. 1474)

10 Cf. Jn 16:12.

WHAT IT IS NECESSARY TO DO TO ENTER INTO THE PATH OF *ANÉANTISSEMENT* (II)

My dear daughter, do not be discouraged about this state of complete death to self. It is not in any way the creature's work, but the work of God's omnipotent hand which causes the soul to enter into it, in the measure that it is stripped and renounces all that occupies it and fills its depths. This is the pure and holy state which you vowed in baptism. It is the one which makes us cease to be what we are in order to allow Jesus Christ to be and live in us.

This death appears cruel and very harsh to nature and to the senses; but it is very sweet to the soul. And a soul which has even a little esteem, love, and reverence for God willingly sacrifices her life and being to His greatness, out of a deep desire to see Him live and reign in us, and to glorify Him according to His good pleasure.

The longer I know you, the more I am certain of your call to this pure path. It is not that you have to be led into it just now; but you must always keep the desire to attain it, and tend toward it according to your grace and ability. In order for us to see from afar the dispositions of Jesus Christ, we must not fail to aspire to them, and to do all that the Providence of our good God has put in our power, abandoning all the rest to His mercy and love.

The remoteness from this blessed condition in which you find yourself at present comes from a very great light which shows you your miseries and unworthiness. You must not know your progress in this path; instead you must walk blindly, submitting to the guidance God has given you, without allowing your soul to reflect on itself to see its progress. Everything must tend toward death. I know that you are still far from this state; but patience and grace amend everything, and Our Lord will make you enter into it by a route you do not guess. Always remain very abandoned. Do not leave the state of sacrifice in which He keeps you. Allow yourself to be led by His divine Spirit.

I am very consoled by your confidence in God, and by the peace and tranquility which you have in view of your distance [from the goal] and the many obstacles you meet in that pure path. The one who, from all eternity, did you the honor and favor of ordaining you to this perfection, will be your strength and virtue by which to enter it. Never be discouraged. Continue to sacrifice yourself, since you feel yourself urged to do so, in view of your obstacles and your cross.

Now is the time for fidelity; you must be constant through the constancy and fortitude of Jesus Christ. Allow yourself to be slain since you are a victim. Adore the precious and loveable hand which crucifies you, and beware of considering anything according to the conduct of creatures. View all events within God's conduct and submit to them reverently. His work must be accomplished.

You will never be a true Christian if you are not on the cross, and if you do not spend your life like your divine master Jesus Christ. What are you afraid of, my child? A little shame and embarrassment from the side of creatures? And are you not afraid of the insult you give to God and His grace? For the sake of vanity we put ourselves in danger of losing a blessed eternity. Alas! If creatures could sanctify us, then it would be necessary to consider them; instead they cause us to perish and are constantly opposed to our sanctity. And since you give me the liberty to speak to you according to my opinions and experience: I only ever tasted true happiness in death to creatures. Would to God that you could know the harm they do us. Let us give them up willingly, not preferring them to the love of Jesus Christ.[11] We cannot serve two masters, God and ourselves.[12] We must of necessity leave the one for the other. Is it not right to leave everything for Jesus?[13] The one who does not renounce himself is not worthy to be His disciple.[14]

My God, my daughter, how I want to see you perfectly submissive to the action of God and entirely full of His divine Spirit! And that you be truly generous in [bearing] your crosses—that human fears and concerns not cause you to withdraw from the holy resolution you made to be entirely God's! Would you be so wretched as to give me the death blow of seeing you return to creatures and leave the true path that leads you to God? Alas! If you have the will to do it, ask God that I may die rather than see such frightful baseness in a soul for whom I sacrificed my own a thousand times, and for whom I prayed and still pray to God with such ardor.

---

11 RB 4.

12 Mt 6:24, Lk 16:13.

13 Mt 19:27, Mk 10:28, Lk 5:11, Lk 5:28.

14 Mt 10:37–38, Lk 14:26.

Oh, how true it is that the love of fathers and mothers is so much stronger than that of children! I know it by my own experience. But after all, I must be deprived of you according to God's good pleasure. You are more Jesus Christ's than mine. I do not have you except through Him and I do not want to have you except to give you and sacrifice you to Him. I do not care to have you in any other way, or to become the proprietor of someone who is a prize of Jesus's blood, whom His providence entrusts to me.

I hold you and I do not hold you. I have hold of you by command of Jesus Christ, and nevertheless I leave you most perfectly to Him, not wanting to occupy your thoughts for an instant with any product or sentiment of my affection. Alas! Would I be so wicked as to profane the temple of the Holy Spirit, to take the place of the divine Master in your heart, and to appropriate what must be uniquely His? I assure you that I feel no such desire or inclination; on the contrary, I have a passionate desire to see you be all His. (n. 2258)

Detachment from Created Things[1]

MY DEAREST LADY, YOU ASK ME ABOUT very important lessons for perfection, and about which I myself would like to know in depth in order to teach you them from my own experience and to better impress them on you; but I give myself to Our Lord to tell you what will please Him.

If I must speak about the bad effects which creatures have on us, I can tell you that they cause us numberless disorders, that they defile us and distance us from Jesus Christ, and that the soul which is totally empty of them is blessed. I entreat you to ask for this grace for me from Jesus Christ our Lord: that I may live in the detachment and in the continual death that I must have with regard to all creatures according to the law which was given me[2] and the vow that I made, which comprises many things, these among others:

1. An active and passive contempt for all creatures.
2. Never to take pleasure in any creature.
3. Never to claim their affection.
4. To despise their esteem and praise as if it were mud.
5. Not to commit the sin of human respect, in our words or actions.
6. Not to desire their approval.
7. Never to say or do anything in order to put oneself forward in their minds or to attract their affection in the slightest.
8. To take no support from them.
9. To desire nothing from them, to ask nothing of them, unless God or our neighbor urges it.
10. Never to intend or hope to obtain anything from them.

In short, we must use creatures as if there were none; and we must be so detached from them that the use or privation of them does not affect us; and we must use them as if we did not use them,[3] always keeping ourselves separate from everything, at least in affection; and

1 In the manuscript this section is entitled "About the bad effects that every kind of creature has on the soul."

2 By her spiritual directors.

3 1 Cor 7:31.

serving creatures only from charity and from necessity, whether with regard to our neighbor or ourselves. A soul who is not properly on its guard against creatures is constantly wounded by them.

Now, in order to understand this better, I distinguish between three types of creatures. First, evil creatures; second, rational creatures; third, simple and innocent creatures.

The first kind of creatures are those who lead us to sin and these are detestable, and we must flee from them more than from hell, for their malice is so dreadful that it would turn us into an abomination. Now this first kind of creature must be rejected without any mercy and we must never have any connection with it.

The second kind of creatures, which I call rational, is not as bad as the first; but nevertheless it has a malignity so great in its depths that ordinarily its conversations sully us—whether through the [fallen] natural inclination we have to be profaned, or through the creature's instinct to cast its venom on those who are connected to it and rely on it. And this in such a manner that it requires a marvelous grace of prudence to be secure against the vices into which they cause us to enter.

Oh! We must be vigilant and stay on guard! The angels themselves could make us stumble, not that they are evil in their nature, but because indeed we are in ours, in such a way that we corrupt the most holy creatures and our vanity causes strange abuses of them.

If we are capable of being sullied among the saints and the most elevated souls, what do we do in conversation with the more imperfect ones and those whose viciousness corresponds to ours? Oh how many miseries and impurities do we contract in such an encounter! A vain pleasure, a conceit, a satisfaction with ourselves, a seeking of approval, a bent toward esteem and praise—how many subterfuges to make creatures enter our senses, and to make ourselves enter their minds! We have within us a horrible tendency. And in conversations, what do we do? Useless things, trivialities, vanities, murmurings, dissipations, and so on. In the end, creatures lead us imperceptibly into sin. Therefore, it is right to have a desire to flee from them. Alas! I am describing merely the shadow of their malignity and some disorders that they cause in souls who are bound and entangled with them.

And I am not surprised that souls who seek God with great ardor and faithfulness retreat into the deepest deserts so as not to be distracted or corrupted by creatures. Oh! If you understood the harm which creatures do you every day, you would be completely astonished. O my God! When will it be that we have enough strength and courage to destroy and annihilate them? Or to put it better, to allow grace to cause their destruction in us.

Rational creatures have in them this evil, that they have in themselves a capacity for sin and for causing others who are attached to them to fall into sin. Oh what humiliation! To be an object of sin, and to be capable of corrupting the most holy persons. When I see what I am in every way, I have reason to be eternally ashamed. For it is true that creatures cause me to sin. But I can also, by an equal and possibly greater depth of malignity, corrupt them too. O my God, when will You give me the grace to know myself to the depths, so that I remain, if not humiliated, at least forever lost in the abyss of my nothingness? Alas! What blindness there is on earth! What will become of these unfortunate creatures who take so much pleasure in drawing others into sin, who toil and torment for the sake of pulling them into it? O abomination of desolation, who can understand it without dying?

The third kind of creatures from which it is necessary to be detached as well are those which are simple and innocent. Despite their innocence and the fact that they are without malice, we have the evil in ourselves which they do not have, and thus we can misuse them and be polluted. I am considering, then, this quality of innocence in inanimate creatures. In themselves they are not capable of offending God; but the use we make of them very often debases them, and causes us to fall into great sins. We see this, by too much experience, in those who use them to excess—some for eating, some others for luxury, and so on. Thus we pervert the simple and innocent creatures by bad use, and our soul remains harmed by it.

It requires a great habit of mortification to remain pure in the constant use of creatures. We must tend toward a continual death, and without respite, and not make a truce before we have destroyed all of them. I do not mean by this destruction to condemn uses that necessity and our neighbor require of us, but we must use them, as the Apostle did, with such detachment that our soul is ready at every moment to be separated from them.[4]

It is necessary to use them purely out of necessity and not out of sensuality; as if in passing and not with attachment. For our souls must not have life except in Jesus Christ, and nothing must bind or captivate it except His love. This life is a passage, it is not the permanent dwelling of our soul. If the soul is to pass on, then it must not be attached to all the created things which we use constantly, whether for the preservation of your life, or for relaxation, or out of necessity. Creatures must not remain in your mind beyond the time you are required to make use of them; and then you must forget about them, and use them only, as I said, with detachment, with prudence and discretion.

From the time Our Lord granted me the mercy of being without desires, without choice, without will, and without inclination, creatures have not had much sway over my soul. But we must remain in death. Otherwise, if we leave it, we meet them at every moment; and they will cause us much disturbance.

Be silent inwardly and outwardly, and love recollection, and you will free yourself from the tyranny of creatures. Oh! How miserable is a soul who is taken captive by them. It is impossible to have true peace in the midst of the turmoil of creatures. In conclusion, they separate us from God. For insofar as a soul enjoys creatures, it cannot completely enjoy God. This one point alone, properly considered, is capable of withdrawing us from them, and we must frequently ask God for their destruction in us, that they may be reduced to nothing in us and that we may be so for them, that we may have no more share in them and no more life in them.

Oh, how difficult it is to die there, if Our Lord Jesus Christ does not slay them by His divine virtue! We have too much pride to strike that blow. Let us wait for it from the pure mercy of Jesus Christ. In the meantime, let us keep our souls free and detached as much as possible for us. Let us not voluntarily admit creatures into our souls. Only make use of them out of pure necessity and charity, as much

4 Phil 1:23; 1 Cor 7:29–31.

with regard to your neighbor as with yourself, without ever seeking satisfaction or enjoyment or pleasure or praise or vanity or anything else for which our fallen ground gives us an appetite, and which would take too long to write to you.

Let us come to the use of creatures, and see how we must use them without being polluted by and immersed in them. In the first place, you must know that you are obliged to use creatures by God's command. For example, you must drink, eat, speak, and the rest. This is a necessity for you, I acknowledge it, whether for the preservation of your life, or for the affairs of your condition as a rational creature, which require you to be in society. In these encounters, you must do as I have told you many times: use creatures soberly, without thinking about their taste or pleasantness, but about the command of God's good pleasure which compels you, and only make use of them more or less according to need.

But you can use creatures out of charity with regard to your neighbor, entertain him, and do the same for yourself through this motive of pure charity. But you must never make use of them out of sensuality, purely for your satisfaction or pleasure; otherwise you are acting like the beasts which use things in that way.

One of the greatest obstacles to our perfection is the wrong use of creatures. They divert us and stop us on our path; and ordinarily they consume a great deal of our time quite uselessly. They defile us. The make a wall between God and our soul. They weaken us. In short, they lay waste our interior depths, profaning our grace and drawing us away from God. Oh, what misery and what desolation! Why are we always so unmoved on this point? Alas! Instead of lamenting our woes, we willingly plunge into them. And the trouble is that we look at the creature in the use we make of it, rather than at God's command and His divine will, which imposes it.

It is necessary to loan yourself to the creature out of charity, according to the needs it has of you, but you must not give yourself to it. For after you have done in its regard what God requires of you, you must forget it, not thinking any more about it or being polluted by returning to it, which often causes you to fall into unfaithfulness by indulgence, pride, or hidden vanity; and possibly also through vices which are even greater. As soon as you have made use of a creature, of whatever kind or quality it may be, withdraw your thoughts from it and lose yourself again in God. This is how you must act in order to keep yourself unsullied with creatures and to be soon detached from them. For if you leave creatures, creatures leave you. And over the course of time, you will no longer be captive to them.

I know a soul who defied and overcame them in some manner. She makes light of them and has no more worries about them because Our Lord showed her by her experience the nothingness of all things. She no longer has trouble enduring creatures' contempt and rejection; I think that she has even made these reasons for her glory and satisfaction.

In reality, it is only God who is; everything else is nothing at all, that is to say, nothing but vanity.[5] Now if all created things are nothing but vanity, can they have enough power to trouble us? What, a puff of wind will knock us down, my daughter? Oh! Such weakness which comes only from our blindness! We do not want to know the truth and thus we dwell in falsehood, in fickleness and vanity. And after this, are you surprised at our miseries? As for me, I am surprised that Our Lord does not forsake us, when He sees our voluntary malice. We have put our finger on the truth I am telling you; and if I pressed you to tell me your opinion, you will confess without hesitation that all these things are true. However, we are content to confess the truth and then remain in our old habits. Alas! If God does not take pity on us, death will catch us having some sort of good desire that will never have its fruits.

Therefore, set your hand to the work, and let us begin to be undeceived about creatures. Let us no longer see them according to what they present to the senses, but let us see them through the eyes of Jesus Christ, so that you can see in truth what they are. For created things must be valued only according to Jesus Christ's estimation of them; and since you are ignorant of His ways and cannot see into His judgments, you must suspend your own when it is a question of judging and assessing what you think to be good and holy; because you do not know how Jesus Christ judges it.

5 Eccl 1:2.

I think it good to leave everything to Jesus Christ, but still to fathom the nothingness of all things by His light, in the nothingness of their being and their natural capacity. If you had once truly understood your nothingness, you would have no trouble separating yourself from everything. You could not live one moment separated from Jesus Christ. My daughter, I pray to Him to give you this knowledge in fullness and that it may be a motive for your complete conversion.

I have said too much about this, I am not able to finish. However, I want to end by asking you to make a little reflection on the use you made of creatures in your past life. Doubtless, there you will find much impurity and much to humiliate and embarrass you. Did you use any out of pure obedience and submission to God? Did you consider His commands and His guidance? Did you use any in the purity of love, having no other aim than God? Did you not pollute creatures in many ways? Are you certain of never having caused a sin in others? Or that your wickedness did not leap out on creatures, even the most innocent? Did not vanity and self-satisfaction normally have the upper hand? Can you truly show one act in your whole life that was not corrupted and polluted by your senses? In sum, the extremely impure pursuits of our pride are continual. Oh what humiliation! Creatures always lived in us and we always took life in creatures. Behold the fine life we have led, a life which was more in vanity than in the truth, which had more of our own interests in view than the most pure glory of God.

Alas! We still do not know what it is to love God for love of Himself. We say something about it with our mouth, but our actions give the lie to our words. We look at ourselves ceaselessly; and if you pay attention to your mind, it is a hundred times more fixed on you than on Jesus Christ. We are very vigilant about our interests and we are rarely content with the circumstances in which Providence places us. We always have something about which to pity ourselves, sometimes our darkness and helplessness, and sometimes our poverty. And if our senses do not have some satisfaction, there is always some covert grumbling. Finally, we must see ourselves. Do you not find this tendency quite detestable? Oh! How I despise it in you and in me!

I pray Our Lord to turn us away from ourselves, in order to attach and unite us very closely to Himself. Let us deal with ourselves as with the wickedest creature on earth. Let us make our dwelling in God. There is the place of true and genuine solitude which you can have in the midst of the world and all the business to which your state in life binds you. In the deserts, your mind very often brings creatures, but when you retreat into God, the divine power annihilates them.

Oh, what happiness to have God for all! And how great it is to have Him in our souls! There is no need to leave your interior to find Him: as soon as you turn to Him, He turns to you[6] and you have Him and embrace Him in the secret of your soul. No one sees you and no one can prevent this holy and heavenly commerce. My daughter, do you not find this an infinitely great privilege? For you can enjoy it at every moment.

This is the lesson which was given to a soul who loved and desired solitude, and could not have it outwardly because of the work at which Providence kept her. But it was shown to her that the true solitude is in the divine essence, and that the better retreat was to be recollected in God, to dwell in God and never leave Him, as much as possible for us. From that time this soul learned to find her solitude in God and to possess Him with a very great peace and tranquility of mind. She also found a peace that the world cannot take from her. Oh! Who can say what a faithful soul receives in this loveable solitude! I am not worthy to explain it further. All that I suppose about it is that the soul possesses something which cannot be said.

Let us leave these souls to enjoy their heaven on earth, and let us try to follow them by withdrawing from created things, at least in our heart and affections, if we cannot do so in fact and by an exterior retreat. Let us find our solitude in Jesus Christ; let us dwell alone with Him alone. Let us learn to find all our sufficiency in Him and we shall see that His grace will be very favorable to us.

Taste, my daughter, this dear solitude, and ask Our Lord Jesus Christ to grant me a small share: I have an extreme need to be protected from the creatures which you see come to attack me. Alas! If I were well hidden in that divine solitude, I would not be found. But

6 Zech 1:3, Tob 13:6, Jas 4:8.

misfortune has willed that I find myself a vagabond among creatures; and the creatures did as they did to that poor bride who was not faithful enough to open the door to her Spouse: as she left in order to find Him, the city watchmen (who represent creatures) mistreated her and took away her bridal cloak,[7] which symbolizes the robe of innocence. Oh, what loss! Ask Our Lord to repair it in me, and that henceforth the wretched creatures have no power over my soul; and that I may begin to live a solitary life in Jesus Christ and through Jesus Christ. (n. 3086)

---

7 Cant 5:4–7.

Silence

MY DAUGHTER, I WANTED TO WRITE TO you today, but Our Lord did not second my little desire and His Providence has made it sufficiently clear to me that it consents to the privation, in which you and I must take pleasure as well.

You say that yesterday I gave you some great lessons, especially on silence. It seems to me that you understood little, and this is what made me determined to write to you more fully when Providence grants me the leisure for it.[1]

O my child, it is a great secret for making much progress in prayer to know well how to keep silence in Our Lord's presence. It is through silence that we are reduced to nothing before that adorable Majesty and it is in profound silence that in a wonderful manner He makes Himself heard.[2] I pray His Holy Spirit to make you understand it, or rather, that you be immersed in it without knowing it, so that your self-love does not pollute the grace.

Yes, I deem it good that you work at silence according to your present ability; meanwhile, I am making you repeat your lesson and writing you more about it. I hope that Providence will give me the grace and the time. Therefore, let us begin to work profitably, as you say. Let us only dwell on eternal things. What are the grounds for loving what perishes? Let us withdraw and subsist only on things that are truly solid. I desire that your nourishment be God Himself, and that everything else be pleasing to you only for Him and through Him. Taste the divine sweetness, be filled with God, and you will see that everything else is tasteless.

You say that it is to make me do penance that God gave you to me. Oh! How sweet and pleasing that penance will be for me if it grants me the privilege of giving you to Him and if it gives me the consolation of seeing you faithful. Yes, I say it before God and His angels, that your soul is more precious to me than your understanding

---

1 This appears to be a short note, which was then joined to the letter it announces, which begins with "O my child."

2 Wis 18:14.

can comprehend. It is infinitely more dear to me than a hundred million lives; and because it is more intimate and dear to me than all I am saying to you, think what joy I would receive to see it completely united with Jesus Christ, and how greatly I would like to obtain graces and blessings for it if I could. But alas! I have only good desires: you know my extreme helplessness. My child, I assure you that physical presence does not unite us more. Heart and mind are indissolubly joined through Jesus Christ. Neither life, nor death, nor the sword, nor hell, nor persecutions, nor height, nor depth, nor angels, nor any other creature will separate us from the charity and union we have in Jesus Christ and through Jesus Christ.[3]

You say that it is not enough to be near my heart; you desire to enter into it, in order to be sacrificed there and made a victim with me. O my child, how impure is the altar of my heart! I welcome you there, despite my unworthiness, since our miseries serve as a throne for Jesus Christ's mercy. I want to hope that His goodness will receive our sacrifice and that He will consume it one day by the sacred fire of His pure love. These are the desires of two hearts which are made one in Jesus Christ. (n. 894)

INSTRUCTION ON SILENCE

Since your life must not be anything but a continuation of Jesus's life, you must learn to keep silence, and to speak, and to act, like Jesus. This is a lesson we often reiterated to you, but since you do not tire of hearing the things necessary for your perfection, I will begin to tell you about the silence of the mind and the tongue.

It is not without reason, my daughter, that we have so frequently exhorted you to silence, to speak little and to weigh carefully what you should say; because, according to Scripture, "in much talking you will not avoid sin."[4] And St. James says that "the man who does not sin in speaking is perfect."[5] We have almost infinite examples of the tongue's bad effects; but I will not stop to tell you about them. Suffice it to say that you yourself have enough, if not too much, experience; and there are few souls who do not become sinful by much talking.

---

3 Rom 8:38–39.

4 Prov 10:19; cf. RB 6, where this verse is quoted.

5 Jas 3:2.

I know and I can say with sorrow and regret that I have sinned countless times through the tongue; and seeing myself so unfortunate as to offend God at every hour by speech, I asked God for many years for the favor of being mute, since my weakness was so appalling and the evil of my ground so dreadful that I cannot be protected from its vile effects. But I was unworthy to have my desire fulfilled. I am forced to bear this extreme misery in myself, and a great many others, which my pride deserves to experience.

But since necessity urges us to speak sometimes, it is necessary to speak like Jesus Christ and be silent like Jesus Christ. You know that He kept a profound silence for thirty years. St. Joseph spoke little and the holy Virgin still less. Here is a wonderful example of silence, which must move you, and confound your self-sufficiency, and the pride which causes you to speak and act. Can you speak in a way better than Jesus Christ and say things more holy and more righteous? And yet the Gospel says, "Jesus was silent."[6] He kept silence in order to earn for you the grace to observe it on such occasions. Therefore, you must learn to be silent. Also it is for the Master to speak and the disciple to listen.[7] You are a school girl, my daughter, and a student of Jesus Christ: therefore, listen to your divine Teacher.

I told you that there are two kinds of silence, one belonging to the mind, and the other to speech. The one belonging to speech must be observed exactly in two or three ways:

1. Never speak needlessly.

2. Speak with a moderate voice.

3. Speak with prudence and presence of mind; that is, without busyness or rashness.

One often falls into a fault, but a very important one, for not having sufficiently weighed one's words. We must ponder what we ought to say in the presence of God, especially the most important things, and be attentive to God in order to speak according to His mind and for His glory.

If words that are merely vain will be punished so strictly,[8] how much more rigorously will those words be punished which have more malignity and are more voluntary? There are many motives for you

---

6 Mt 26:63. 7 RB 6:6. 8 Mt 12:36.

to keep silence; but the most pressing and the one which must move you the most is that it will purify your soul and render it more fit for God's presence. It will give you more facility with inner recollection and dispose you to receive God's gifts. If an idle word pollutes your soul, how many sins will you avoid through silence!

Love silence. Listen much and speak little. Before you engage in lengthy conversation, and about something important, raise your mind to God, begging Him to speak through you and to preserve you from offending Him through speech. It is difficult to speak much without sinning! Weigh well this truth taken from Holy Scripture and put it into practice. Speak without scruple about necessary things and about your obligations, and in those encounters where charity requires your speech; but speak as little as you can about superfluous things.

Try to make all your words honor God, as the words of Jesus Christ honored His divine Father. Always have the desire to manifest Jesus Christ through them, to make Him known, to make Him loved by the souls with whom you are required to converse and communicate. Beware, in a multitude of words, of injuring your neighbor. This is a very delicate matter and we fall into it unawares, even often, through laxity. Never speak of the faults of others; and in company, when someone says something like this, prudently watch over your silence or, if you can, skillfully turn the conversation away, so as to avoid the sins which we may easily commit on such occasions.

Never argue with anyone when it is just about your own interest. Yield on everything that is possible for you, without trespassing on prudence and the authority you must keep to govern your domestic servants. And this, not as a severe mistress, but as a Christian, filled with the charity of Jesus Christ, who, being the master and lord of all, became the least and the servant of all.[9] Mix oil with wine, like the Good Samaritan in the Gospel.[10] Be both grave and affable; but above all, always see your strength, your grace, and your ability in Jesus Christ.

In conversations, speak about yourself as little as possible. It is impossible to speak much of oneself without putting oneself forward, without being polluted with many other infidelities. Self-satisfactions,

---

9 Jn 13:13–14.

10 Lk 10:34.

vanity, and our sense of superiority play their cards well in the proliferation of discourse.

Pay attention to God, and you will see that what I am telling you is important and very true. Never have such an unfortunate obligingness that you displease God in order to please the creature. When you recognize that God desires some fidelity from you, be immovable with regard to everything that can distract you from it. Let God always be first in your thoughts, your words, and your intentions; let Him always be God most powerful and reigning in you. Prefer nothing to His love.[11]

My dear daughter, I am admonishing you most insistently on these matters. Perhaps these will be the last instructions I give you? I pray Our Lord to inscribe them on your heart for His glory. I am most unworthy to express His will to you, but I must do what He commands me in simplicity, waiting until He gives you an interpreter more capable of making you understand and of expressing His intentions.

Oh! How many things I would have to say to you in view of your remoteness, not only about silence, but about many other very important points. I hope always that Our Lord will be your Teacher and that He Himself will reveal to you His good pleasure. But in order to be prepared to receive such a grace, you must enter into inner silence and begin to be more present to Him and more attentive to the movements of His grace. In order to reach this you must put yourself in a condition more worthy to receive your adorable Master's divine teaching, dismissing everything useless in your mind; the thoughts and unnecessary conversations and even the follies of your mind. You must renounce the complacency of your thoughts and learn to be silent, since you are before your Master, your Judge, and your King.

Silence, love, and respect are needed, and without these three points, you will learn nothing in this sacred school. Silence disposes you to listen. Love makes you embrace the instructions which God's Spirit gives you. And respect keeps you in a profound reverence for the knowledge of Jesus Christ. Consequently, be attentive to God who is present, with love and respect. Never forget these three points, which must never be separated from each other. For if you are attentive

11 RB 4:21.

without love and respect, Jesus Christ's words will not have the results they must have in you. If you are without attentiveness, you do not hear His voice. If you are without love, your action is without life or soul. Thus, love and respect are bound inseparably to attention. This is the reason I have so often recommended loving attention to God who is present. Remember God with love and respect.

Therefore, be silent in your mind in order to hear God's voice, who speaks to the soul in various ways: sometimes by distinct words, at other times by touches in the heart's depth; sometimes by delicate invitations which He makes felt in the apex of the soul, other times through His divine inspirations; sometimes by some words or actions, even outward, which we see or hear from others. God has voices everywhere: in the flames, in the waters, a voice in virtue, a voice in splendor, and so on, according to what David teaches us.[12] And the great secret of the interior life is to listen well to these voices and to yield oneself to what they teach us. It is also necessary to listen to His voice in afflictions, in insults, in contradictions, in sorrows, in disturbances. "*Vox, Vox, Vox.*" Voices, voices, voices everywhere, in heaven and on earth. An attentive soul listens only to the voices which invite it to love, adore, and glorify the One who is.[13] All these voices are calling you to see and to know God in all things, to make you worship His holy hand which applies to you the cross, the nails, and the thorns, which tells you to suffer for pure love, which invites you to humble and reduce yourself to nothing beneath all creatures, which exhorts you to fidelity on all occasions.

My daughter, listen to this divine voice, and let us beware of hardening our hearts, as Scripture says.[14] Be yielding to His loving warnings. Leave everything to follow Him.

Possibly you will ask me, "What is the inner silence of the mind and how can we observe it?" Silence of the mind consists in keeping the three powers of the soul silent. There are two ways of being silent: the first is to reduce to nothing all the operations of the powers, doing everything we can on our part, aided by grace, to place our whole selves in an emptiness. And this way is called active *anéantissement* because of the work the soul performs to arrive at it:

---

12 Ps 148, Dan 3:57–87. 13 Ex 3:14. 14 Ps 94:8 (95:7).

First, it silences the memory, according to its ability, by not accepting all the objects that it presents to the understanding. It ignores them as much as it can in order to empty this faculty and hinder its productions which distract the soul from the simple remembrance of God by faith, which is more precious to the soul and more glorious to God than all the imaginings the mind can produce. Thus, the memory keeps silence because we do not permit it remembrance or being voluntarily occupied with anything created.

The understanding is likewise in silence when we do not welcome its images or its reasonings. We must ignore all it produces in order to become attentive to God in pure faith, without clothing Him in our imaginings. You must abolish its natural curiosity and be satisfied with God alone, who will indeed know how to illumine you when it will please Him.

Your will is in silence when it has no desire, no inclination toward created things, when nothing on earth any longer engages it — not even concerns about its perfection. It is entirely in God and leaves itself entirely to Him.

In your prayer right now, your memory must simply recall God; your understanding must believe in Him, that is, it must be raised toward God in faith; and your will must be in pure and simple love, allowing yourself to be gently pulled by the powerful attraction of Our Lord's grace, which will draw you in the way that pleases Him, more or less according to your soul's purity and fidelity or according to the good pleasure of the divine Master, who sometimes purifies souls for a long time in conditions of pain, darkness, and privation, in order to prepare them to receive high graces and mercies which He wants to communicate to them. My child, you must be very faithful in all the different dispositions to which Providence will bring you.

If, in your prayer, your memory presents things to you which only serve to distract you and wipe out the simple and loving remembrance of God, you must disregard them and pay them no attention. I say the same with regard to your understanding, which sometimes wishes to bring in its own natural activities. Ignore all this exuberance and impertinence, raising yourself gently toward God above all those things; and if the din and uproar is so great that you cannot eradicate it yourself, then remain peaceful by surrendering yourself to the divine permission which desires to crucify you through these things. This *anéantissement* is called *anéantissement* of the will, which is the most excellent of all; for once the will, as the lady and mistress, is reduced to nothing, the other faculties do not have much power. Now, you cannot always reduce to nothing the operations of your memory or your mind; but as for the will, you *can* reduce it to nothing; for on account of your freedom, you only have to will this. When you say, "I do not want this or that," the will is made to obey. Now, your will is reduced to nothing by your inclination to leave yourself entirely to God, abandoned without reservation to His good pleasure, not wanting to choose anything in heaven or on earth except His divine will. (n. 2549)

With Jesus on the Cross

THE EXCELLENCE AND GOOD EFFECTS OF CROSSES

My dear daughter, I acknowledge that you press me, without forcing me, to find in myself some means for not deserting you. Our bond is very close and all these little squalls only serve to purify it and make it more intimate. It requires a few misfortunes in life to detach us from many things which would sully us and to which we have vicious attachments.

I am carried away with joy to see you perform this heroic act, which makes you say "may I do what God will have me do" — that you want to respect it and abide in your sorrow, since the cross is your portion!

Weigh well what you are saying: yes, the cross is your portion as a child of God or as a Christian. If you want to understand it better: it was the portion of Jesus Christ who received it from the hand of His Father. Do you not want to have a share in it? I answer for you and say that you will always choose the cross as the *preciput*,[1] the light of faith having shown you its excellence. Jesus Christ your divine Master would have had to exalt it [the cross] far less than He did for Him to disdain the dignity He placed in it.[2] Our sanctification is attached to it, for it is impossible to be holy without being on the cross. Purity of life is in the cross. All the virtues are in the cross: profound humility is in the cross, holy *anéantissement* is in the cross, death is in the cross, and life itself is to be found there.[3]

O precious cross, O most adorable cross which mortifies, vivifies, and sanctifies! Powerful cross, having the power to make saints, to convert sinners, and in short to consume souls in the sacred love of Jesus Christ! What soul would wish to be without a cross, knowing

---

1 In juridical Latin, the *preciput* is the right to take certain goods from a common mass. In this context, it seems that Mother Mectilde considers that the Countess will choose the cross as the best good willed for her by God.

2 In other words, since we know that Christ could never disdain the dignity He placed in the instrument of the redemption of the world and the perfect sacrifice of charity to His Father, the high exaltation of the cross for all Christians follows necessarily.

3 1 Cor 1:18, Gal 6:14.

its excellence? A soul who does not want the cross must renounce its salvation, for there is none except in the cross. The name of the cross is so loveable to favored souls that they bear it engraved on their hearts. And if they were made to live without a cross, they would be terribly crucified at not being on the cross. Let us follow these great souls, even at a distance, but according to our strength and the ability Jesus places in us. If you do not have such a great love for the cross, at least do not reject it. It is the only treasure Our Lord had on earth and it is the inheritance He left for His elect. If we gave up our share, we would be renouncing our eternal happiness.

Therefore, on the cross I cherish you and I embrace you out of love for it, fastening you there with Jesus Christ, and sacrificing you there, to be completely united and consumed on it. That is where I leave you without separating myself from you. (n. 901)

MAY JESUS CHRIST BE ETERNALLY IN YOUR HEART!

My dear daughter, I see you are in a spirit of despondency. I pray Our Lord very much to support you. Certainly, you need help from on high to endure what God, creatures, and yourself cause you to suffer.

It is a question of great fidelity to leave oneself totally surrendered to the divine action. Although your heart tries to give itself to God generously, your poor nature suffers from it, and sees very clearly that little by little it is being led toward death. That is why its pain is great. It is not necessary to crush it entirely. You are required to give it some little relief, not to give it life, but to give it the strength to endure the most harsh and painful crosses. You must fortify it a little to give it more time to die. That is how the saints dealt with it. You must imitate them, and like them offer yourself at every moment of your life to be immolated and consumed for Jesus Christ and with Jesus Christ. If God makes us live, we must be even more attached to the cross and imitate His death on the cross more. Let us have great courage — we are only beginning. We must go much farther, we must find death; we are still very far from it, because we still find life in everything.

I want you to be God's in such a pure and holy way that if I were able to obtain for you the most pure seraphs' love, I would give a thousand lives, if God gave me as many. Provided that I see you truly God's, it is enough for me. The love I have for your soul is not because of earthly grandeurs, which I regard with St. Paul as filth and rubbish.[4] I love you for the sake of the blessed eternity which God prepares for you in His mercy. That is why I can desire for you only what will make you worthy to possess it.

What is there in heaven or on earth more precious than Jesus Christ?[5] It is Jesus Christ Himself that I would like to introduce into your heart and tear out all the rest. Oh! How good it is to have nothing but Him and to be poor in all the rest; to have no longer any attachment to creatures, no more inclination toward earth's honors, no more share in the world and all that it contains. Oh! Holy and sacred poverty!

Give yourself to the spirit and grace of Jesus Christ, the poor one, so that His holy poverty may give you the strength to endure the impoverishment His love produces. May it please God that we be poor with the poverty of Jesus Christ! Oh! If His love pierces us once, it will strip us of all creatures and ourselves. We have only to let it do so, it will work miracles if we do not hinder it. (n. 1819)

I FIND YOU IN A SEA OF SORROW AND TEARS! WHAT has pierced your heart so painfully? Is nature not prevailing over grace? If you are suffering in the capacity of a victim, [remember that] the victim does not utter a word: it is led to punishment without complaining, notwithstanding that it may be charged with the crimes of the one for whom it becomes a victim. This you see symbolically in the Old Law, and you see it much more clearly in the person of Our Lord Jesus Christ, who was sacrificed to His Father's justice for the sins of the whole world. You offered yourself, it is true; but your sacrifice had no other goal than the glory of the eternal Father and that of Jesus Christ His Son. Would you have enough courage to offer Him your dear Isaac?[6] You give him with one hand and you keep him with the other. Begin to open the eyes of your mind a little, which the light of faith has illumined, and see your *N.* as your only

4 Phil 3:8. 5 Ps 72(73):25–26.

6 As the letter continues, it becomes clear that the Countess's daughter, Françoise, is the person in question.

Isaac in the adorable hand of Our Lord. She is under His divine protection, and this divine Lord loves her with an infinite love—not as earthly fathers and mothers love their children, to advance them in the fortunes of the age, to make them great on earth, and fill them with the miseries of life, which our vanity and blindness make us call delightful and happy.

Jesus Christ loves us with too holy a love for us to love in that way. He loves us in order to give us a share in His glory. He loves us for eternity and in order to make us taste divine truth. He loves us in order to unite us to Himself and make us, by His grace, absolutely one with Him. And we do not want to respect His love. Why? Because it is not a love that satisfies the impurity of our self-love, which is plunged in the vanity of this life as if into eternal felicity. It [self-love] fills itself with all the human aims. It does not value anything except what pleases nature and satisfies our mind. In our eyes the light of truth does not shine: vanity and deceit are the torch which guides us, and imperceptibly leads us into sin. But because Jesus Christ's love crucifies our feelings, we cannot esteem it or endure it. Consequently, we prefer creatures and the pleasure of sin to the purity and holiness of Jesus Christ's love. Decide, my daughter, if we are not truly blind. Be more clear-sighted from now on: prize the share your dear daughter should have in the love of Our Lord Jesus Christ. She is not created for earth: she belongs to Jesus Christ and He desires to make her a worthy object of His eternal kindness. And for this reason, He fills her with His graces in attaching her to His cross, wherein it is necessary that you help her to be sanctified. Love your child as Jesus Christ loves her; love her for eternal beatitude, love her according to the holiness into which God wants to lead her. Desire more that God be glorified by her fidelity than to see her delivered from what is crucifying her.

I have many things to write you, but it is time for Mass. I will write you afterward if Our Lord gives me the grace. However, you may receive Communion if Providence grants you the means to do so, offering your cross to Our Lord in order to receive the grace you need to carry it. And since you see that there is no human help, have recourse to divine help, which is Our Lord Jesus Christ, so that He may draw His glory from this harsh cross, who is moved more deeply by it than you are yourself, although you be deeply affected by it.

I pray God to bless the mother and the child. Take courage, He will bring His glory from this. He does nothing without design, He is adorable in His dealings. Bear them with respect and submission to Him. Farewell. (n. 1815)

MY GOOD SISTER, WHEN I RECEIVED YOUR NEWS, I WAS expecting it or you yourself. It will be this evening, then; but if you see that this causes even the slightest annoyance, then you must forego this little consolation, abandoning yourself without reserve to God's guidance. Beware of lowering your arrow by, in that meeting, attributing this little vexation and opposition to the creature. It is God who purifies your inner depths and gives you matter for sacrificing your Isaac. (I can name your desire in this way, since the defeat of it is so costly to you.) God will accomplish it when its hour comes.

I only carry in myself the sentence of death and yet I am not able to be entirely dead. I ask you to pray Our Lord to grant me the grace to die without holding anything back.

Do not grieve over what is happening. If the continuation is useful, God will move... Remember that you are the child of Providence, that you must no longer have desire or will. Your satiation and delight must be God's good pleasure. Plunge into His holy will and take your sweetest satisfaction in it. You must be God's in the way He desires, and not in the way you think. Allow yourself to be guided. Respect the outcome, although it mortifies you. Adore the secret judgments of God and His adorable designs in everything. Be completely abandoned to the divine will and if His Providence deprives you of coming, remain peaceful. See all this as being God's loving action, which purifies you and strips you, and to put it briefly, detaches you from the hidden attachment you may have, under the pretext of your perfection.

The whole of sanctity consists in being a victim of God's good pleasure and I beg you to sacrifice yourself completely to Him. Do not take trouble about anything except being faithful. Providence, who is your good mother, will take care of the rest and will give you what is necessary for your sanctification. Do not be grieved about anything in this world except being opposed to God. Also, you must control your sorrow, for fear of self-love. Entrust yourself to God, and rest in the arms of His loving kindness, without being disturbed about anything. All the things affecting you are merely creatures; allow yourself to be affected and pierced with pure love. Your greatest concern is to be entirely God's—but in the manner He desires and not as you may suppose. Open your heart to little pains and Our Lord will one day grant you the grace of being worthy to suffer greater ones for His love.

(n. 2152)

LETTERS OF CONSOLATION ABOUT A LOSS SUFFERED IN A FAMILY

My dearest. I am not writing a particular response, you have too much sorrow in the great affliction that it pleased Our Lord to give you today, by which I am moved with you, knowing the loss the family suffers according to the world's reckoning.[7] But why? Everything is God's. He is Master of all and He deals with His creatures in the way He pleases. We must endure it with respect and submit to it. That is what you must do, my child, giving back to God the creatures He loaned you for a time, without being proprietary about them.

This is a misfortune that will have surprised you, especially since it seemed that you wanted to have a hope of life. A soul is surprised by what it does not expect; but a soul who has nothing and who leaves all creatures in God is not surprised by His providential dispositions for them.

My child, adore the cross which Our Lord presents to you through this death, prostrate yourself on the ground to receive it, and submit to it. Consent humbly and lovingly to God's designs and remember that you are offered to Him as a victim. Therefore, adore God's counsels and His judgments concerning this soul and learn to give yourself to God at every moment of your life, so that you are not surprised at the hour of your death.

7 It is possible that it was the death of her grandson which distressed the Countess so much. He died in youth. This group of letters and notes may have been written in various circumstances and later grouped together by the Countess because they are on the same subject.

While desiring to instruct you about how you must deal with your affliction, I also feel deeply affected and share your sufferings with you. But it is in such situations [especially] that we must be faithful. And you ask how must you be abandoned to God? This is an excellent occasion which crucifies you and your whole family in submitting to this cross. Of the cross, on the arms of which you hang again, let us say with the holy apostle: "*Salve, crux pretiosa.*"[8] You must not withdraw or be moved in too natural a fashion. Instead, bear the cross with fortitude, constancy, and fidelity. Farewell, my dear daughter, I entrust you to Jesus Christ's strength to endure your affliction.

(n. 1248)

MY CHILD, THE SHARE I HAVE IN YOUR AFFLICTION IS so great that from the moment I received the news, I was not parted from it for one moment, offering you ceaselessly to Our Lord, to ask Him for the grace for you and your family to bear in a holy way the cross He places on you. I see that it is great according to the world's thinking, but yet all adorable in the hand of Jesus Christ, who does nothing except by a very particular command of His divine wisdom. You must view it from this angle, and have respect for it.

It is here you can have recourse to faith beyond your [natural] lights and reasonings, to submit in the humble conviction that the action of God and of His good pleasure is good, and that you prefer the divine will to all earth's felicities and grandeurs. My child, let us be detached from everything else, regarding nothing as worthy of our love except Jesus Christ. You promised Him this fidelity in your baptism; and you must put it into effect when there is a need, demonstrating that you are a Christian. What good is it to have fine sentiments about the cross and suffering and, when you meet them, not have the courage to endure anything? After we made a thousand declarations of fidelity to God, He receives our good will and does not fail to test us through events; and if we are so wretched as to disregard our grace, then we deserve to be deprived of it. This is an event which demands heroic acts from you, and these are capable of sanctifying you:

8 "Hail, O precious cross!" From the first antiphon for the office of St. Andrew. This is how he accepted the cross on which he was martyred.

1. A total abandonment to God's good pleasure.

2. A respect so great for the accomplishment of His divine will that you prefer it to all your interests.

3. Do not be too natural, do not let your mind be much occupied with a thousand human reasonings.

4. Endure God's designs being accomplished according to His divine pleasure in the person of your friends.

5. A trust in God which is unshakeable, regarding all created things as nothing, and believing that Our Lord will pour forth grace for the sanctification of the family, to bear this affliction.

6. Do not grieve over the earthly fortunes which seem diminished by this death. Love your children in the degree of greatness in which God placed them, without desiring anything for them but the grace of Jesus Christ.

7. Ponder the power of a God who brings everything to nothing when He pleases, without anyone being able to resist Him. Submit to His sovereignty, without finding fault with it. God is the absolute master of His works: He makes them and unmakes them according to His good pleasure.

8. Remain at peace in the midst of war and endure the carrying out of God's orders.

9. That, then, is what you can do if Our Lord does not give you other lights. I would be glad, when you are free, to know your dispositions in this encounter. Meanwhile, be strengthened through the grace of Jesus Christ. You still have many more things to bear. But it is a glory for a Christian soul to be immolated and consumed on the cross of her most adorable Jesus. You must not be daunted, He will be your strength and your virtue.

When you can, give me word of your news. *Adieu*, I assure you that I am with you on the cross, and possibly, I take too much part in it. I see in this that I love you deeply and more than I can express.

(n. 1894)

MY CHILD, YOUR LETTER FROM THIS MORNING BOTH consoled and edified me, and gave me reason to adore the mystery of the divine mercies on your account, and made me hope for many graces for the rest of your life.

Come, my child, let us carry our cross generously. Let us give Jesus Christ evidence that we are His victims gladly and that we desire to spend our lives in the love of His divine will. I do not condemn you for having shown your sorrow outwardly or even for having stirred it up; charity requires these sentiments of your kind heart, imitating the Apostle who wept with those who were afflicted.[9] It is right to show your sorrow, indeed you can shed tears, but beware of becoming totally softened and throwing yourself into feelings that are too natural. This would lower the flight of your arrow too much; it would be a lack of fidelity.

Everything must be sacrificed to Jesus Christ: your husband, your children, and your friends. You must not become their proprietor, or desire on their behalf what might cause the loss of their soul, under the pretext of affection. Love your friends more for eternity than for the present life, which is very short and very strewn with thorns and sufferings. You have cause enough every day to notice its wretchedness and vanities, to make you loathe them and to oblige you to obtain for your children a better fortune than the one for which the world wishes them to hope.

Everything passes, there is nothing permanent except God. All the rest can be possessed only for a moment, and yet, during the little time we enjoy it, we are put in great danger of losing the inestimable treasure of grace. There are too many who are blind about this point. Do not be, my daughter. Our Lord having opened your eyes, do not be willingly mistaken. Let us pass from earth to heaven. You are no longer allowed to have a share in it; your grace and your Christian confession separate you from it. It would be a kind of sacrilege to be tied to it again. Our Lord already broke one part of your chains, which are the great bonds of sin. I pray Him to finish breaking all, so that being free you can, with the holy prophet, offer a sacrifice of love and praise,[10] which will last for eternity.

Yes, yes, my child, creatures are very harmful to you. You are still a child and very weak. But take courage, wait for your deliverance and bear the weight of your misery with confidence and humility. I suspected that family interests would attack you and that the establishment of its fortunes would affect you; but it is God's and God

9 Rom 12:15. 10 Ps 106(107):22.

will raise it as high as He pleases. You have to relinquish much, and see in the light of truth that all such grandeurs are only nothings all filled with extreme misery.

The cross is salvation to the elect. It is the inheritance of the children of God. Be happy to have a share in it and may this one serve to prepare you for a greater one. I do not think He will leave you long without bestowing new ones. Do not be afraid of them, I beg you.

(n. 2985)

YOUR LETTER FROM YESTERDAY CONSOLED ME VERY much. I ask Our Lord to continue giving His graces to you and to give you the strength to be perfectly submissive to His good pleasure. Without a doubt, He is preparing you for some special visitation. Be faithful, fear nothing. Remain in God beyond all things and leave all things to God; do not be occupied with them. Do not be disturbed about future things, but rest sweetly in the arms of divine Providence. Everything God will do will be done very well. Begin to have a high esteem of His plans concerning you, my child, and have a loving submission of mind in this. I wish that we could always be concerned with pleasing and loving God, and that we no longer had any desire except to lay hold of life continually in Him. My God, how I want to see us totally separated from the world and from creatures! How much we are buried in ourselves and in human interests! I pray Our Lord to deliver us from this. (n. 2896)

MY DEAREST, IT IS TRUE THAT *N.* WAS VERY SICK. BUT it was not thought opportune to tell you, because of the fear of losing mother and child. It was for this reason that you were not told everything about it. Our Lord is wonderful in His arrangements for His elect. Yesterday I urged you to a holy and loving satisfaction with God's good pleasure. Oh! How good it is to see nothing outside of Him and to receive everything in Him! You see how much this holy practice keeps you at peace above your senses. This is the way we must lose ourselves so that God alone may be in us all that He must be. At length He gave you back your child. I ask you tomorrow to make a new sacrifice to Him, in thanksgiving to God for her recovery.

(n. 491)

DEAREST, YOU EDIFIED AND TOUCHED ME WITH YOUR abandonment and submission to God's good pleasure. I ask Him, if it is for His glory, that He be content with your disposition, as He was with Abraham's good will at the sacrifice of his Isaac.[11] Remain abandoned in this way. Despite the fact that your child receives life, do not take her back to appropriate her. You gave her to God, do not take her back, for fear that the infidelity you might commit would oblige God to snatch her from you. You must remain in the detachment which the command of His wisdom caused you to enter. Do not leave His guidance. Remain steadfast without fearing anything.

The person who has God has everything, and a soul who possesses Him is assured of its happiness for all eternity. O my child, we must not be content with anything less than God, since creatures are too paltry to satisfy us. Leave, leave willingly what ties you to earth. The life of the world and the senses is too low and ignoble for a soul of grace. Each must live according to his lineage and dignity. You are a Christian, live like Jesus Christ. Alas! You have only the moments of the present life to arrange for your eternity. It seems to me that nothing created should stop us, however small it may be.

Oh! If I were faithful in doing myself what I am telling you, I would be in reality what I am not. Ask God to change me and I will pray Him to do His holy will in you and in your beloved daughter.

(n. 3085)

MY CHILD, SEE FROM YOUR OWN EXPERIENCE THAT IT is impossible to know ourselves truly if Providence does not put us on the cross. The real gold is known by the touchstone.[12] God's hand must fix us to the cross of Jesus, to contradictions, and so on, to teach us what we are. Your weaknesses will be very useful to you and I am not sorry that you sometimes fell, provided that your soul is not anxious and discouraged about it. Humility is never solid if it is not founded on a long experience of our miseries. Love

---

11 Gen 22:1–15.

12 *pierre de touche:* a variety of black jasper used to make tests with the *touchau*, a set of small plates of gold or silver alloy of different titles, arranged on a star-shaped support, allowing one to determine the title of a jewel by comparing the impressions left on the touchstone.

this condition which humiliates you, and be humbled at the sight of your feelings which often have no other motives than causes which are purely human and natural. Alas! It is not always God's interests which move us! We are creatures and it is seen clearly in our actions. That is why I have reason to say that we must have pure actions and not just good feelings.

As for me, sometime I told you that if I am not on the cross, whether inwardly or outwardly, I am not content, even though we must be content in every state. With regard to God's good pleasure I am, but not with respect to myself, because apart from the cross I do not know myself, and I should suspect some hidden good opinions which the creature's impurity produces in itself. However, when I see myself continually unfaithful on such occasions, there is no way to have a good opinion of myself. Thus, a fall is sometimes very beneficial to a soul who should only be humbled and abased.

As Our Lord said, you must have the dispositions of a child, with regard to purity, innocence, and humility; but you must also follow St. Paul's advice, who said that you must be a man and walk generously in the ways of God.[13]

You have sufficient instruction; it remains only for you to be faithful. Our Lord will not forsake you, my child. Open your heart to Him and allow Him to establish His pure love in it in the way He pleases. If He crucifies you, He will be your strength. I implore you to be completely abandoned to His good pleasure, and then allow Him to do all that He wishes. He can do nothing except what is holy and most right. Pour out your sorrows into His adorable Heart; suffer in His holy presence and beware of too pressing an anxiety and of [your mind's] activity. You can weep and lament before God, but beware of your sentiments being too natural. Rise again by a complete submission to the guidance of God, who gives you trials in order to perfect your sacrifice. (n. 3166)

SINCE IT PLEASED DIVINE PROVIDENCE TO ARRANGE A cross for you, on this occasion, which is one of the most painful that can happen to you, show that you are a Christian and that your will

13 Mt 18:3, Mk 10:15, Lk 18:17; 1 Cor 13:11, 14:20.

is completely reduced to nothing in the love of Jesus and His good pleasure. It is His adorable hand which presents the cross to you. I beseech you to receive it worthily, as a soul clothed with Jesus Christ's sentiments and love must do: with respect and submission, revering God's dealings with His creatures. Beware of your mind running off on this occasion where God wants to test your faithfulness. (n. 2556)

MY DEAREST DAUGHTER. SINCE PROVIDENCE HAS FURnished you with matter for sacrifice, I bid you to give yourself to it very faithfully and remember that it is a favor in the interior life to meet with such opportunities, in order to prove to Our Lord your love and fidelity; His wisdom sends them to you for this reason. I encourage you to make use of them and to expose yourself often to Jesus's holiness so as to destroy in yourself the impurity of creatures and your senses.

The lack of firmness which I observe in you often gives me very great worries about your perfection, and it seems to me that I am almost obliged to hold you by the hand and always push you, I have so much fear of seeing you turn back. And I fear that for lack of a little courage and fidelity, you may be wretched enough to remain in want of an infinite happiness, rendering yourself incapable of tasting the divine sweetness which is found in God and which the faithful soul has the honor to experience. Would it be necessary that the nothingness of everything created deprive you of this privilege? I cannot allow this for you.

Since Our Lord grants you the mercy of calling you to the feast of His divine love, do not refuse such a remarkable favor. In the midst of your turmoil keep a continual desire for God, a hunger to possess Him and to be perfectly united to Him. Whatever crosses and afflictions life gives you, do not retreat from them, since they are the means to sacrifice yourself more fully and purely to God. Prostrate before God's majesty, willingly say Jesus's words on the cross: "My Father, I commend and give back My spirit into Your hands."[14]

Through these words you sacrifice to the eternal Father, with Jesus, all that you are: not only your spirit, but all your actions, all your

14 Lk 23:46.

crosses and all that you can be. Have this intention of giving yourself completely to God and of remaining purely abandoned into His hands, and endeavor to make this sacrifice with understanding and with the intention of surrendering yourself entirely to God through Jesus Christ. You will do this little penance three times a day; I leave the times for it to your convenience. (n. 2536)

MY CHILD. I WRITE YOU THIS LITTLE NOTE TO HAVE the consolation of learning your news, since I will not have that of seeing you today. Send word to me, if you can, how your spirit is in the cross which Our Lord Jesus Christ Himself imposes on it. Be very faithful on it and adore the ways of God's loving conduct regarding His chosen ones, and the admirable inventions of His Providence to sanctify them. Have patience on the cross. Detest everything you encounter there which dishonors God, but bind yourself to what crucifies you, and remember the three dispositions with which Our Lord Jesus Christ suffered, which I have explained to you in the past:

1. He suffered in view of His Father's orders.[15]

2. He suffered for His pure love.

3. He suffered with a disposition of eternity; that is, He was willing to suffer eternally if such had been His Father's good pleasure.

(nn. 1248, 1745)

15 Is 53:10, Mt 26:39, Mk 14:36, Lk 22:42.

Nature and Grace

INSTRUCTIONS FOR KNOWING IF INNER REPROACHES ARE FROM GRACE OR NATURE

I have read your letter from this morning, in which you complain of your scant progress, your poor memory, and your ignorance, not knowing, from what you say, what your disposition is except confusedly, and everything in you reproaches you, without your being able to discern whether it is grace or nature.

I believe it is both the one and the other. Grace reproaches the impurity of your depths, not in order to trouble, disturb, or hamper you, but to humble you. For in the past, you never knew yourself in truth. That is why you lived with a secret self-regard; and you had so much support in your works, that you believed you could have more from them, thinking that God still owed you much on account of them, and that you increased the Church's treasures greatly.

However, in order to do away with this esteem of yourself and this vain presumption about your works, Our Lord had to open your eyes and make you see your ground and its impure fruits, in order to undeceive you and detach you from that hidden pride and to overthrow your esteem for yourself, which was in place for such a long time and was so deeply rooted.

It was necessary that the awareness of your miseries be built by a long experience of your corruption; otherwise you could never be undeceived. For we have a natural instinct to excuse ourselves, to believe there is more good than evil in ourselves, and a terrible inclination to elevate ourselves. We cannot acknowledge our sins and our nothingness, unless we are very deeply convinced of them; and this can happen only if you experience what you are and by groaning under the weight of your infirmities. And despite the feelings and experience we have of them, we always have a tendency to conceal them, so true it is that we live in a lie; we willingly retreat from the truth to avoid a little abjection. This is the first reason, in my opinion, why your actions reproach you: it is to make you consider the depth of your impurity.

The second reason comes again from grace, which, wanting to pull you from your own operations to cause you to enter into a greater detachment, causes you to loathe your productions in order to strip you of them and to enter into a great contempt of self and of everything that comes from you.

The third reason proceeds from the same grace, which cannot permit the impurity with which you act, because this grace calls you to a very great sanctity and consequently demands much purity of you.

Now to know if it is grace which gives you these reproaches, you must see if its effects are contrary to those of nature: for grace humbles without disturbance, it abases without discouraging, it casts you into a holy loathing of yourself without making you impatient; and finally, little by little, it reduces you to nothing and makes you leave your self-regard in order to surrender yourself without reserve to Jesus Christ.

The reproaches which come from nature have other effects, you can easily recognize them:

1. They disturb and pull down the spirit.

2. They cause uneasiness with discouragement.

3. They are always bent toward human interests. They cause frequent returns to self, to make us anxious, saying that we are not advancing, that we are making no progress in the interior life, that we are not advancing in grace. Then, little by little, they propel us into a disgust for the interior life, saying that we will never do anything. Here are the effects of pride and there are many others that it would take me too long to explain.

However, it is not enough to state the effects of the one and the other, let us say a word about how you must act in this:

1. During these continual reproaches, you must learn to be calm.

2. You must consider your imperfections in order to humble yourself about them. If you say this does not humble you, I know in fact that it at least pulls you from and opens your eyes about your opinion of yourself.

3. It causes you to notice the corruption of your ground.

4. And to see your need of grace to be purified, and your dependence on Jesus Christ, in order to act properly; therefore you must surrender to it.

5. You must have great patience in your miseries.

6. Recognize that you are unworthy to act properly, and that it is a grace merited for you by Jesus Christ, of which you are not able to make use. In order to act here with more simplicity, you must surrender everything to the divine justice and mercy, hide yourself in God, confessing that there is nothing pure or worthy of Him except Himself, and thus remaining in your nothingness, darkness, and helplessness, and without ceasing to do what you are obliged to do. But you will do it with less pride, less complacency, and with more indifference, confessing that our actions are unworthy to glorify God; and nevertheless do them with as much fidelity as if God must receive an eternal glory from them.

This is how you must act without attachment and without possessiveness; and after you have done everything you could have, say that you are a useless servant.[1] In truth God does not need you. He subsists through Himself. But He wants you to put yourself in a disposition to glorify Him in every moment of your life and in all your actions. You must become faithful to this according to your small ability, and His grace and love will make up for your inadequacies. Therefore do not be discouraged, always be steadfast, and endure the tyranny of your pride. Bear with humility and patience the reproaches of your impurities. You are not worthy to have higher graces. Make use of your talent and the *paterfamilias* will give you more.[2]

I recommend patience with yourself. Beware of your natural activity and being overly zealous for perfection. You must die to everything, even to desires which are too eager for this, being content in everything and everywhere with the divine will which must be the rule for your life and for all your perfections. You must not desire anything except what it pleases Him to desire for you. This is a great rest for the souls who know how to find and experience it.

You say you desire everything and do not desire nothing. My daughter, desire what God desires for you. You cannot err in desiring Jesus Christ's desires, because He can desire only what is just and holy. All the plans you form about yourself—the majority are useless: entrust yourself to God to arrange for you as He pleases. And everything that

1 Lk 17:10. 2 Mt 25:14–24.

your affairs require you to plan, you must do this with a great submission to the orders of Providence, so that you are ready at every moment to stop doing them and to enter into the plans of Our Lord when it pleases Him to manifest them to you. It is always necessary to be in a state to break your will out of homage to the divine will, and out of fidelity to the promises which you solemnly made in your baptism.

You say that you feel the impurity of your actions without being able to say it. I am not surprised. One must suffer and see oneself destroyed without being able to complain. God sees you and He alone can console you, He is enough. You will go through many other troubles yet. Courage, allow yourself to be truly crucified in order to be truly purified. Let us suffer as long as we can, this is the best we could possibly achieve. The rest is in the hands of Jesus Christ, it is for Him to carry it out. (n. 725)

DEMONSTRATING THAT THE WILL IS MISTRESS

Will you come tomorrow, my child, so that I can make preparations to speak with you and reiterate what I already told you? For I think it right that you understand its importance for your peace of mind and the tranquility of your conscience.

Yes, it is appropriate that you know how your will is the mistress of your soul, and that it is this [faculty] in you which causes sin or virtue. For if the will does not adhere to the temptation, the temptation will not be able to harm you, though it is as evil as all of hell. And this truth should calm your soul in the midst of the storms and troubles of life. As an example: if your mind is distracted, you suffer much from its wanderings, but you do not sin if it is not voluntary, that is, if your will takes no pleasure in it. Now as long as you see that your imperfections are painful to you and crucify you, this is a sign that you do not consent to them. For when the consent of the will is united to the temptation, all is in agreement and the soul does not suffer the pain it feels in spirit. Be at peace, my child, your soul is not always polluted by your mistakes and thoughts. The battles you endure will win crowns for you.

Have a little constancy on your cross; your ills will not last forever. And God will know how to reward you for them. And when you see that you do not know what to do or what to decide, instead of being disappointed and thinking about your ignorance and misery, say to Our Lord along with the Prophet: "*Domine, vim patior, responde pro me.*"[3] Lord, I suffer and I can do no more, answer and act for me. And despite the continuing trouble, leave yourself to this suffering for as long as God pleases, and trust in His goodness, that He will bring His glory and your perfection out of it. (n. 2922)

MY VERY DEAR DAUGHTER, I REMAINED YESTERDAY IN my little solitude where it pleased Our Lord to make me feel the effects of His very great mercy. This was not without thinking of you, and I observe that you are too little focused on one truth, and there still is in your depths a hidden bad habit of knowing, and imperceptibly it happens through attacks of your self-love.

You say that your weakness is so great that you cannot even give an account of yourself. As for me I tell you that in your weakness and darkness, I find you illumined; and your condition in that disposition is much more solid, since your pride has less share in it.

I give you enough lessons—and I suspect too many—because of your mind's activity which is feeding itself and does not allow you to remain steadfast, in order to fill yourself with the truth that is shown to you.

You say that you do not know if you consent or not, if you sin or not. There is no difficulty about this. You are conscious that you have a higher will, that is to say, one which is mistress of your senses, to accept or reject what they present to you which is opposed to God. You cannot prevent the feeling, which you have in common with the animals. But you can reject the evil, though it may have the feeling of sin. But in spite of feeling this, you do not consent. You are very confused in the interior life, and by wanting to be too enlightened about it, you do not see anything at all. Your mind is insatiable: it devours everything. And knowing it to be inclined to spiritual gluttony, it is sometimes good to make it fast and bear being content with its darkness, wretchedness, and poverty.

You say that your desire to receive instruction is only for the sake of finding God better. But I say that the majority of your desires are

3 Is 38:14.

nothing but the productions of your self-love, which, as I already told you, has a very great penchant for searching so as to fill itself. What! My child, if you seek God in spirit and in truth, do you not possess Him through faith? Did you not learn that there is a God worthy of your love? No, no, the interior life does not require many things; but only that we believe and abandon ourselves in love; that is to say, to believe in God and be entirely abandoned to His love. If you search too much, you will find little. Faith does not consist in much knowing, but in believing and submitting to the truths we are required to believe.

For a long time I have been exhorting you to become simple in your mind, and to be content with God's good pleasure in everything, and above all to be less focused on yourself. I find you too busy for your own good, and you reflect too much. This is a great infidelity in the pure life of grace, because to the extent that you are focused on your own interests, even spiritual ones, you are less elevated and united to God. For we must be more God's than our own, and have more zeal for His reign and His glory than for all the rest.

I bid you to be very faithful in your darkness and forsakenness. Find it good that God is doing His work and do not think about whether the lower part [of your soul] is content with it. Remain firm, that is, firm in your precious abandonment, even without feeling or seeing it in your senses. It is your will which accomplishes this, as lady and mistress of your soul. You have the liberty; you can use it by taking it prisoner to the holy direction of Jesus, which you cannot see in the midst of your darkness. Your mind gets confused for wanting to do too much. Simplify yourself and remain at peace. Someday you will know what you are ignorant about at present. Have patience.

(n. 966)

Pride and Humility[1]

LET US SAY A WORD OR TWO ABOUT YOUR letter. I notice in many places in it that you have a great desire to know and be pierced with a horror for the sin of pride, so as to convince your mind of it and have a true opinion of the dreadfulness of its evil. You will understand it in depth only to the extent that you enter by faith and love into esteem for God. You must know God, His holiness, His goodness, and the rest of His divine perfections, to truly fathom the wickedness of pride. Your understanding of this will be more or less according to your understanding of God. I think I already wrote and spoke something to you about the rest that can be said, such as its qualities and its effects.

If we had one tiny mite of humility, we would not be so blind. What makes you recognize your pride so little is the fact that you were always on its side. You were not opposed to it, and, being in agreement with it, you made it your friend, because the love of yourself found its life and its satisfaction there. You see by experience the wretchedness of the soul who clings to it.

It is true that I told you that your pride has some resemblance to that of the devil. He is cunning and subtle for his own interests, to satisfy himself, and so on. The secret esteem you have always had for yourself—what is it but an elevation of yourself which placed you on God's throne, making you esteem creatures?

Alas! that for so long God was reduced to nothing in you, that He endured humiliations, insults, and rejection! How often you have thought about yourself so as to take pleasure in yourself and in creatures! Oh! How few are the souls who are illumined about these truths! But since He gives you the grace to be in the number of those by whom He wills to be glorified, be submissive to the lights of His Holy Spirit. Surpass yourself. Enter into these truths by faith, and little by little the experience will make you learned.

1 In the manuscript, this section is entitled "Of the sin of pride and its evil consequences."

As for the essay in which you made the declaration about your whole life, if you think to say something to your disadvantage[2] in reading it, you will demonstrate by it your greatest humiliation and the embarrassment of your pride.

I feel very well in my soul that yours is not much penetrated with the pride and vanity that has reigned in you up until now. I pray God to grant me the grace and light to be able to show you something about its malice, to oblige you to hate it as you must.

Other sins have to do with God indirectly, but pride has this evil: it is directed toward the divinity itself. Oh! How terrible it is! I am not at all surprised that God hurled the [bad] angel from paradise to hell and drove Adam from His place of delights where He created him in justice and holiness. I am much more surprised at His divine and incomprehensible mercy which does not condemn me to the abyss. After having received the grace to be a Christian and the lights which accompany it, I am so presumptuous as to raise myself by a detestable pride up to the throne of God. Yes, my daughter, pride is so wicked and so abominable that it chases God from His throne and takes His place in order to be worshipped.

Oh! My God, but we do not know this abomination! We would have endless horrors from it [if we knew it], and we would choose rather to die a thousand deaths than to commit such a sin and dishonor God so presumptuously. It requires the light of God Himself to understand and be penetrated with this truth, which we are explaining to you. I hope one day it will be given to you abundantly and that you will understand your blindness in depth. Have patience and persevere always in the will where I find you to be all God's. The rest will not be lacking to you. (n. 356)

I GIVE MYSELF TO OUR LORD'S SPIRIT TO ANSWER your letter.

Regarding the first section containing the instructions: I indeed recognized that you always had nothing firm or true in the inner depths of your soul; and that this is what hindered your true and genuine grounding in the Christian principles, and which surprised you today

2 Certain manuscripts have: "to your advantage."

by the knowledge that the mercy of God pours into your soul, which shows it something of its extreme miseries. I can assure you that you still see only a shadow of it, so from that, judge what it is.

I told you yesterday about a truth with which I myself was pierced, lamenting in my soul over our blindness. Oh God, what impurity of life, to live from creatures and for creatures! Oh, what a profanation of the grace and holiness of the Christian life! Does it have any resemblance to Jesus Christ? Yes, you have deceived creatures by defiling yourself with their vain praise, esteem, and good report. You gave them a conviction of perfections in yourself from which you are very far in reality. You took the appearance for the reality, and satisfied yourself with that, without considering that God was not at all satisfied, but frequently very offended.

Here are the masterpieces of your past life, which you must regret from the bottom of your heart, since your pride and vanity preferred creatures to God and through so much clinging to them, you placed yourself in opposition to God, doing in your own way what Lucifer did in his, raising himself to God's throne through esteem of himself and an odious presumption. Alas! How many times do we put ourselves on God's throne within ourselves, worshipping ourselves, making an idol of our senses and our inclinations? I am not surprised if souls who know and revere God are sometimes even so moved as to die of sorrow at the sight of a God of infinite majesty, grandeur, and holiness not being honored, at least by Christians who have received the faith in baptism and who must be acquainted with these truths. I pray the pure and holy Spirit of Jesus to pierce us keenly with these truths, so that, at least one moment before dying, we may enter into ourselves once and for all, to mourn and ask for mercy about our darkness and our ignorance, and begin to pay our respects to Him, giving Him our love, homage, and reverence. And since you have a little light on this matter, and God grants you the very great grace of understanding it, become very faithful to its pure attraction. Do you know that this will not [turn out to] be the last occasion on which He will present it to you to sanctify you?

Open, open your heart which you often closed to God in order to give it to creatures; and live from now on with a humble opinion of yourself. And in the encounters where your mind was accustomed to take flight, you will be reduced to nothing in your soul in view of the abyss of your miseries and you will speak only with humility and respect, seeing before God how you fool the world with your discourse. Remember that you are a schoolgirl and a disciple of Jesus Christ, and that you must really know and practice your lesson before teaching it to others.

We will write, when it pleases God, what you wish regarding the loathing you must have of sin (supported by Scripture and its truths). In the meantime, simplify your mind, and receive within the ordering of God the laws imposed on you by Him.

Regarding the ill effect which Adam's sin causes in us, I think this requires less explanation inasmuch as our own wretchedness so often makes us experience its malice and corruption that we are all capable of preaching about it. Our depth of pride, our vanity, our pursuits, and the products of our self-love and all the rest would fill volumes, which I leave unsaid, for who would listen? Do we not feel it at every hour? Or else a wretched powerlessness to give ourselves to God and be subject to His good pleasure? Oh! How immense is the misery of sin! It is too little known, that is why we do not dread it. (n. 994)

WOULD TO GOD THAT YOU COULD FATHOM THE EXTREME and terrible evil that it is to sin. Oh! Sin, sin, what harm you have done to us! Alas! Who will be able to repair your ruins? Jesus Christ alone has the power, the will, and the capacity for this, and He did it in a perfect manner through His blood and through His death. It is Jesus Christ who ransomed me and gave me back the possession of my rights. He redeems every moment of my life, because after committing one [mortal] sin, we deserve not only spiritual death, but bodily death too. And if God executed justice, it would destroy us irretrievably.

Therefore, I owe Jesus Christ every moment of my life, all the operations of my soul's powers, all my time, all my work, all my ability, all my thoughts, in a word, the use of my senses and all my faculties. And as many acts are for myself, or for creatures, these are so many thefts I perpetrate against the blood of God's Son. All is His, we are purchased at that inestimable price, and we have no right to use or spend our life's moments except for His love and glory. Otherwise, we make a dreadful profanation of this precious blood and render ourselves guilty of it.

Oh! Blessed is the soul who is preserved in innocence and who is not subject to feeling in itself the stings of sin! I confess to you that I am moved, and doubly so when I see the character of the divinity effaced. O Jesus, divine Reparator, by Your omnipotence, grace, and virtue, repair that adorable image! I hope for this from Your pure mercy.

If a soul understood the evil and abomination of one sin, she would have such a horror of it, that, however wicked she might be, she could not bring herself to commit it. You must confess that our blindness is great and worthy of compassion. (n. 2476)

YOU WANT TO KNOW THE ESTEEM I HAVE FOR YOU according to Adam and according to Jesus Christ.[3] According to Adam, my child, I believe you are abomination, sin, and the object of eternal Justice, irretrievably worthy of hell, opposed to God, resistant to God, and most unworthy of God. I know you, according to Adam, to be a true fiend, entirely full of malice, entirely corrupted in impurity, and finally, more abominable than any comparison I can give you. This is the regard I have for you and for your origin from Adam. Here are the excellences, or to put it better, the dreadful traits you have inherited from your first father. See if you have a right or reason to draw any glory from them, and when you examine them thoroughly, if you do not rather have reason to be continually ashamed. However, I am only telling you a little, and I do not say how, in your capacity as a daughter of Adam, you are cursed by God and forever cast out of His holy presence. Our misfortunes according to Adam are shocking and beyond understanding. They are so extensive and so bad that faith produces better understanding than words.

In virtue of Jesus, however, you are a daughter of God, spouse of Jesus Christ, clothed with Jesus Christ, renewed by His grace. You

---

3 That is, according to derivation from Adam and according to association with Christ.

are a member of His Body and you bear His image and likeness.[4] You are the beloved of the Holy Trinity.

Your desire to pull down what your pride and vanity built among creatures comes from God; but you must work at it through His Spirit and not your own, otherwise you will only bring about a new corruption.

To the extent that you will reduce yourself to nothing before God, He will imprint in you the true lights to establish your nothingness. It is not by the effort of your natural mind that you must enter it, but rather in giving and entrusting yourself to God to be led there.

It is good for you to be more reserved in every way about putting yourself forward. However, you must take care of your household affairs and it would not be a virtue to neglect them. You know what I told you about this. When you are more firmly grounded, you will do better and with more detachment. In the meantime, bear your falls with humility and learn that your whole capacity consists only in being contrary and opposed to God.

Abandon yourself often to God, above your miseries and weaknesses, and with a loving confidence in His goodness, that He will grant you the grace of drawing you from yourself to be completely His one day.

Only be faithful to God's light and attraction, and sacrifice your solitude to Him, since His Providence does not give you the means to have it. You must wait on His good pleasure and, nevertheless, always work. The little you can do with difficulty will always be very beneficial for entering into the path where God wants you.

Courage! Do not think about the obstacles so much. Say with St. Paul, "I can do all things in the One who strengthens me."[5] With Jesus Christ you can do everything. (n. 3041)

THE ESTEEM I HAVE FOR YOU IS SO GREAT THAT IF I did not view you as a member of Jesus Christ and as the prize of His Blood, you would be unbearable to me. It is not yourself that I esteem in you, but His grace and mercy, which I see shining in a manner beyond words. Beware of neglecting it voluntarily. If you stop, I do not know if you could ever pick yourself up again.

---

4 Eph 2:1–11. 5 Phil 4:13.

After God has waited a long time at the door of our hearts, He goes away, as we see with that slothful spouse;[6] and when we seek Him, we do not find Him. This is the punishment which is typically applied to our meanness and our negligence, which always delays until another time. Oh! Wretches that we are! Can we vouch for the times? Are they ours to dispose of? Behold our miserable blindness.

Hodie si vocem Domini audieritis. If today you hear His voice, beware of hardening your heart.[7] Do not delay in giving yourself to God. Be vigilant with regard to His holy attractions. He says in St. Luke that He will come like a thief at the hour when no one expects,[8] to teach us how we must be inwardly attentive to be able to hear His voice and give ourselves to His divine invitations, and so that He does not find us sleeping in the love of self and creatures. Alas! How often we are dozing in that wretched sleep which makes us unable to respond to God. *Vigilate et orate.*[9] This is the counsel Jesus gives us to deliver us from this sleep of death.

The disposition you have in regard to the desire you had for death is good, you can make use of it and work in that spirit. (n. 2087)

DO NOT BE SURPRISED TO SEE SO MUCH MISERY AND corruption in yourself. After you will have really understood by experience what you are and what you would be if grace did not sustain you, it will be necessary to *not* be occupied with yourself and, to begin to be detached from everything you are in order to remain closely united to God. However, you must still for a long time experience the depth of your own misery. You must be really convinced about the truth of the nothingness of your being.

You know the nothingness of your being through the presence of God, about which I spoke to you yesterday; this shows God operating in all things and all things subsisting in Him. The light of faith shows you that it is only He who is in truth. He said it to the great St. Catherine of Siena in these same terms, when she lovingly asked Him to tell her who He was. "I am the One who is and you are the one who is not," He said. Oh, the holy truth pronounced by the

6 Cant 5:2–7. 7 Ps 94(95):7. 8 Lk 12:39–40.
9 Mt 26:41. Watch and pray.

lips of Jesus! Listen to this and profit from it. Here, then, is the nothingness of being.

But the nothingness of sin is much worse. The former[10] is not opposed to God, but the latter fights Him as much as it can. And its malignity is so great that it is powerless and unable to have any being in good or virtue. The first nothingness regards our soul's being,[11] but the nothingness of sin regards the being of grace—and destroys it. Oh! Cursed and abominable nothingness! The first keeps us in the view of non-being. It is simple and is a truth that does not shame us, in a certain way; but sin's nothingness always humiliates and embarrasses us.

When a creature leaves its nothingness in order to commit a sin, it falls into a double nothingness which makes it infinitely more incapable of the simple nothingness which is not resistant to God. And it is a great cause of humiliation for the soul to see itself capable by its own malice of such a great disorder. (n. 2551)

YOUR LETTER FROM TODAY GAVE ME GREAT CAUSE FOR blessing God, seeing the insights He gives you about your depth of misery and nothingness. Regard this light as a very high grace, because it is infinitely more useful to you than to work miracles and be full of ecstasies and revelations. Oh! My child, the lovely enchantment of being absorbed in one's nothingness! Blessed is the soul who allows herself to be lovingly led to it by the sweet attractions of grace.

No, no, my child. You are not acting more impurely than in the past, rather, you have much more understanding, and you see a bit better the depth of your corruption and weakness, and your inability to do anything worthy of Jesus. Remain in this condition as long as it pleases Our Lord to keep you there and experience the impurity of your ground. But really experience its malice and horror, so that you can never forget it. Become learned in self-knowledge through your own experience. Be wise at your own cost, that is, be humble through the destruction of your pride.

---

10 That is, nothingness of being: the creature as lacking self-existence and totally reliant on God, who exists in and through Himself.

11 Mother Mectilde writes *l'être moral*, which can mean mental or intellectual being.

Oh! How great was your blindness when hidden vanity and self-regard persuaded you to make an account of your life in order to have it admired! Without a doubt your thoughts are different now and your feelings have taken a very different direction. What would you say now if you were asked to write your life? Oh! My child, you must confess that until now your lights have been darkness and when you believed yourself to be very righteous, you were very sinful before God. I compare you to the Pharisee in the Gospel who had so much esteem for his works that to make their excellence known, he blamed the poor publican, saying that he was not like him.[12] Alas! My child, how long did you think and perhaps believe in your heart that you did better than so-and-so? How much did you prefer yourself to your neighbor?

My child, receive the lesson that I give you today, and do not forget it. Here it is in brief: You will be more to the degree that you want to be less. "Do not be anything at all and you will be everything in fullness."[13]

Remember this little lesson well; it is short but efficacious. And so that it has its effects, love to be nothing in everything you do. Be glad that Our Lord grants you the mercy of pulling you from the darkness of your ignorance and that He causes you to see and feel your continual dependence on His goodness, and how you can do nothing without His very particular help. This truth is important and fundamental for our spiritual edifice.

Our natural bent toward elevation, that is, to our own excellence and to vanity, requires Our Lord to keep us a long time, and sometimes our whole life, in the awareness of and in sentiments about our lowliness. Although we feel, by a too evident experience, the abyss of our miserable corruption, and our conscience reproaches us at every moment for our impurities and infidelities, we are so attached to our self-regard that we cannot bear to be condemned or insulted. We cannot endure the rebukes we deserve.

We are sufficiently convinced that we do nothing which is worthy; however, we admit and we have a hidden satisfaction when someone approves of what we do. We are abominable before God and often

12 Lk 18:9–14.

13 St. John of the Cross.

we say this about ourselves; but in encounters where we must endure a little scorn, it kills us.

It is a very rare thing to see souls who live in truth. We all live, but alas, the greater number lead a life of illusion and feed themselves on vanity. We take the shadow for the body and we make what is subordinate the principal thing. Let us mourn our blindness and see how you and I lived in darkness and falsehood up to the present. The soul who does not have an understanding of itself does not have the truth at all. In order to live in truth, we must live in humility, or to put it better, in nothingness. A soul who lives in truth is so abased that it cannot be found, even in the center of hell. It exists no longer and abides in its nothingness, creatures can no longer find it.

O blessed loss, O saving loss! May we be lost in this way, my child, where we can find nothing except God! Oh! If you knew that sovereign happiness, you would wish to suffer a thousand deaths to have it. Oh! If I were permitted to speak, or rather, if God gave me the ability, I would tell you what you still do not know, but which you will experience some day if you are very faithful to God.

(n. 2984, n. 356)

The Word Incarnate

ON THE MYSTERY OF THE INCARNATION

Yesterday I had many thoughts to write to you, and the same tonight while awaiting the hour of the adorable Incarnation of the Word.[1] But two things distracted me from those thoughts.

The first is that Our Lord Jesus Christ is a great Master, most adorable in His divine teachings. It is He who instructed St. Paul in the desert[2] for sixty-six years, where he lived as a solitary without human conversation. It is He who taught Mary of Egypt and countless others, who for His pure love willingly separated themselves from creatures. And I saw that these great saints were sanctified through solitude, through silence, through *anéantissement*, and through a profound death to themselves, living as though dead, in forgetfulness of the whole world.

Oh! How holy this life seems to me! I revere it in you—not that it is established there, nor that you live in this way, but from the vantage that Jesus is your divine Master, that He can make you learned in all His holy mysteries, by Himself. And I asked Him to teach you those adorable lessons of His divine love. And as I have a great respect for the hidden workings of grace in your soul, I honored them in silence tonight, worshipping the adorable Incarnation (in a certain manner) of the Word in you, and desiring that your soul be completely melted and liquefied[3] in love for His *anéantissements*.

Oh! How adorable is this mystery! How great it is, how holy and heavenly! Our minds are not worthy to comprehend it. But we must be linked and united to the grace it confers, desiring that it take effect in us, according to the intentions of Jesus Christ. And let us

1 Mother Mectilde established in the Benedictines of Perpetual Adoration the custom of reciting an act, written by her, in homage to the Word becoming incarnate in Mary. This act is recited on March 24 at midnight, before the night office of the Annunciation.

2 St. Paul the Hermit lived in the deserts of Egypt in the Thebaid. He died at the age of 113 in the year 342.

3 Cant 5:6.

remain at the feet of the most holy Virgin, our Mistress, to share in this extraordinary mystery of a God reduced to nothing in her virginal womb. Imitate His humility and submission, and today say three times in a spirit of love, reverence, and abandonment, "*Verbum caro factum est*,"[4] and say three times, "*Ecce ancilla Domini*,"[5] adoring the humiliations of the Word made flesh, and honoring the humility of the most holy Virgin. Never depart from this disposition. Always humble yourself before the greatness of God, consenting to His good pleasure.

The second reason I abstained from writing to you came from my own side, because of the disposition in which I found myself yesterday the whole day, and in which I still am today.

I delight in seeing that you are entirely filled with God, that all the parts of your body, soul, and spirit are full of Jesus Christ.[6] Allow yourself to be filled with His love for you by emptying yourself, remaining in silence and reverence before God. It seems to me that God is giving me very holy desires for your soul. But, alas! I have only desires; Jesus Christ contains in Himself their realization and it is He alone who can sanctify you. (n. 1562)

THE DISPOSITIONS WE MUST HAVE DURING THE HOLY SEASON OF ADVENT

I beg you that in this holy season I may have some share of your prayers, inasmuch as I have received many mercies from Our Lord in this sacred time. I wish to be renewed in the faithfulness which I owe Our Lord Jesus Christ and to begin a new life in a state of complete death, but I am infinitely far from this.

This holy time is precious to me in various ways, but especially because the Church engages us in adoring the profound mystery of the Word's *anéantissement*. It seems to me that it is a time for death to ourselves and for life in God. The Church also focuses us on rendering homage to the coming of Jesus. His advent is of three kinds: first, His coming in the flesh; second, the majesty of His glory; and

---

4 Jn 1:14. The Word became flesh.

5 Lk 1:38. Behold, the handmaid of the Lord.

6 1 Thess 5:23.

third, accomplished mystically in souls. We must adore the first two, but to this third we owe attentiveness, profound humility, and a loving obedience to be prepared for His coming in us.

From time to time, let us say with the most holy Mother of God, answering the angel, "*Ecce ancilla Domini, fiat mihi secundum verbum tuum.*"[7] Let us be the slaves of the Lord, so that He may accomplish His most holy will in us and we may be attentive and obedient to the inspirations of His Holy Spirit.

I entreat Him to bring about in us the destruction of everything contrary to Him and that He may make me worthy in His holy love to be all yours forever. (n. 1813)

THE DISPOSITIONS WE MUST HAVE FOR THE NATIVITY OF OUR LORD JESUS CHRIST

My dearest daughter. Not being able to sleep because of my cough intensifying, you desire me to spend a quarter of an hour with you in spirit, to share with you some little thought about the dispositions which your soul must have to receive in itself the newborn Jesus.

If I thought about it, I would preserve a deep silence about so profound and adorable a mystery, which contains the *anéantissements* of a God clothed in our flesh and the excess of love which the eternal Father bears to us in giving us His Son.

God so loved the world that He gave to it His own Son.[8]

Alas! I confess my unworthiness and my ignorance! Also, I do not aspire to tell you about the excellence and holiness of this mystery. I imagine that you are not ignorant of it and that your preachers open for you those divine treasures hidden and contained in the infant God. In simplicity let us say only the dispositions you must have for the sake of not hindering the effects of this heavenly birth.

The first is that your soul be empty of creatures. "There was no room in the inn" to accommodate Jesus, we are told in the Gospel of St. Luke.[9] Created things occupied all the places, and the interests of our pride were preferred to the welcome of Jesus and His most holy Mother in the little village of Bethlehem. My child, if you desire

7 Lk 1:38. Behold, the handmaid of the Lord: be it done unto me according to Thy word. 8 Jn 3:16. 9 Lk 2:7.

Jesus to come and be born in you, make room for Him in your heart. Empty it of every creature and of your own interests. The stable of Bethlehem was found unoccupied and God lodged in it as in His palace and there made His entry into the world.

The second disposition is faith. Jesus was born in the middle of the night, in darkness, without any other light than that of His divinity. Be detached from your senses and remain in faith if you want to receive the grace of this mystery. You must be in darkness with respect to your senses and your own mind if you want to receive the divine light, and Jesus will be born spiritually in you.

The third disposition is silence. Jesus makes His entry into the world in a time of peace, at an hour which holds all creatures in silence to teach us that He is the king of peace, that He loves silence, and that it is when all our passions, senses, and powers are calm that He makes His profound communications to the soul, that it is in recollection and inner solitude that He makes His divine voice heard. Oh, how happy is the soul who orders everything in itself so well that its adorable Lord makes it the place of His birth.

However, there are three kinds of silence which we must try to practice, according to our ability. First, the silence of our passions. This is produced through a faithful and constant renunciation of ourselves, so that our passions, being mortified, make no more noise. Second, the silence of our senses, which always wish to see and feel what is happening. They make a racket and disturb the soul's peace, which must have a great attentiveness toward God. That is why souls must keep the senses in silence without listening to them or taking their side. The third silence is that of the soul's powers; these must be reduced to nothing. Your understanding must be in silence, not allowing it much superfluous reasoning or the many useless productions which proceed only from self-seeking. It must remain in silence gazing at God with reverence. The memory must be in silence, not willingly receiving any image or memory of creatures, but remaining simplified in God's presence. And the will must be in silence, without desire, without inclination, without passion, without constraint, without preference, and without attachment to anything except God alone.

In short, the best and most holy disposition, and the one for which my soul has the most attraction, is profound death to ourselves, which we call the true *anéantissement*. It is this holy disposition which drew the Word from the bosom of His divine Father to become incarnate in the virginal womb of Mary. God had regard for the humility of His servant.[10] God regarded the lowliness and nothingness in which the most holy Virgin was immersed. Nothing is more capable of attracting God into us than for us to be reduced to nothing beneath all things. A soul in her nothingness is enchanting to God's eyes and we can say that He is so enamored with love for her that He forgets His greatness, lowering Himself to her, and raising her up to God.

Oh! Pride must be such an abyss of dreadful malice, to blind us to the point of being unable to discern the beauty and holiness of *anéantissement*. How long will we be surrounded with darkness, so that we do not see that our happiness and felicity consist in being nothing in ourselves or in creatures?

Jesus came to be born into the world in the most extreme poverty of all creatures in order to teach us how much we must be separated from them, if we want to have the honor to see Him be born and reign in us. God and creatures are incompatible in one heart. Creatures want to share the kingship with God and God wants to reign alone in the soul, and possess it by His love. Is it not right that Jesus Christ be the Master? Can you do Him the affront of refusing Him your heart in order to give it to creatures? He asks to make His entry and to take possession of it anew. Give yourself to Him with humility and reverence for the grace of His birth. Have a disposition of emptiness, silence, faith, and *anéantissement*. Everything must be destroyed and reduced to nothing, so that God alone may be.

Be, then, O adorable Jesus, be born, living, and reigning perfectly in us. May everything in us which is opposed to You be consumed by the power of Your divine love. May we know You for what You are and may we be the victims of Your good pleasure, sacrificed in homage to Your divine Infancy.

Oh! My child, can you think about the holiness of the mystery of a God reduced to nothing without being moved by love and reverence?

---

10 Lk 1:48.

Oh! My divine Master, how Your greatness is humbled and our lowness is raised! It is in this adorable mystery that You made God man and man God. Work in us the unfathomable mystery of Your marvels and make us worthy of the grace You desire to communicate to us. (n. 2238)

REGARDING THE PEACE WHICH THE ANGELS PROCLAIMED TO THE SHEPHERDS

Since Providence does not allow me the necessity of sleeping, I want to use this moment to proclaim peace to you along with the angels who proclaim it to the shepherds: "Glory to God in the highest, and on earth peace to men of good will."[11] My child, peace in your soul, peace in your memory, peace in your understanding, peace in your will; peace with God, peace with men, peace with yourself. Peace, peace, peace, in heaven and on earth. Peace in the depth of your heart. This is what the Child Jesus grants us through His birth. He reconciles us with His Father and gives us power to triumph over our enemies and enjoy peace in the midst of war.

How did you spend this holy night, my child? Did you have the honor of finding the Mother and Child? Were you there in the darkness, in silence and in the emptiness of creatures and yourself? Have you worshipped the incomprehensible and adorable *anéantissements* of the Infant God?

O what love, O what grace, O what holiness this mystery produces! But this must be in a faithful soul, a detached soul. Adore with a lofty esteem the Child Jesus's humiliations, the helplessness of this mighty God, of which Holy Scripture makes mention in Isaiah, saying He shall reign with a kingdom that has no end.[12]

Let us see a little how this Prince of peace comes to establish His reign, to display His power over all souls, and to occupy the estates of His kingdom. He is born in a stable, in the greatest want with regard to everything, to show us that the most powerful way to establish in ourselves a profound peace, which is the throne of this peaceful king, is true poverty in everything: poverty in greatness, honors,

---

11 Lk 1:14.

12 Is 9:1–6. First reading from the night office for Christmas.

and pleasures; poverty of earthly goods, of consolations, of men's affection,[13] poverty of desires and inclinations, poverty in our senses, poverty of thoughts, poverty of will, in a word, poverty in everything. For a soul which is stripped and bare of everything is in perfect and profound peace, and nothing in heaven or earth can rob it of this precious peace. Such a soul has God, who rests in it as on His couch of delights, and hell with all its fury could not disturb it.

O secret so little known and so poorly practiced! How many graces and heavenly blessings are we deprived of because we are too filled with those wretched possessions which only adorn the soul with impurity and peculiar corruption!

Our adorable King builds His dominion on humiliations and on crosses. In these He is magnificent, and this is what makes Him today an object of astonishment to our minds.

A God becomes an infant and is reduced to the weaknesses of our flesh. "He bore our weakness and was burdened with our sorrows," says the Prophet.[14] He is powerful in our weaknesses and commences His reign in *anéantissement.*

Oh, what miracles are contained in an Infant God! He comes to rule in your heart in a manner that cannot be understood. He was reduced to nothing in order to captivate souls, and He does in us and for us what we should be doing if sin had not destroyed the grace for us to do it. He comes to repair His Father's glory and conquer our rebellion, but in a way very opposed to the senses and the human mind. He does everything opposite to what we continually do.

We live for ourselves, but He lives for His Father's glory and from His divine life. Our continual tendency is toward the elevation of ourselves in us and in creatures—a horrible longing to have the esteem and affection of creatures, to have applause, honor, and approval. Jesus comes to be the disgrace of men, and the outcast of the people, comparing Himself to a worm.[15]

O my child, can our vanity and ambition still have room in our hearts? What? The criminal will be raised to a throne of glory and

---

13 The primary manuscript has "affliction," which perhaps can be understood in the sense of compassion. Parallel manuscripts have "affection."

14 Is 53:4.

15 Ps 21:7 (22:6).

majesty, making an idol of himself and making creatures into idolaters, while the divinity, clothed in our flesh, is in contempt on a little hay! Are we not moved to see our Judge taking the place of a criminal, beginning to do penance for our sins and impurities? Alas! How insensitive we are with respect to God! A father, a mother, a child moves us, but Jesus Christ, the true God reduced to nothing, does not affect us at all. Let us be humbled to see that flesh and blood prevail over Him.

I confess to you that I am a bit grieved at the little love and reverence we have for Jesus, and by the ignorance in which we live. You want me to console myself by telling you about my trouble. Yesterday in your letter you told me that I am all your consolation and that you pour out your thoughts and sorrows into my soul. Allow me the same liberty in your place, not that I want to use it now (I would fear complacency and self-love from it), but when my weakness gets the better of me so as to complain about the reason for my suffering, bear with me in patience, but always with the fidelity you promised me of telling me frankly what may cause you pain or offence. It has been a long time since you cheered and consoled me with your sincerity and frankness in this matter; think about this from time to time when you will be unencumbered.

Further, I brought you not only into the royal palace of Bethlehem, but into the adorable Heart of Jesus, and you are and have been so present and pressing to my mind that I think I dare to say that I offer you to God and sacrifice you to Him continually. Inwardly, I am constrained to pray for you unceasingly, waking and sleeping, and in managing our little affairs. There is the principal part of my soul which offers you to God and it is impossible for me to withdraw from it or be distracted from it. Never did I find myself in such a condition with regard to any soul. I can neither remove you nor draw back, you are so firm in your place that it seems to me that my arms do not have enough strength to tear you away from it. I wanted to test this tonight in some encounter, but in vain: it is necessary that you endure it for as long as the command of God keeps you there and that I reduce myself to nothing about all this.

Do not take the trouble of writing to me, you cannot do it today. Do not be in a hurry about anything. Leave yourself gently and peacefully to God. I hope that He will bless your crosses and that they will not be as heavy as imagined. Have an absolute confidence in God and wait in peace for the results of His Providence and the graces He desires to grant you for giving yourself entirely to Him.

Good day, my child, I leave you at the feet of the Infant Jesus. Ask Him to reduce me to nothing and that I might begin today to live a life of death, without any return or reserve. For God to reign in us, everything which is from us and from creatures must be reduced to nothing. These are the desires of a heart which, in Jesus, is more yours than its own. *Adieu.* (n. 2540)

THAT IT IS NECESSARY TO TAKE THE CHILD JESUS AS OUR MODEL

My dearest, I reply to your letter which I received this morning and to which I could not reply because of Mass and Communion, at which I gladly offered you in sacrifice and I received increased hope of seeing you, before death, all Jesus Christ's. This is what consoles me and makes me exhort you to have a great courage and to persevere in the labor and in the combat, if you want to win the crown.

Regarding that quality of a child that you desire in yourself, I give you the Child Jesus as a model for your childhood. Be formed as much as possible on this divine model and let your soul be filled with His holy dispositions. Be pure with His purity, be gentle and humble with His gentleness and humility. Be simple as He is simple, be little as He is little. In a word, be reduced to nothing like Him. Be submissive to the guidance of His Spirit as He is subject to His heavenly Father.

And this same Jesus says to us that unless we become like little children we will not enter the kingdom of heaven.[16] We must submit our minds to our divine Master's adorable words. Pray to Him to cause an emanation of His grace of childhood in your soul, and to reproduce there the purity and innocence which sin destroyed; pray that He impress on you an effect of His divine suppleness to His Father's will. May you be so subject to God's good pleasure that your joy may be to do His holy will, through likeness to Jesus. May all your care be to rest with Jesus on Mary's virginal heart.

---

16 Mk 10:13–16.

Children love those who are like them: if you are a child in littleness, namely, in humility and lowliness of spirit, and in innocence and simplicity, you will be beloved of the Child Jesus.

Be in His holy company at the feet of His most holy Mother in the stable; and as she has the power to give Jesus to the world, ask her humbly to give Him to your soul and to give your soul to Jesus. It is through her ministrations that we enter into the holiness of the interior life. For just as Jesus gives us to His Father, likewise Mary gives us to Jesus. "No one can come to My Father except through Me,"[17] says Our Lord in the Gospel. And no one can go to Jesus if His most holy Mother does not lead that one to Him. Renew your devotions, homage, and respect toward this gracious Virgin, and if you cannot formulate some particular devotions to honor her, remain in the disposition of being everything you ought to be with regard to her.

Do not be that child who amuses himself with trifles. Lay aside all the foolish things which distract your soul. Go to what is solid, be filled with what is holy, feed your soul on that, without filling it with many vanities. You need a generosity from grace which lifts you to God; you are sufficiently moved, but Jesus is not the strongest power in you. I observe that in you creatures still conquer and carry the day with the triumphs which belong to Jesus Christ alone.

There are three things which cast my small understanding into an abyss of astonishment. The first is that the times and moments of our lives, being given to us to trade for the blessedness of a sweet eternity—this is the least of our thoughts. Further, without reflection about the brevity of our days, we do not realize that upon leaving this life we will be required to give an account for our smallest vanities. What will a soul who has spent its life among creatures do at that meeting? O dreadful misfortune!

The second thing which astounds me is that we live, breathe, are moved, and act within and in God,[18] and meanwhile we are not at all focused on His presence and we live the majority of the time as if there were no God, without respect, without love, and without fear of His majesty which is present.

---

17 Jn 14:6.

18 Acts 17:28, 2 Cor 6:15.

The third is that having Jesus Christ really and truly present in the Most Holy Sacrament and, where He is, all three divine Persons, we are so little moved by the mystery of His divine love, which He communicates to us in all its immensity, and this, without reserve. Is it not loving us truly [for Him] to desire to be converted into food for the sake of incorporating us into Himself? So that we may become completely one with Him in a most ineffable and incomprehensible manner? We search for relics, we want to see saints.... Let us go to the Most Holy Sacrament, let us consume this adorable Host. We have not just relics, but the source of all sanctity, who sanctifies us. We have eternal goodness itself instead of the saints, and we converse with Jesus Christ! Oh! Awesome mystery! Who can comprehend or understand this holy mystery without being seized with amazement?

Here are the three matters by which I am overcome, seeing the terrible blindness of Christians. Acknowledge with me, through your own experience, that the cause of so many evils comes from the very poor use we make of our senses, a miserable use which deprives us of an infinite grace. Do we not have reason to weep over our blindness? Let a soul who is pierced with these truths suffer from sorrow to see her divine Master so little known and almost not loved at all.

My child, when will we be moved, and entering into the interests of His glory, offer ourselves as victims in the desire to repair His glory in His creatures? You must pay for yourself before making satisfaction for another, I confess it, but without reflecting on yourself. These insights cause a soul who loves its God to die, and I deplore my hardness at not being moved. What? Do we have no love for the One who for love gives Himself without reserve? Must it be that creatures still have the power to distract us from Him—some interest, vanity, pleasure, or human respect?

Let us make a solemn profession at Jesus's feet in the stable, in the future not to live in creatures, not to pursue vanity, and not to live in falsehood. Since a God is reduced to nothing, it is a matter of justice that our pride be vanquished and cast down. How does it look to raise ourselves when a God humbles Himself, and to sustain in ourselves the enemies of His glory, that is, our sins, when He came to earth to destroy them? He came to deliver us from the tyranny of

Satan. He came to overthrow the reign of the devil. Finally He came to take possession of what was His. Your soul is His, your entire being views Him as its creator. And we must confess that everything depends on Him, by creation, redemption, and conservation; but also by other rights which are infinite.

Let us rejoice in the birth of our King. Let us render homage to His sovereignty, submitting to His divine powers. Let all our glory consist in being reduced to nothing so that He alone reigns perfectly. Let our life be hidden in Him and let us continually depend on Him. Finally, let us live from His life, so that we may be animated with His love and that He alone may be living in us.

See how I am forgetting myself: intending only to write you a few words, I find I cannot stop, throwing me into a jumble of thoughts that fell into my mind. If you find something here useful to your soul, very good. I surrender all to remain in my precious nothingness.

I wandered very far from what I meant to say to you; it is necessary to return to the subject of your letter.

I wrote to you this morning that I found the order you keep for your exterior devotions very good, and that with regard to the interior, you must be dependent on the Holy Spirit's touches which occupy the soul as it pleases Him. If you are in a state of death, then everything gives homage to the Child Jesus. Your helplessness will be offered to Jesus's helplessness and captivity, your darkness to that which He wants to endure in the place of His birth, your poverty of grace to His poverty. Thus you will find that nothing happens which does not give glory to Jesus. But just as He gives Himself entirely to you, so likewise, without reserve give yourself all to Him.

The temporal birth of Jesus will not happen again, but the grace of His birth will last eternally. And He is born mystically in our souls continually when there is no opposition to this on our part, when we are not filled with creatures and our own interests, like the hostelries in Bethlehem, and when we remain in faith's luminous darkness so that our senses are reduced to nothing and we are in silence and solitude, detached from everything which is not God.

I am imposing silence on myself, and recommending it to you. I do not know if it is God's Spirit which presses me but if I follow my thoughts I will not finish, and yet all of it is superfluous, being only repetition. Your humility, or rather, Jesus's charity in you, will excuse everything. (n. 1389)

ON THE MYSTERY OF THE EPIPHANY

This adorable mystery of the Epiphany must produce great effects of grace in our souls.

First, it must cause you to adore Jesus Christ as King with the Magi. Today He begins to rule, today He is recognized as King and given the homage worthy of royalty. It is on this day that the first public adoration and honor were given to Jesus. The first homage in the name of the whole world was offered and the first fruits of the Gentiles were consecrated to Him.

Enter into the interests of Jesus your divine King and rejoice to see that He establishes His reign, that He manifests Himself, and draws to Himself those souls who are most distant. The grace He gave to the Magi is very great, but those He gives us today are no less great. He called you from a very distant country,[19] that is, the region of sin. He wants you to be faithful like these holy Magi, leaving their country as they did to go to sacrifice to Jesus. They left everything in order to seek their King and be subject to His dominion. Do the same today. Depart from the land of yourself, your own house, and the place of your knowledge. Give up your interests as they did and go to find Jesus in Bethlehem. Follow inspiration, which is the star. Leave the old habits of your senses and your own thinking, and abandon yourself to God's guidance.

If the Magi had not been submissive and had not done away with human views, they would never have found Jesus. They walk by faith and trust. This is what you must do. They follow a star: see which star you must follow and become faithful. They came into a foreign country. That is, into grace, which is not in us, but very remote from us, since in order to have it we must leave ourselves.

They bring gold, myrrh, and incense. This is what you must bring: the gold of a pure love, the myrrh of a generous mortification of everything in you that displeases God, and the incense of a fervent

---

19 Lk 15:13, 20.

and very simple prayer. The incense raises you to God, the myrrh detaches and separates you from creatures, the gold and love unite you most intimately with God. Behold the three effects which the gold, myrrh, and incense must produce in you. This is what you must bring to Jesus. The incense confesses and honors Him as God; the myrrh testifies to Him as man; and the gold owns Him as King. May Jesus be to you God, man, and King: God, in giving you being, conserving and vivifying you; man, in showing you the path of *anéantissement* and of the cross which He came to set up on earth for us, to smooth the way for our reunion with Him; King, in submitting to His dominion and power, to His love and authority.

In conclusion, imitate the Magi, who, after finding and adoring Jesus, returned by another path. That is what you must do: return by another path. Oh! How much this says and contains! There are very few who return by another path. We have a wretched inclination which always makes us walk in creatures and in ourselves. We must take a different and hidden path, far from Herod who symbolizes pride. And what is this path? It is pure faith, by which pride and vanity find their downfall and are cheated in their expectations. This path makes us leave behind our feelings, forsaking our interests and satisfactions for the esteem and interests of God Himself. The Magi left Jesus to go and bring forth Jesus, and we must leave ourselves to glorify Jesus, to publish Him and make Him known. But to succeed, we must walk by another path, which is that precious faith. I desire this for you, my child, and the grace to be faithful to it.

Here are some little thoughts which may divert you. If they are useful to you, very good. If not, I will always have grounds for humility. Esteem highly the grace God gives you, for fear that He may be obliged by your negligence to deprive you of it. Be very faithful; I cannot recommend faithfulness to you enough. Watch over it; temptation will assail you. Be strong with Jesus's strength and do not be discouraged by your weaknesses. Never cease and you will see the happiness which comes to you from it. (n. 120)

Death and Resurrection[1]

ON HOLY SATURDAY

My dearest, I placed myself before Our Lord so I could tell you something concerning the profound and terrible mystery of His death. But alas! I find myself seized with an inability to speak of it. I am too impure to converse with you about the most prodigious charity that was ever exercised. One must burn with this same love which consumed our divine Master on the cross to speak about the excess of His sacred dilection.

The angels are mute at the sight of that sorrowful spectacle. They are plunged into an abyss of astonishment to see a God die for men — for abominable sinners, among whom I am numbered. A God reduced to nothing, not only in the image of a sinner, but who assumes the sins of the world, and becomes the victim of God's just anger, bearing before His Father's majesty the crimes of all men, and in that state rejected by God.[2] This is the most dreadful suffering and humiliation which Our Lord Jesus Christ accepted in His death.

Oh! How sorrowful it is to endure being rejected, rebuked, and condemned by God Himself! This is what our adorable Lord suffered for you, for me, and for all men! Oh! You cannot comprehend that intense and dreadful humiliation! The holiness of God hidden under the corruption of sin, and all His divine attributes as if annihilated.

To understand truly these profound and terrible pains, we would have to fathom the infernal abomination of sin, its malignity and how much it dishonors God, how opposed it is to Him and how He abhors it. But alas! Our minds are too weak to plumb these truths. We must revere them in faith, and imitate the silence of the angels and saints, being lost in astonishment, love, and reverence. Oh! How wonderful and ineffable is God in the inventions of His love!

---

1 In the manuscripts this section is entitled "On the Mystery of Jesus Christ's Passion"; another manuscript includes the note "On Holy Saturday."

2 These lines from Mother Mectilde should be understood as following St. Paul's meaning. See especially 2 Cor 5:20–21, Gal 3:13.

My child, I do not dare to follow my thoughts, since they would launch me into a long discourse. I must allow the Holy Spirit to act in you. All I recommend to you is silence and recollection of spirit, adoring in faith—that is, without understanding it—the holiness of this mystery, remaining in deep reverence for what God does there.

In the ground of your soul have a disposition to adore everything our adorable Lord did and suffered in His Passion. Desire that everything which happened in Him may happen spiritually in you, since you must be similar to Him. Adhere to all the designs of Jesus on the cross for you, and surrender in a spirit of continual sacrifice to pay homage to His holiness, His power, and His love.

Love to suffer some pain of body or mind in honor of the sufferings of Jesus's holy soul; and to adore His holy Humanity, you will say tomorrow and hereafter, thirty-three times, "*Adoramus te Christe, et benedicimus tibi, quia per crucem tuam redemisti mundum, qui passus es pro nobis.*"[3]

Also adore the three hours of agony in the garden and the three hours of agony on the cross, and for that you will say the *Pater Noster* three times, prostrate. (n. 1008)

HOLY SATURDAY AT NIGHT[4]

My child, receive Communion tomorrow if you can, and may the dead Jesus enter into you as into His sepulcher.[5] Give Him the

3 Response for the feast of the Exaltation of the Holy Cross (September 14); also said on the feast of the Finding of the Holy Cross (May 3): "We adore Thee, O Christ, and we bless Thee, who suffered for us, for by Thy holy cross Thou hast redeemed the world."

4 In the manuscripts this section is entitled "On the mystery of the resurrection."

5 This phrase may seem surprising to modern readers. Mother Mectilde held, with the rest of the French School, that Christians are meant to share in all the states and dispositions of Christ. According to St. Thomas Aquinas, the Lord of glory present under the consecrated species is the Christ-who-suffered, *Christus passus*. In the *Commentary on John*, he writes: "Since this sacrament is of the Lord's Passion, it contains within itself Christ who suffered. Hence whatever is an effect of the Lord's Passion is wholly contained in this sacrament, for it is nothing else than the application of the Lord's Passion to us.... Hence it is clear that the destruction of death, which Christ accomplished by his death, and the restoration of life, which he accomplished by his resurrection, are effects of this sacrament" (*Super Ioan.* 6, lec. 6, §964; cf. *In IV Sent.*, dist. 8, qu. 1, art. 2, qa. 2; *Summa theologiae* III, qu. 66, art. 9, ad 5 and qu. 73, art. 5, ad 2).

power to fill you with the holiness of His death and desire to have a share in the grace of His resurrection. As a member of His body you have been crucified with Him, so you must rise with Him.[6] These are the Apostle's words.

We must begin a new life, a life which is not of the earth, a life which must be completely detached from the senses, totally purified and raised to God. St. Paul says, "If we are risen, let us seek the things which are on high."[7] A resurrected soul can no longer delight in earthly things. Creatures are a cross to such a person, and everything the world views as most delightful is a hell to him.

Do you want to know if you are mystically resurrected? See if you bear the marks of it and if your soul is adorned with the marriage portions of the blessed, as Our Lord's divine humanity was at the moment of His resurrection.

1. It was rendered impassible, for the Apostle says, "Jesus, risen from the dead, dies no more,"[8] and after this He can no longer suffer. You must imitate this spiritually through a firm resolve, made by His grace, to never again die through sin, to no longer adhere to your passions, to your senses, or to temptation.

2. It received agility, by which He could transport Himself in one moment from one place to another far away. You must be spiritually agile by a prompt obedience and correspondence to all the movements of grace, saying with Samuel, "Speak, Lord, Your servant is listening to You."[9]

3. It received subtlety, by which He went through material things, as when He rose from the sepulcher without moving the stone. You must be spiritually subtle in being detached and remote from all clinging to your own will, to your own understanding, to low and perishable things, or to anything which is not God or does not tend toward Him, passing through temporal things in such a way that you are always longing for eternal ones, saying with David, "What do I have in heaven, and what do I desire upon earth, but You, my God?"[10]

4. The fourth inheritance of Jesus's glorious body is that He was arrayed with a glory[11] and splendor which obscured that of the sun.

---

6 Rom 6:5.
7 Col 3:1.
8 Rom 6:9.
9 1 Sam 3:9–10.
10 Ps 72(73):25.
11 *clarité*, from the Latin *claritas*, often used as a synonym for *gloria*.

But it was not visible to the still-mortal eyes of the apostles, whether by the nature of this light of glory, or by Jesus's intention so that He could still converse and interact with them. You must be spiritually clear and resplendent through a pure intention toward God; this is the eye of the soul, according to the words of Our Lord, who says, "If your eye is simple, your whole body will be full of light."[12] This makes us consider only God in all our actions. It is also the light of living faith and prayer, by which God illuminates our darkness and reveals His divine counsels and prompts us in His ways.

My child, I was not planning to tell you these things. I was intending to tell you them in person without writing them. I would have many other thoughts about the ceremony which the Church celebrates today; but I fear loading your mind with too much. That is why I will be content to tell you that you must have a great respect for everything the Church does, and to abandon yourself to Jesus's Spirit, who directs and guides her, desiring that the grace of all the ceremonies, and the holy mysteries which they represent, may be infused into your soul and that it may be adorned with their holy effects.

At last, behold a day altogether new: Jesus Christ makes all things new.[13] Ask Him humbly to renew everything in you and that you begin to live a new life. (n. 279)

12 Mt 6:22. 13 Rev 21:5.

Complete Surrender

REGARDING YOUR WRITINGS GENERALLY, here is what Our Lord gives me to understand about them.

1. There is more show than substance.

2. It is all mind and no heart.

3. The greatest obstacle you will always have in the spiritual life is your mind's curiosity.

4. An excess of human light blinds you and the blindness must enlighten you, inasmuch as you are in the number of those whom Jesus Christ speaks about in the Gospel of St. John, who are blind because they suppose themselves to have good eyes. In order to see properly, however, they must put them out.[1]

5. The inner irregularity which appears constantly in your writings is a sign of God's vocation and of your infidelity. You do not need to search for reasons to do penance outside yourself, because for a long time you gave reasons for this to God through your flights and resistances; He is also weary of watching you flee.

6. You have good reason to say that your mind goes too fast, because in fact, it goes ahead of God's, and wants to decide what it should suffer.

7. Regarding prayer, you will never succeed if you continue doing as you have done, through an excessive desire to do well. This is because your prayer has only been the exercise of a mind loving beautiful truths, and these it pursued only to be perfected by the knowledge of what is lofty in our religion, as I observe most particularly in article 27 of the essay.[2]

8. And, to succeed in this, you were not content with your own industry, you employed and sought the help of others, which, either because you did not penetrate it well enough, or because you followed the common mistake of making a labor of devotion, made you lose a great deal of time; and this is what I regret, especially since God

1 Jn 9:39–41; Mt 5:29.

2 It is not clear what essay Mother Mectilde is referring to.

has given you great capacity for true good. It is absolutely necessary for you to let God do a little more in you and that you put yourself in a condition to follow Him.

9. Learn to defer to the guidance of the Holy Spirit, attending to Him and acting in submission to the grace He has given you. For what is positive and what serves as the foundation of the spirit of Christianity is to remain with Jesus Christ under the control of the Spirit of God, waiting until He speaks in order to act and ceasing when He no longer employs us: "*Spiritus Domini super me.*"[3]

I beseech you to give a little attention to the above, in the form of an examination of conscience, and you will see what God's Spirit will reveal to you about it.

10. With regard to the presence of God, you did not understand it as is necessary. Moreover, because it is a gift of God, which one receives in prayer first, it cannot be acquired by effort. Instead of you putting yourself in a state where God comes to you, you want to go to Him by the path that pleases you, and have the liberty of choosing your path—not having, up to now, entered into the dependence you must have on God's action that He wants to set up in you. (n. 2804)

IMPORTANT INSTRUCTIONS

My very dear daughter in Jesus Christ, I pray Him to make me worthy to tell you His holy will and make you understand and note most particularly the truths I have already explained concerning the general condition of your life. I repeat them to you in writing, to waken you through reading them and to incite you to a new fidelity; and you will be all the more culpable before God's judgment if you have neglected to observe them.

I. The greatest distrust you must have is for your own mind, whether for its own investigations, or for the supports it labors to find in itself; but above all, for its extremely malignant vanity and presumption of spirit. I already told you that you must distrust yourself generally about everything that your mind generates; never base anything on your natural lights. In short, you must tend toward a total detachment from yourself, always depending on God's lights

3 Lk 4:18, Is 61:1. The Spirit of the Lord is upon me.

by a faith that is simple and stripped of supports and of the senses.

II. One of the greatest obstacles for your soul in the path to which God does you the honor and favor of calling you is that you are not abandoned enough to God's action, to His grace and power. Your trust in Him is not complete in the ground of your soul. You do not strip yourself enough of your natural strengths and industry. You do not lose yourself in the complete surrender you owe to God. And this failure comes from a secret self-regard which makes you think about your dispositions through self-love; and everything you find in yourself which seems to be good you turn into a support, and this is your difficulty—especially since you clothe yourself with yourself still, keeping whatever it is that gives you life in your own operations and dispositions. For the sake of withdrawing from this evil, which you still do not really understand, and which causes you endless delays in arriving at the pure path or state to which you are called, do the following:

Do not attach any importance to what you experience in yourself, whether it be light, good will, good works, good sentiments, fervors and resolutions, and so on. Rise to God above all these things. Do not be attached to the gifts which the divine mercy grants you, but avail yourself of them in order to rise to God and be united to His love. It is not experiences or favors that you should seek, because these are not our goal, they are only means to make the road easier which should lead us to Him. Divest yourself of everything so that you may be filled with God alone.

III. Never have an attachment of affection to any creatures, however good and holy they may seem to you, inasmuch as a gold plate placed before your eyes impedes the view of the sun no less than a lead plate. You must be on guard, then, against this great imperfection, which is found in the majority of spiritual people and very often ruins their perfection.

Remember what I told you many times: God is jealous of your heart; He desires to possess it entirely. It must not be divided in any way. Your love is for Him alone. He cannot bear a rival. You must be all His or belong entirely to evil and vile creatures. Jesus Christ says, "No one can serve two masters."[4] You cannot be all God's and

4 Lk 16:13, Mt 6:24.

live in creatures and yourself. Of necessity, you must leave them. You cannot remain in them without being polluted, by seeking them, by producing them and being planted in them, by attracting them to you, and you being introduced into them. And all this wicked commerce produces only contamination. It fills you with darkness, errors, anxieties, desires—in short, a thousand distractions, and you spend a great deal of time on such trifles, nonsense, and strange vanities.

You have the experience of this at the cost of your own perfection. Oh! How many moments have you lost! Only one is needed to merit eternity, and yet you have made such profane use of it, employing it so unworthily in creatures! Remember that a moment costs the blood of God and that you can employ it only for the interests of His glory. Otherwise, you become a criminal, committing a theft against that adorable Blood. Work constantly at being detached. Never cease from tending toward God and think about how much we are delayed from this by our diversions.

My child, if I forbid you so particularly about having an attachment to creatures, even those who have a reputation for sanctity, for fear of your being diverted even the slightest bit from God, who desires to be the only one in your heart, then judge how much more I forbid you and condemn in you all other affections which are less pure. If I do not permit you to become attached to a good person, that is all the more reason I must order you to beware of all others, keeping your heart for God alone.

Reflect often on the hindrance for your soul, and on the wretched condition into which it would fall, if it were entangled again in its attachments of affection. Is it not a terrible offense to God if you place an impure creature on His throne? That is what you do when you draw creatures to yourself and love them, you prefer them to God—you make them your idol. Alas! How many times a trifle, a nothing, has occupied your mind and you have left God an infinite number of times to cling to it, following your mind's inclination, without reverence for God who is present. Oh! How adorable is the divine patience to endure from us these disgraces, which we continually give to Jesus Christ.

IV. The fourth piece of advice I give you, and which you must receive as a command given by Jesus Christ, is never to rate highly the praise and applause of creatures. Remember the words of Holy Scripture, "*Omnis homo mendax.*"[5] All men are liars. God alone is truthful. "I am the truth," Jesus says.[6] Everything men say comes from them and since creatures are nothing but falsehood and vanity, we must have an extraordinary blindness to take satisfaction in their discourse and in the regard they testify to having for us. To take even the slightest satisfaction in this is to live in darkness and ignorance. How can you be fed on wind? How can you be supported by praise which has no other source than blindness and ignorance? Can you make a crutch of human opinion? Do you not know the truth that I put before you: all men are liars? If you believe this as faith requires you to do, then why do you prize their vain praise so much? One must be very blind to be satisfied with it and take pleasure in it. To be filled with such vanity is to live in deceit. Creatures ordinarily approve what God condemns. They speak only from their senses and by the extremely impure light of their own minds; and all of that is not inside God's light. For myself, I do not understand how we do not tremble with terror when we are praised, when we are applauded.

We do not know what is worthy of love or of hatred.[7] This creature exalts you and God who is Truth, Holiness, and eternal Wisdom, who cannot be deceived, condemns you. And it may be that the creature in whom you take satisfaction for his flatteries and snake-whistling will be eternally in flames. What deceit! What blindness!

But after all, what utility do you find in the deceitful praises of men? Do they make you more pure, more holy, more faithful, and more reduced to nothing? In short, do they unite you to God? Alas, far from it! They separate you from Him, so as to occupy you with this creature which covers you with its corruption, not being content with being corrupt in itself: it casts its venom on you and tends to kill you. This is what pride and vanity do in us. They not only ruin the sanctity of our intentions, but also have a unfortunate tendency to ruin it again in another person. See the terrible malignity.

That is enough on this point. I see that I am saying too much about it, and that I cannot draw back, finding myself deeply moved

5 Ps 115:2 (116:11). 6 Jn 14:6. 7 Cf. Eccl 9:1.

by the blindness of countless souls, and particularly by yours, which was fed and lived on this horrible corruption for such a long time. Our Lord granted you a very great mercy by making you feel your misery; but that is not enough. You must be absolutely secured from it. One must not return to one's vomit.[8] Remember that this wicked complacency and vanity destroys holiness completely. It pulls you from your blessed state of *anéantissement* into which grace leads you and to which you owe a faithful correspondence; and since this is your weakness, your tendency, and your inclination, be on your guard.

1. Never put yourself forward except for the needs of charity or by a very particular order from God.

2. Never willingly and intentionally give a reason for being praised.

3. If men approve and exalt you, tremble in uncertainty about God's disapproval and remember that creatures see only the exterior of your actions, but God sees into their depths. "Man sees the face, but God sees the heart," says Holy Scripture.[9]

4. Withdraw to Our Lord's feet, adoring in silence, humility, and respect the estimation He has of you. Gently rise toward God in this way, separating yourself from all creatures who tend to corrupt you by their vain praises and impurities.

5. Never say anything that can turn to your praise and glory, at least directly.

6. Do not reveal the graces Our Lord gives you to anyone except to those who accepted from God the direction of your soul, or those to whom you are led and incited by a very clear motive for the pure glory of God; especially since your tendency to elevate and esteem yourself, in your mind and in that of others, will sometimes provide you with occasions which appear to be very good. But live as one reduced to nothing; beware of everything. Be content that God sees you and knows you. Renounce creatures, having neither any hope nor claim on them since you are and must be, without any reservation, entirely Jesus Christ's.

V. Be very circumspect and reserved about communicating and revealing your state. Beware of confiding indiscriminately in all sorts of people who have power and jurisdiction. If you are not faithful

8 Prov 26:11. 9 1 Sam 16:7.

on this point, you will confuse your soul and fill it with a multitude of things which will cast it into darkness, trouble, and temptations.

Be content with the directors that God will give you, be very faithful to them and listen to them as you would to Jesus Christ, and obey them the same way. If Providence deprives you of the one you have now, who is full of grace, doctrine, prudence, and light, do not choose another according to your own inspiration: you must ask for this from God fervently, so that He will give you a guide who will lead you according to His Spirit. A good director, one who is disinterested and who is filled with Jesus, is a great treasure. I confess to you that they are very rare. Many have a hand in directing souls, but I do not think they all have the grace for it. However that may be, make use of the advice you are given and remember that there is only too much experience of the misfortunes that happen in a soul when it falls under the guidance of a director who is not endowed with the interests of Jesus Christ.

Your soul, being weak and full of the corruption of creatures, as it is now, has need of good direction which will extricate it from itself, from creatures, and from the senses. And I beg Our Lord that His grace will provide for you in this very important matter. Your need is very great, inasmuch as there is still nothing solid in you. You begin indeed to understand the truths of Jesus Christ and of His holy Gospels, but you are not grounded in the perfection which they set before you, seeing that you are still not fully convinced. And this is what makes me distressed seeing you without guidance—if you are so in the future—although I trust that God will not fail you; but I doubt your faithfulness in persevering, finding yourself on the one side without support and on the other surrounded by creatures, the world, and the vanity they can offer you. Be immovable. God is more than all that these creatures, the world, and vanity can give you. Bear their persecutions and tyranny for the sake of Jesus Christ, and He will be your strength to overcome them.

Therefore, never confide your state to any except souls who are very enlightened and truly filled with God's Spirit and who have experience of the different states by which God leads souls, above all the ones who have the grace and spirit of prayer. Try to find the ones who are firm in true and solid piety rather than in doctrine alone. The Spirit of God does more in one moment, as you know, than all human knowledge will do in many years. Be sincere and candid when you discuss your inner dispositions, but never think about the creature, only Jesus Christ who shows you His divine will through this way of submission and direction which He set up in the Church.

VI. I exhort you most solemnly to the fidelity which you owe to Jesus Christ in the state to which His grace calls you. Remember what I have told you many times. Jesus Christ says, "Walk while you have the light."[10] Do not neglect the mercies God offers you, for fear that you may lose them forever. I see no other path for your soul except the one that Jesus Christ has shown you for some time; and if you desist from it, I see a miserable shipwreck encompass you—one you will not avoid if you are not faithful. You know the reasons for this, which are in yourself:

1. The natural weaknesses of your mind.

2. The inconstancy that accompanied you in all your past states, which was so great that it did not allow you to ground yourself in any solid path until now. Did you ever do anything but change? Did you sometimes want one thing and then another? Have you given place for a moment to the Spirit of God to direct you? Alas! Jesus Christ never reigned as king in your heart. You looked upon Him as a slave who has no power or authority in His house, and when He wanted to exercise His rights over you, your own mind and creatures were opposed to it. Oh! My child, there are such reasons for humiliation in you—if your soul were a little more penetrated by them!

3. You have an insensitivity to the things of God, occasioned by your mind's inconstancy, which makes them seem insipid, causing you to be easily disgusted with them, and casting you into a certain inner meanness and idleness which has no taste for God's service. This trouble comes from your lack of esteem and lack of respect for God and the poor foundation of your soul in the interior path. And if you wish to search into your interior ground without flattery, you will find that there is nothing at all there, and there was never anything there, except yourself and the vanity of creatures, and that you built

10 Jn 12:35.

the palace of your soul on shifting sand. But this must be entirely demolished. It must be beaten into ruins; God wants to place His throne there. He has the right to reign there. That is what He is doing now and what He will do perfectly if you are not opposed to Him.

4. If you stop doing what God requires of you, you will fall into inward miseries, into disgust and discouragement; and further, into an evil even more peculiar. For according to what I understand about your soul, you would come to a willful carelessness, and—if I dare to tell you what I see—to a contempt of God's ways and the holy workings of His grace. Alas! I have seen many more elevated than you, and seemingly much better grounded, fall terribly. What becomes of a soul when it leaves its God? Its wretchedness cannot be expressed.

"If you stand, take heed lest you fall."[11] Now, you will not fall from your present state all at once, but little by little. Today by a neglect, tomorrow by a little aversion, afterwards by some liberty you will give to your senses, then by some satisfaction, after that vanity, and thus, bit by bit, your soul will be emancipated and your chief misfortune will come from neglecting the attention you owe to God who is present, and to the movements of His grace in you.

Thus, your soul, letting itself go into this frightful disorder, forsaking your God, will remain without strength and without help, exposed to the power of the demons which have made it their plaything. And for you to rise again would require a very great miracle and I do not know if God would do it, after the many mercies He gave you. As for ordinary means, there is no need to speak of them. Your soul would be insensible to them, since infallibly it would become hardened. And unless by some miracle, I do not see it drawing back from this.

Avoid this disastrous and appalling misery. Keep yourself very closely tied to God. May neither hell, nor demons, nor creatures ever be able to separate you from Him. Regard with the highest esteem the grace given to you and never cease your continual tending toward Jesus Christ. Be faithful to Him.

Now if you ask me what constitutes fidelity, I will tell you that it consists in becoming very punctual and very submissive to the orders of God's good pleasure and the promptings of His grace; in preferring

11 1 Cor 10:12.

to die rather than to transgress the smallest of His commands. It consists in seeking the pure glory and interests of God in everything, in seeing all things in God, whether it be pain or rest, peace or war, good or evil, sweetness or bitterness.

Everything is in God and within the organization of His divine Wisdom. There are no accidents in God and in the ordering of His divine Wisdom. He foresaw from all eternity your paths, your crosses, and the misfortunes in your life. Jesus Christ says, "A hair does not fall from your head without the order and permission of the Father."[12] This being so, as we have no reason to doubt since it is eternal Truth who says it, appreciate the goodness and Providence of God over the means of our sanctification, and how much your heavenly Father will support you if you know how to be completely abandoned to Him.

1. Maintain a humble opinion of yourself before God and men. Always be ready to see yourself dashed under everyone's feet, if God's good pleasure reduced you to that.[13]

2. Esteem nothing except God and prefer nothing to His love.[14]

3. Do not prefer yourself to any one, no matter how imperfect he seems to you.[15] Respect inwardly what God secretly works in the ground of souls.

4. Never judge the actions or intentions of others.[16] Remain in your nothingness and leave the judgment of all things to God.

5. Always hold fast to the presence of God.[17] Do not willingly let yourself be pulled away from it. Act simply out of this perspective, and once you have done what Providence has indicated, return within yourself and give yourself over to this simple and loving gaze fixed on God.

There, my child, you have what I can say to you for the moment. I believe that Providence would not have me say anything more. In a few days we shall see what will be given us in order to pursue what remains to be said, as much with regard to the points you proposed in your note to me as with regard to other things which seem to me very necessary.

---

12 Mt 10:29.
13 RB 7:49–50; Ps 72(73):22–23.
14 RB 4:21; RB 72:9, 11.
15 RB 7:51–54.
16 RB 4:42–44.
17 RB 7:10–11.

It seems to me that I must give you all the precautions I can so as to preserve you and cause you, by the grace of Jesus Christ, to persevere. I always fear that your mind may be discouraged and that it may revolt through unfaithfulness. I understand in depth its wretchedness and weaknesses and that is what makes me doubt. However, if you follow the advice you are given, I certainly believe, supported by the power of Jesus Christ, that you will not cease to tend toward God.

I thought about what you said to me recently, about your need for us to speak often, especially since I was pulling down what creatures were building in you. There are still other subjects which make me know it necessary [to speak often], but above all you must keep your mind in check and under control, since it will cause you great difficulty if you let it run away.

Meanwhile, this silence in which He places you right now, according to what your letter from this evening indicates, requires something. You must try to understand it and be faithful to it. It is perhaps a disposition remote from any separation. Do not be occupied with it. Leave everything to God's Providence and the Holy Spirit's guidance. Alas! If I had to leave you now, it seems to me that I would have an endless number of things to say to you, and a great many others to give you for the rest of your life. But I think that it will not be yet, and that we can see each other again many times before Providence arranges that [moment]. Do not stop, do not be grieved. When we must be separated, Our Lord will provide a good guide for you. He will take you from an impure hand in order to place you into one capable of bringing about sanctity in you. All things have their time. Remain in peace and pray to God for me.

Adieu, my dear daughter—to God in God for the eternity in which I lose you and immerse you, withdrawing to the center of my nothingness.[18] Alas! You have made me leave it; but Providence will make me enter into it again, and there keep the love that He gave me for your soul and the union that Jesus caused in us. I will be eternally all yours in Him. *Adieu*. (n. 389)

18 RB 7:62 to the end. We should not forget that for Mother Mectilde "the center of her nothingness" is "the place of perfect humility where God Himself comes to pay court."

Twenty-Four Counsels[1]

TO BE FAITHFUL TO GOD IS TO PREFER nothing to His love, it is to take up His interests; in a word, it is to do nothing that is contrary to Him. Fidelity demands from you a determined resolve to be completely God's, whatever it may cost, and to never cease tending toward His love and serving Him faithfully. "For love of Himself" means to serve because He alone is worthy to be loved and served. It means to serve diligently, willingly, and sincerely, with all your heart, striving only to please Him. It means being very prompt in executing His holy will, very docile to the movements of His divine Spirit, and lovingly consenting to all His plans concerning your soul. This is to give life to Jesus Christ in yourself, to kill all that is opposed to the holiness He desires in you. It is to forsake creatures and one's self in order to be surrendered entirely to Him. In short, it is to follow exactly the prompting of grace. When you are told that you must be very faithful, you are being told briefly that you must do all of this: that you must continually give yourself to God, that you must fulfill the promises you made to Him, that you must give Him everything you owe Him, that you must not in any way usurp His rights over you or appropriate what belongs to Him. Consider what fidelity is between two people who love each other; you have this experience from your past life.

To be unfaithful to God is to do the contrary of the above. It is to turn your back on Jesus Christ in order to look at creatures, to please yourself, and so on. It is to prefer your own thoughts and satisfactions to the simple attention you must have to God's presence in acts of charity or those you are obliged to do. Doing them for human views or considerations is to be unfaithful—thinking about oneself or seeking one's satisfaction or interests in them, whether interior or exterior.

1 In the manuscripts this section is entitled "Instructions on some propositions." The archives of the Rouen monastery preserve no trace of the twenty-four "propositions" from the Countess to which Mother Mectilde is responding.

In indifferent actions, the intention must be to elevate them and make them divine through a divine principle. You must do everything you do out of obedience to God. "Whether you eat or drink, do all for the love of Jesus Christ."[2] Do everything through (His) submission to His holy Providence which requires these things of you, and, remaining detached from your action in your mind, stay focused on God in the highest part of your soul. Give your body what it needs out of obedience to God who wants to preserve your life for Himself.

2. FEW PEOPLE MAKE PROGRESS IN THE INTERIOR LIFE because there are very few who want to abandon themselves unconditionally to Jesus Christ. They are abandoned to a certain degree, but being there, one sees few souls who go beyond this. Especially since we do not give up ourselves as is necessary; something is kept back in the abandonment, it is not complete.

The inconstancy of your spirit comes because you have little or no *anéantissement*. The soul changes its disposition often according to the diverse workings of grace, but it does not change its state often. Dispositions are passing, the state is permanent. If your soul ceases to give itself to God, after such a particular call of His divine mercy, it would put itself in clear danger of being lost; inasmuch as I do not foresee, short of a miracle, that you could rise again. And the reason for this is that you would enter into a state in which you would not be able to be moved. Therefore, you must dread more than hell itself an evil from which you suspect you could never deliver yourself. There are an endless number of passages in Holy Scripture which confirm this truth. If you doubt it, you can read them.

3. EVERY MOMENT OF YOUR LIFE HAS COST THE BLOOD of a God. You must give them to Him faithfully, using them only for Him and for things worthy of Him. Yes, it is to commit a dreadful profanation to use them for something that is not for Him or for love of Him. That is to prefer the nothing to the All, the creature to the Creator, corruption to holiness. Remember what I said and wrote to you about this.

2 1 Cor 10:31.

4. AT EVERY MOMENT OF YOUR LIFE, JESUS CHRIST MUST be brought forth in you. That is, He must take up [His] life in you, and your tendency must be toward producing Him in all creatures, by your fidelity to grace, by holy words, and by good example. That is, everything in you must be affected by the fragrance of Jesus Christ.[3] In this way, you bring Him forth in souls, impressing in them esteem, love, reverence, and imitation of Him. Thus, through you as an intermediary, Jesus Christ is formed in souls. This is how you bring forth Jesus Christ.

5. YES, IT IS GOOD TO SAY YOUR *CONFITEOR* IN A SPIRIT of penitence before Holy Communion, and confess yourself a sinner before God and His angels and, consequently, most unworthy of Communion. You can also say, "*Domine non sum dignus*," but if your soul is focused inwardly in faith on this idea, or on the sentiment of its unworthiness or its nothingness, that is sufficient; there is no need to say it.

6. AT CONFESSION, YOU MUST GO WITH PROFOUND humility, as a criminal presented before his judge. You must accuse yourself humbly, sincerely, and succinctly; listen respectfully to what God tells you through your confessor, receive the penance, and put yourself in a condition to receive absolution which is nothing but the power of Jesus Christ's Blood applied to us. This repairs in your soul the disorders of sin and reunites you with God, making you worthy of His graces.

Jesus Christ made full satisfaction for you, but He desires that you do some small thing on your part, as a little tribute which you pay to His justice, acknowledging that you are indebted to His mercy. And your penance always must be united to that which Jesus Christ did for you, whether in His holy life or in His death; but especially in the Garden of Olives, where He presented Himself before the face of His Father bearing our sins, and where He made an act of contrition so holy and so perfect that He merited for us the grace to share in it. He bore His Father's rebukes as a sinner, without ever sinning or ever being able to sin. In His divine Person, sin was condemned.[4]

---

3 Eph 5:2, Cant 1:3. 4 Rom 8:3, 2 Cor 5:21.

Place yourself before the feet of the priest like Jesus prostrate before His Father and, in view of His holy and profound humility and confession,[5] make your Confession. After having done the above, withdraw in silence and in reverence for the grace you have received through Jesus. See how He delivers Himself to death in order to give you life and how His precious Blood washes you and reconciles you with His Father.

Esteem the sacrament of Penance very highly, it is extremely important; and beware of polluting yourself instead of purifying yourself. Always accuse yourself in the sight of God, as if it were directly to Him. After Confession, do not waste time talking idly with your confessor, even about good things, unless there is a great need. Withdraw and remain recollected, so that the grace of the sacrament takes its effect in you and the horror of sin takes hold of your soul, in order that you may detest it and experience an antipathy toward it not sought for in your senses, but received in the ground of your soul.

7. SPIRITUAL COMMUNION IS MADE THROUGH DESIRE. The soul receives great graces from this when she endeavors to have the desire for it as a state; namely, when she has continually in her heart the requisite disposition, which is nothing but the desire to be entirely Jesus Christ's, as we told you with regard to sacramental Communion.

---

5 The writers of the French School looked to Our Lord as the exemplar of every virtue, including penitence. This did not mean, according to their thought, that Our Lord had sinned, but rather that He completely identified Himself with sinful man and showed sinful man the way of return to God, that is, penitence or repentance. Christ confesses no personal sin to the Father, but assuming the likeness of sinful flesh, in a double confession of sin and of the Father's mercy He shows sinners how to turn to the Father. The confession of Christ is essentially the state of "facing God" that was His from all eternity: "In the beginning was the Word, and the Word was with God [*pros ton Theon*, toward God], and the Word was God" (Jn 1:1). Christ confesses to the Father all the sins of the world for which He is immolated as the sacrificial Lamb; in so doing, He makes our sins His, not in the sense of pretending to have committed them, but in the way that an advocate so identifies with his client's plea that, in representing his client, he makes the client's plea his own. A description of Christ's confession may found in the Epistle to the Hebrews: "Christ, during his earthly life, offered prayer and entreaty to the God who could save him from death, not without a piercing cry, not without tears; yet with such piety as won him a hearing" (Heb 5:7).

The soul who is habituated to living in the presence of God and to living with His Spirit has no trouble making a spiritual Communion; because at every moment it is in a state to receive Communion, since it has a continual desire for God and would like to give itself to Him eternally.

Again, to communicate spiritually is to receive everything from His holy hand. For receiving everything from God's hand, you receive in your heart His divine will, which orders all things. Now the divine will is God Himself. You abolish the sight of creatures so as to give entry to God's good pleasure in your soul; thus you receive Him mystically at every hour and on every occasion. And when we are unfaithful in this matter, we deprive God of a very great glory, because He takes delight in being received in this manner, and we deprive ourselves of an infinite good. The soul habituated to this holy practice, who does it without an effort of mind and by a simple gaze toward God, is marvelously purified, being emptied of creatures and a thousand imperfections.

8. WHEN YOU MAKE JUDGMENTS ABOUT YOUR NEIGHBOR, you contaminate yourself with another's imperfection, taking a creature into yourself and being occupied with its imperfection. Detach your mind from such things. "Do not judge and you will not be judged."[6] It belongs to Jesus Christ to judge and not to you. Be very circumspect on this point; very little is required for it to be a sin.

9. THE PROPER DISPOSITION FOR HOLY MASS IS NOTHING other than your prayer which makes you Jesus Christ's victim, having in your soul a desire to be a victim in Him, immolated to His Father's glory, and a simple disposition to adore all that Jesus does in the Mass for His glory and our sanctification; abandoning yourself to all the designs He has concerning your soul in this divine mystery, remaining in silence, attention, sacrifice, and reverence. Remember that you are member of Jesus Christ and consequently you are sacrificed with Him. Do not draw back from this immolation, remain there in desire and you will be consumed.

---

6 Mt 7:1.

10. THE SACRIFICE OF THE CROSS IS FOR ALL MEN AND the one at the altar is for many. That is to say, Jesus died for all men on Calvary. He poured out His Blood and His life for the salvation of all mankind. It was His intention that all participate in it, St. Paul says.[7] On the altar, there is a mystical shedding of blood, it is shed "for many,"[8] namely for all those who want to become worthy of it and receive it in a holy manner. For in communicating, the blood of Jesus is mystically poured out on our souls.

11. YOU MUST LOVE YOUR NEIGHBOR AS YOURSELF—this is your obligation. But it is difficult to accomplish this well if we are not truly clothed and filled with Jesus Christ. In order to love your neighbor as yourself, you must view him as a member of Jesus Christ, just as you are. In this capacity, out of justice you will do to him the same good you would do to yourself, since he belongs to Jesus Christ, like you. When your interests and self-love are reduced to nothing, you will have no difficulty in loving your neighbor as yourself.

12. THERE ARE TWO MANNERS IN WHICH YOU LOVE God in creatures and creatures in God: seeing them in God and seeing God in them. Both the one and the other are good. To see all creatures in God is to see them engulfed in His divine essence. This is to go beyond creatures in order to see them in that immensity where they have their being and their conservation, and outside of which they are without subsistence.

You must see yourself always and continually in God and see Him in all other creatures. Your dwelling place is the divine essence, your abode is the immensity of God, and your palace is the divinity itself, from which you can never depart. David assures you of this in one of his Psalms: "*Quo ibo a spiritu tuo* . . ."[9] O blessed necessity of

7 Col 1:19–20.

8 Mother Mectilde alludes to the Roman liturgical formula for the consecration of the wine: "Hic est enim calix sanguinis mei, novi et aeterni testamenti: mysterium fidei: qui pro vobis et pro multis effundetur in remissionem peccatorum" (For this is the chalice of my Blood, of the new and eternal testament, the mystery of faith: which shall be shed for you and for many unto the remission of sins).

9 Ps 138(139):7. Whither shall I go from thy spirit? [or whither shall I flee from thy face?]

remaining in God and never being able to leave! This necessity must be beneficial for you, since it facilitates your awareness of His divine Presence and keeps you in reverence, attention, and submission. Faith obliges you to believe this truth, do not neglect to make use of it.

As for creatures, you can see them in God also and sometimes God in them. You see them all in God as in their center. When it is a question of making use of them or serving them, see God in them. Serve God in His creatures, and if they cause you some irritation, you will see God's hand, which crucifies you through this creature. In this way, you disentangle yourself from creatures, so that you are continually occupied with God alone, who alone must occupy and possess you.

There is still another manner of seeing creatures in God, but it is not yet possible for you; it must wait till the time of very great progress. This way comes about through a complete death of all creatures in the soul that, being transformed into God, can no longer see anything except God, as if without the ability to discern creatures. To such a soul, God is so much everything that it cannot any longer see anything but Him in everything. And the soul in this state no longer has any life in creatures, nor can it be defiled in them.

This is a very purified state. There are few souls who reach it, because there are few who want to let themselves be stripped in order to be clothed with God. We often say, "I want Jesus Christ to have me, to be everything in me." But when He wants to drive impurity from your soul's ground and sever your heart's attachments, you turn away from Him. O the blindness of the human heart, to prefer filth to the grandeur and nobility of Jesus Christ!

13. THE [PRACTICE OF THE] PRESENCE OF GOD WITHout constraint is done by a simple regard of God in faith. The soul very simply believes this without making a great number of acts [of faith]. The soul remembers Him as continually as it can; and when it finds itself distracted, the remembrance of God alone, believed to be in us, places the soul again in His holy presence, without the effort of its own mind. If your mind is too distracted, you can make some simple act, that is, without a lot of complexity, so that the soul is

less encumbered and full of creatures and consequently more able to receive in itself God and His holy operations.

14. THE SOUL PRAYS FOR ITS NEIGHBOR ACCORDING to its degree of prayer. Some pray vocally, others mentally; and others, more simplified, pray by a simple regard toward God. Sometimes God prompts a soul to pray for the troubles of another person; when you feel this inclination in yourself, you must pray in the way given to you in the prompting.

The most ordinary fashion in which you must pray is in faith, by a simple regard toward God, who knows the needs of His creatures. Pray that He will sanctify them all. And if your neighbor has particular needs of which you are aware, you may offer these to Our Lord, without being much occupied with them, for fear that under the pretext of charity, you cast your mind into dissipation and the wanderings of your senses and imagination.

We must be surrendered to God's good pleasure in all our prayers, as much for ourselves as for our neighbor, adoring the profundity of His holy and adorable counsels over His creatures and the paths He uses to sanctify them. Love your neighbor as God loves Him, in the condition in which His eternal Wisdom has brought him or keeps him.

15. YOU CAN HAVE PARTICULAR INTENTIONS WHEN YOU have Masses said, and it is good to tell them to the priest, so that he can join his intentions to yours, and that, being united in will, you experience more fruits. It is necessary to make novenas and pilgrimages, and to give alms according to the prompting God's Spirit gives for these. It is not possible to make rules about this, since it must be done according to need or according to God's earnest promptings; and at the time one acts on them, seeking only the pure glory of God everywhere and in everything. It is good to have an interior command from God for them, or obedience to someone from outside, in order to avoid the illusions of our own mind. It is necessary to always try to have direction.

16. WHEN YOU RECEIVE COMMUNION FOR YOUR NEIGHBOR, you must not take pains to explain your intention. Our Lord

knows quite well that you intend to pray for that person. You have only to expose to Him the affection and desire which you have to pray for him and offer him to Our Lord according to your ability, without laboring to explain to Him all your intentions.

17. YOU CAN, WITHOUT SCRUPLE, PROPOSE SOME PARticular need capable of making you obtain Communion, since Providence holds you captive in this respect.[10] But if you were quite free, it would be more useful to do otherwise, because your directors could and even should oblige you to receive Communion often. I charge you again to withdraw from it as little as possible.

18. ATTEND MASS AT YOUR PARISH AS OFTEN AS YOU can. It is to be preferred to other devotions, except that occasionally Providence requires us to do something else. You are obliged to give this example and edification. Therefore, attend at your parish. As for sermons, you can go sometimes where you think there will be more elegance; but beware of deceiving yourself, for if you are faithful to God, God will nourish and sustain you everywhere. Beware of curiosity and indulging your senses.

19. IT IS GOOD TO GIVE ALMS TO THE POOR OF THE streets when you have the prompting. In your acts of piety, always beware of self-satisfaction, ostentation, vanity, and the corruption that can be mixed into them. Act purely in the sight of God, and give alms as to Jesus Christ Himself, returning to Him the goods you have on loan from Him.

20. WE CAN RECOGNIZE GOD'S INSPIRATION BY THE effects it produces in our spirit. If it tends directly toward glorifying God—if it has for its effect leaving us detached from our own concerns, in peace and in pure abandonment—we can follow it in the

10 At the time when Mother Mectilde was writing, it was normal for a directee to ask his or her spiritual director or superior for permission to receive Holy Communion on a given day or for a given period of time. The director/superior had the role of ascertaining the presence of the right dispositions and appropriate motives.

desire to give ourselves more fully to God. But when the inspiration brings us to something important, it is necessary to have recourse to [spiritual] direction.

21. DISCOURAGEMENT COMES FROM A GROUND OF pride, because if the soul does not have hidden supports in itself, it will never be discouraged. The confidence it has in its own powers is thrown down when the soul finds them insufficient for attaining the point where it desires to be.

The soul is always subject to discouragement until it has understood thoroughly the abyss of its wretchedness, nothingness, and weakness, and that it is lifted up again by Jesus Christ's power and virtue; until it sees by its own experience how it constantly depends on His grace. When the soul has understood this truth, it remains firm in its nothingness, not at all surprised by its weaknesses, but leaving itself to Christ's power. The soul waits for His help with humility and confidence, knowing that it can do nothing without Him.[11] And faith and its own experience showing it this truth, it remains steadfast without disturbance in the midst of temptation, abandoned without reservation completely to Jesus Christ.

22. DISTRACTIONS ARE CALLED VOLUNTARY WHEN THE superior part of the soul notices them and becomes occupied with them; and then, they are more or less sinful depending on the place, time, and subjects.

23. IT IS NECESSARY TO DESIRE TO HAVE SORROW FOR our sins when confessing them. It does not need to be sensible; it is enough for it to be in the reason. And you will recognize it when you have in your interior ground an aversion to sin, not wanting to commit one for anything; and this, only because it is displeasing to God. It is enough that you have this disposition in the ground of your soul.

24. YOU MUST DO YOUR ACTIONS WITH GREAT SIMPLICITY. When they are not done well, the conscience cannot bear it,

---

11 Jn 15:5.

and God cannot be satisfied with it. This is better understood by experience than by explanation. In thinking about your actions, you must fear appropriating them and stealing the glory which they must give to God. You must distrust your malicious subtlety which steals everything, pollutes everything, and appropriates everything for itself.

At the very time you do your action, leave it in God, and humble yourself regarding the impurities you have committed in doing it. Then detach yourself from your action so as not to fall into something harmful. Be distrustful of your [fallen] ground. It is sufficient that God is pleased—you have no need to be. On the contrary, it is quite helpful for you to be without any satisfaction and that your pride take no part in it. It stole too much in the past, so it must make restitution for it and be left in want as a penance. (n. 421)

Answers to Difficulties

In the state of darkness, is it better to remain in this disposition even though one has nothing to show that one sees God in faith except awareness of it?

If the soul is sufficiently generous as to lose itself in God above the senses, the mind, and its natural lights, it can persevere in God's presence through a naked faith, and this is most excellent. But for you, you can renew your mind by a simple act of faith from time to time, remembering that you are in God, surrounded and permeated with the divinity, where you receive it in your simple intelligence, where you will make it [viz., the act of faith] if such a movement is given to you.

It is necessary to notice that in the darkness God has very particular plans for the soul which His wisdom causes to walk there and which require the highest fidelity. In this state, it is not at all necessary to seek consolation from the senses or from creatures. You must remain very simply abandoned and allow yourself to be led blindly. Do not hesitate, you are in a holy and divine hand, you cannot perish there. Therefore, allow yourself to be entirely sacrificed, for the true sacrifice requires darkness as well as weakness and all the rest of it. The sacrifice must be complete, since in the state of darkness the soul offers to God the light of its own mind in order to receive God's. Everything in you must be purified and renewed; that is why you should take heart and allow yourself to be blind as the Spirit of God pleases.

The hidden remembrance of God which is in the depth of the soul shows it clearly that it is not separated from Him. But inasmuch as it does not see Him or experience Him, it does not believe it. You must become habituated to exercising a pure and detached faith: this is your path. But I see that you have great difficulty in this, and, especially since your mind is accustomed to its own light and reasoning, it will disturb you often before being firmly established in this state where God desires you to be. But you must endure these battles and remain steadfast. Fear nothing, the grace of Jesus Christ will not fail you. The more you give to God, the more you will receive from His goodness. Sacrifice your natural lights to Him: you will be filled with His completely holy and divine light.

How does one know when one is acting by the spirit of grace or by that of nature? By what can one recognize the difference?

Grace directs our mind to God's pure glory, while nature thinks about creatures and about its own interests. To recognize in ourselves the impulse of grace, we must be in silence and the passions must be calm. Otherwise, we cannot discern God's Spirit, and instead of the one, we often lay hold of the other.

It is necessary to be very suspicious of oneself in this discernment. In order to be freed from nature's snare, you must keep your soul in a continual indifference toward all occupations, all dispositions, and all choices or inclinations, keeping your soul empty of all desires, so that you are in a state to receive the impression of God's Spirit in you. And when you have received it, in order to act, it is good to simply raise your soul to God present, so that by this simple gaze, you direct and sacrifice your actions to Him.

To the extent that you are emptied of yourself, your natural lights, and attachment to your operations, you will be more able to recognize the movement of grace in your soul. There is an excellent chapter about this in *The Imitation of Christ*,[1] but I think that something more particular than what it says can still be explained, because there are movements of grace for hidden operations. I think you still cannot understand what I would say about this topic. You must wait in humility and patience for the grace of Jesus Christ to purify you completely.

Meanwhile, act as much as is possible for you through the Holy Spirit, that is, always seek God's glory and the accomplishment of the divine will, renouncing all the pursuits of your self-love, the inclinations of nature, creatures, in short, your interests, of whatever kind they seem to you to be. Be detached from all of it for the sake of considering God alone.

I do not know how to tell the difference between a state and a disposition.

Dispositions are very different and variable in souls in grace; for

1 *Imitation of Christ*, III.37.

sometimes the soul has a spirit of sacrifice, at other times of love, at other times of abandonment, at other times of *anéantissement*, and at other times, of respect for God's greatness and majesty.

States are something permanent, they do not vary. This is why, when we say "that soul is in a state of complete abandonment to Providence," it means that that disposition is established deeply and the soul never leaves it, whereas it does not leave that state in order to receive various dispositions and workings of grace. So it is with a soul in a state of death toward creatures.[2]

How is it that we depart from God through our operations?

The soul truly dwells in the divine essence and our body is completely permeated with it, and this is an inevitable necessity of being—to live and act in God in this manner. But this is different from acting through His pure grace. You are in God essentially, and despite this, God does not cooperate in the imperfection or sin you commit. His divine essence conserves your being, life, and so on, but God does not cooperate in the faults you commit, because He cannot descend into powerlessness toward the good. That is why when you commit a sin, you withdraw, not from His essence—you would cease to live—but from His grace which causes you to do the good. And there, you do an act from your own spirit and from pure malice, desired and accepted by your disordered will which turned away from its divine source so as to turn itself toward creatures.[3] Thus, to commit sin, the soul does not leave God's essence (that is impossible for it), but it leaves His grace and the guidance of His Spirit.

"But then," you say, "God cooperates in sin." He cannot cooperate with your evil will. But with respect to the action, there is a concurrence, the theologians say, namely, a preservation of our freedom. And God Himself preserves it in us, giving us the power to do the evil action which is chosen and determined by our wicked will, because He does not violate free will and we are able to choose good or evil.[4]

We sin without Him, but we cannot recover without Him. And it would be blasphemy to say that God cooperates in our sin; because sin is a denial of God which turns us toward creatures, in one way

2 Rom 6:6–11.

3 Rom 1:21, 24–25.

4 Cf. Sir 15:11–17.

or in another; and God who is eternal unity cannot deny Himself. Therefore, note what I am telling you: His concurrence preserves our freedom, but it does not cooperate in sin at all. It is not my hand that commits the sin, whatever I strike; rather, it is the evil of my ground which makes me angry.[5]

Is it better to make a simple act or to have the desire for it in the soul's ground? But since this desire is imperceptible, and the mind cannot exist in a void, it becomes distressed. Likewise for the presence of God, because one does not know or experience in the mind or senses this presence of God. I do not believe it to be constant, although I have prayed for this. At least, if I think about it, I suppose this would be the question.

There is no danger in forming your act if you have the inclination and the prompting [for it], or if it is simple. If the soul is captive and powerless to work, it will be content with the desire in the depths of the spirit. But I think it good that you, who are still not established in the pure ways of the soul, make an act or two at the beginning of your prayer.

First, a remembrance of God in faith (that is, without images), which brings your mind to form an act of adoration, which will include a disposition of the reverence, esteem, and homage which you owe to the supreme greatness of God.

Second, an act of complete abandonment into His divine hands, submitting to His holy action, and offering yourself as a victim for the love of His good pleasure for time and for eternity.[6]

And if you desire, a third that renounces everything which might pass through you, during the holy time of prayer, that is contrary to God.

After you have done this, remain completely abandoned, leaving yourself entirely to God, rejoicing at being consumed in His holy presence, rendering homage to all that He is in Himself and ought to be in you. Remain firm and inaccessible with respect to business and creatures, unless God or charity to your neighbor takes you out of it.

During your prayer, if you are given some truth to revere which moves you, you will allow yourself to be exposed to God so as to

5 Mt 15:18–19. 6 Rom 12:1.

receive the impression through His divine Spirit. You will give yourself to His grace for this. And if you find yourself disturbed in emptiness, remain reduced to nothing. If you bring weakness and distraction to it, be sacrificed. All of this purifies the soul, making it suffer, and God draws His glory from everything, when the soul knows how to truly abandon itself.

When I find myself in a state of darkness, and I cannot perceive this presence of God, I try to put myself there in faith, taking my senses captive, binding my mind. Then, this gives me an awareness I believe to be God's presence, but I cannot make this out. In order to act purely in faith, I think it is not necessary to do all of this; but I worry that it would put me into some carelessness of mind, which easily grows slack and cannot be captive for long.

It is good for you to exercise pure faith so as to put yourself into God's presence, as we said, but you must not make imprudent efforts. For this purpose, you must use a simple elevation which causes you to remember that God sees you and which keeps you reverently in His holy presence. There is no need for you to bind your mind to have certainty that you are in God's presence, for you can take this certainty from faith, which is pure and in no way sensed. If God's presence were discernible for you, it would not be based on faith. Sometimes it does overflow even to the senses, but when that happens you must accept it with a detached soul, without claiming it for yourself or being pleased about this sensible grace; rather, you must make use of it according to God's designs. He gives it in order to fortify you in fidelity, making you experience some little spark of the delight which souls receive in loving Him.

The experience of God through faith is more pure and more holy. But you must humbly receive what God gives you, considering yourself unworthy of the slightest of His mercies. Do not tend toward being elevated in grace, but tend toward leaving yourself completely to the divine disposition. Abandon yourself and God will do with you what He pleases. It is for Him to direct our ways and to straighten our paths;[7] and it is for us to walk in simplicity.

7 Prov 3:6.

Do not worry about untangling your [sense of] God's presence. Do not seek for certitude out of your desire to see and know. Beware of your enemy who will not fail to make efforts to repair the destruction we have tried to cause for him up to now, and who will play his tricks.

Be completely little in your own eyes and utterly simple like a small child in the arms of obedience. My child, God is subjecting you to this very particularly. He desires that, just as Adam took you from God through his disobedience[8] and you have clung so long to the evil of his spirit, you [now] return to God through the most perfect and complete submission of mind to those whom His Providence has given you for your guidance.

Your mind will not become careless and slothful through the practice of faith, because this will impress on you a high regard for God, and meanwhile, by it your senses will be held captive out of respect. If you meet with some drowsiness, rouse yourself with an act formed to remind you of the incomprehensible majesty of the living God; or if a simple remembrance is enough, remain in your recollection without troubling to go beyond it by the acts mentioned above.

When one has Masses said, which is better: to have particular intentions and tell them to the priest, or to have none but those of the Church and to join your intention to that of the Sacrifice?

The intention of the Church and of the Sacrifice is most holy; you may honor and respect them, uniting yours to them. But it is permitted to sometimes have particular intentions and to tell them to the priest. You can also offer them yourself, according to your private and personal intentions, or for the needs of your soul, or for the dead, or for the needs of some affair or of your neighbor. Likewise also for God's interests, asking for the establishment of His reign in you, the grace to know Him, or the grace to be detached from everything which is not Him. Or to honor some saint to whom you have had recourse, or to give thanks for some mercy, and so on. You can do the same in Holy Communion.

But always note that the holy Sacrifice of the holy Mass sacrifices you with Jesus Christ, that it requires you to be a victim and to have

8 Rom 5:19.

a desire to give yourself to Jesus Christ's designs, and that you enter into this spirit of victimhood, entirely immolated to the glory of the Father, the Son, and the Holy Spirit.

At Communion, your sacrifice is even more complete, since then you consent to its effects, giving the three divine Persons an abode in your soul to take up power and authority in you and subject you to their divine reign, abandoning yourself unreservedly to Jesus Christ.

I think I am very sinful with regard to kindness toward my neighbor.

Charity or love of neighbor follows the same path as love of God: St. John assures you of this.[9] I still do not see this love established in you. You are too interested in yourself, too little desirous for the Kingdom of God in all hearts, too stingy for souls. You view them as separated from Jesus Christ, not remembering that they are His members, who make up His Mystical Body.[10] There is a great deal of work for you on this point. But to the extent that God takes up His dwelling in you, the love of neighbor will grow in you and produce its fruits.[11]

In the renewal of my vow of baptism, I note that one gives oneself to God, and you told me the other day that being Jesus Christ's in so many ways, one cannot give oneself again . . .

I think I wrote you that being God's, we are given and sacrificed to Him through Jesus Christ, as members of His Mystical Body and because everything belongs to God. Thus we are of necessity His, but in a manner beyond words, through the sacrifice of Jesus Christ, as much on the cross as on the altar. For on the cross you have been mystically crucified (see what St. Paul says about this) and you are dead with Him.[12] This is why you are obliged to live a life of death, totally detached and separated from the life of your senses, because "your life is hidden in Jesus Christ," as the Apostle says.[13] Accordingly, if your life is hidden in Jesus Christ, nothing must be seen in you except Jesus Christ. You must be a living expression of His virtues, His dispositions, and His sanctity. Everything in you which is from

---

9 1 Jn 4:19–21.
10 1 Cor 12:27.
11 1 Jn 3:23, 4:7.
12 Rom 6:6, Col 2:11, Gal 2:19–20.
13 Col 3:3.

you must be reduced to nothing so that Jesus alone is seen in you. In short, you must lead a crucified life, since you are [crucified] with Jesus Christ.[14]

With regard to the sacrifice of the altar, you know how it is the memorial of the sacrifice of the cross and a continuation of that most adorable sacrifice. There is this difference, that it is not bloody; but [it is no less] efficacious and works its mighty effects in souls to whom it is applied, and who remain in the grace it communicates to us.

I believe I was saying to you last night that I can no longer say, "My God, I give myself to You." If I am given to God through Jesus Christ, is this gift not complete? Am I less obliged to be God's? Since Jesus Christ sacrifices me continually, I cannot disavow it. Is not this gift more than sufficient? We must allow ourselves to be sacrificed and lovingly consent to it, continuing this life or act of sacrifice through a disposition of submission and respect.

And since you were not on Calvary to consent to your crucifixion, Our Lord desires that you consent to the one at the altar in order to make up what is lacking in His Passion,[15] in such a way that, as one of His members, you are offered to the Father with Jesus Christ and by Jesus Christ, and the priest holds you mystically in his hands, and in this way you are in the host.

O dignity of the Christian state, to be made entirely one with Jesus Christ, to be crucified with Him, and to be immolated on the altar every day with Him! O adorable impossibility, where Christian grace keeps us distinct from Jesus Christ, yet makes us one same thing with Him![16] Since we constitute part of His Body, we are thus part of Himself.

In the renewal of your baptism, you do not perform a new act of giving yourself to God; rather, you renew the gift and sacrifice which Jesus Christ made to the Most Holy Trinity. And it is this that I wanted to make you realize, so that you know that all your actions and sacrifices are nothing but the fruits of those which Jesus Christ did and made for you. Therefore renew your baptism in order to be renewed in the sacrifice which Our Lord made of you there. You cannot make a sacrifice of yourself to God more holy than the one

14 Gal 2:19–20. 15 Col 1:24. 16 Rom 8:8–29, 37–38.

which Jesus Christ made of you to His Father. You must continue it and never draw back from it, living thus perpetually in the spirit of a victim, not by your choice, but because Jesus Christ made you subject to it, through His sacrifice. And doing so, you are a victim, not of your own volition, but of Jesus Christ's.

When I want to make the sacrifice of myself to God, in order to be joined to Jesus Christ as His member, I find myself in a quandary...

The sacrifice you make must be very simple, being content with the pure faith which shows you this truth: that you and all Christians are members of Jesus Christ. It is enough to believe this without examining it minutely.

When I consider myself to be a member of Jesus Christ along with many others...

It is good to desire that all members of Jesus Christ may be sacrificed with Him. And we must desire that all souls be pure victims of Jesus Christ. But you are not required to focus on such thoughts. The constant state of sacrifice in the continual presence of God keeps a soul like this.[17]

Regarding sinners, at least those who appear so to me, I cannot...

The sinner, by his sin, separates himself from Jesus Christ. But be careful about judging. Do not be polluted by the sins of another. Sometimes those we think are buried in sins are perhaps already moved by God and completely converted.

I cannot bear that a soul who professed that she loves Jesus Christ is occupied with thinking about her neighbor. Your mind must observe a very strict silence on this point. "Do not judge and you will not be judged,"[18] says Our Lord. Esteem your neighbor the way God does. Do not elevate creatures and do not belittle them.

Maintain prudence and a very great silence based on charity, since this is the sign of the Spirit of God in a soul. For if prudence is lacking, the soul is without guidance. Jesus says, "Be simple as doves and

17 That is, keeps the soul's desire for the sacrifice of the Mystical Body virtually present and active.

18 Mt 7:1.

prudent as serpents."[19] In matters which concern your neighbor, you must be very restrained about speaking. I leave you to think about consequences which would be harmful to them.

Do not investigate whether the poor to whom you give are in a state of grace; it is enough for you if they are Christians. And if they are not [in grace], such an act is for God, and consequently, it is to Him that you give your alms and not to the creature present before you. The intention ennobles and enriches the action. Have in all things the pure sight of God, and you will be at peace in all your actions.

When we are required to converse with our neighbor, what thoughts is it necessary to have?

It is the sight of God that we must never forget. In conversations, we must always maintain gentleness, charitable kindness, humility, and discretion. You must converse with your neighbor as with the angels, with respect and simplicity; and beware of scandalizing the little ones whom Our Lord mentions in the Gospel.[20] The little ones, according to the meaning of Scripture, are the sinners; for they are the smallest in God's sight, since by sin they are doubly reduced to nothing.

In conversations, always tend away from vanities and the world's foolishness. Beware also of talking too much in them and being hasty through [your mind's] great activity. Be considerate and reserved.

Never forget that God sees you, and that He sounds the ground of your heart. In short, converse out of submission to the divine will which subjects you to this law of conversing and maintaining fellowship with your neighbor. Be free without becoming anxious. Never argue unless the pure glory of God and pure charity force you to do so. Only converse out of obedience and charity, for fear that you may become too immersed, sullied, and bound up in it.

The duties to which we are obliged....

The affairs which are your obligation must not be neglected. If they are urgent, you may put them before your prayers. If you know how to keep the interior spirit which must accompany you in all your

19 Mt 10:16, Lk 10:3. 20 Mt 18:6–8, Mk 9:42.

actions, then in doing them you will find that you perform your duties with a spirit of prayer. You will preserve presence of mind in them, so that you can do them as you must. And observing the lessons which I already gave you in similar matters, you will do what you must do at the time, but always out of obedience to God's command which is employing you in them, without losing the awareness of God who is present.

If your duties are not pressing, and you do not have the inclination or readiness to work on them, you may put them off for another time. But beware of slackness! Nevertheless, you may postpone them and busy yourself with reading or in prayer, waiting until God gives you the ability to dispatch them. But note that if they are urgent, you must quit everything else and abandon yourself [to the duties]. Everything is for God—your work as much as your prayer—and it would be an error to want to pray when God wants you to act. We must be altogether in a complete abandonment to the guidance of God's good pleasure.

You must try to yield to God all actions which depend on your choice, and although they are at your liberty, you must nevertheless always and only do them out of obedience to Jesus Christ who inspires you. If the action is good in itself, you must view it within God's order, but if your self-love pollutes it, you must purify your intention through a simple and pure gaze toward God in order to direct it to the pure glory of His name.

Is it not the degree of love which gives merit to the action?

Yes, the more love there is, the more grace there is. But I do not mean here the love which affects the senses. I mean that the more purity there is in your soul's ground—that is, if you have an intention which is more purified and tends toward acting uniquely for and through the love of God—the more grace there is, and consequently, the more merit. That is why the most holy Mother of God when on earth merited more by one turn of the spindle than all the saints by their penances and extraordinary austerities: because she had more love than all the angels and saints together. Thus, if you pick up a straw with more purity of love than another has in taking the discipline, your merit is greater. You can also infer that if two actions, the one small and the other great, are done with the same degree of love, the greater is worth more than the smaller. It is the purity of love which gives the weight.

What thoughts is it necessary to have when one is required to receive some service from one's neighbor?

We must receive such things in a spirit of deep inward humility, being ashamed in ourselves that souls created in the image and likeness of God, His members and His spouses, and who in heaven will perhaps be infinitely more elevated than ourselves, are occupied in serving us — but even more: who are perhaps, on earth, in a very elevated degree of grace. For a soul in a state of grace is cherished and honored by God Himself and by His angels; and these persons are more worthy of esteem than all the greatest monarchs of the earth, since they are worthy to be objects of God's approval. Such a soul is the throne of His greatness wherein He delights;[21] the angels have respect for them, and yet we don't think about this.

We frequently have presumption and arrogance about services which are given to us. This comes from our extreme ignorance, which makes us appropriate to ourselves the services rendered to us. You are not served out of love for yourself, but for love of God in you.[22] Therefore, these services, that honor, this respect which you receive, do not belong to you, but to Jesus Christ; and you rob Him of them when you make them your own, without having the right to do so. This is a usurpation which must be restored, sooner or later. Leave to God what belongs to God, and keep what is yours, namely, to know the nothingness of your being, the nothingness of sin, the ire of God and eternal damnation. This is what you merit. Why do you encroach upon the rights of Jesus Christ?

Furthermore, do you not know that, considered as a sinner, you do not deserve any service from creatures, but rather, continual punishment? For if God executed justice, all creatures would band together against us to avenge the dishonor we have done to God and to the blood of His Son. And that they do not do this is owing to His very

21 Prov 8:31. 22 Eph 6:7, Col 3:22–24.

great mercy, which "does not desire the death of a sinner, but that He be converted and live."[23]

But God's goodness [to us] should not make us forget what we are. You are always criminal enough to stay in your abjection and in the view that you are not worthy of being served by the least of creatures. For myself, I confess to you that I grieve that even animals should be occupied in something for my service. I see that, having sinned, I deserve to be torn apart beneath the beasts; in this way, then, the animals are better than I am and have the right to humiliate me and even crucify me. O profound truth, which powerfully reduces to nothing a soul which is pierced with it! Alas! People and animals serve me and perhaps I will be eternally damned. This prospect is a second torment to me in view of the services which charity renders me. Yet I must endure them since Providence subjects me to them, and humble myself a great deal, returning them to Jesus Christ. (n. 307)

The End of the
"Breviary
of Fire"

23 Ez 18:22 and 32, 33:11; Lk 5:32; 2 Pet 3:9.

APPENDIX I

The "Breviary of Fire": Background & Major Themes

MICHEL DUPUY, PSS

I. MARIE DE CHÂTEAUVIEUX

The reader is already acquainted with Mother Mectilde. We must introduce Madame de Châteauvieux, as much as our sources permit us to know.

In 1651 the civil war was raging in the area of Paris. Mother Mectilde's nuns from Lorraine had fled once more and were taking refuge at the gates of Paris, in the St. Germain suburb. They found only a temporary lodging in the rue du Bac, where they stayed for two months without bread and without blankets, living only on peas. Mother Mectilde was sick. But Jean-Jacques Olier, still curé of Saint-Sulpice, had stirred up in the quarter a genuine spirit of charity. One of his relations visited the poor there. On the last Sunday of August, she brought with her some of her friends—among them a certain Marie de la Guesle, Countess of Châteauvieux. They stopped at the "little nuns from Lorraine" for a moment only, since they had other visits to make.

On September 14, Marie de la Guesle, "extremely inquisitive about spiritual discourse," visited them again, accompanied by a friend. She engaged in conversation with the Prioress, posed some questions on the life of perfection, and stated her difficulties in meditating and in putting into practice what she had read in spiritual books on the subject. At first, Mother Mectilde remained silent, then "said some words that were so substantial and so full of unction" that her visitor was "fully satisfied" by them and admitted, "You have found in a few words what my soul has been seeking for so long."[1] From that time on, her visits increased.

Where was she from? We know the names of her forebears. She was the daughter of Jean de la Guesle and Marie Béraux, niece of François de la Guesle, archbishop of Tours (†1614), granddaughter

1 MS, p. 365.

of Jean de la Guesle, *president á mortier* at the Parliament of Paris, great granddaughter of François de la Guesle, governor of the County of Auvergne... We have her genealogical tree, but we do not have the date of her birth. In 1625 she married René de Vienne, Knight, Count of Châteauvieux and Confolens. Her husband was heir to one of the most illustrious families in the whole Bourgogne and Franche counties. They had one daughter, who had recently married (1649) and a son, Henri, who died young. They lived in the hôtel de la Guesle, called the hôtel de Châteauvieux; it was situated in the Saint-Germain quarter, next to the church of St.-André-des-Arts. René de Châteauvieux was also an earnest and generous Christian. One of his female relations, under the blow of a sorrowful mourning, would shortly retire to lodge with the "little nuns," once they were set up in a less precarious manner, and this provided the Countess with an additional occasion to go there more frequently.

The *Memoirs* report that Mother Mectilde and Madame de Châteauvieux had very different characters. As much as the first was master of herself, so the second was impetuous, active, sensitive, and more inclined to aid hospitals than contemplatives. Therefore, it was not a sister soul that she found in the Prioress, but a superior woman who did not hesitate to contradict her. We would like to know more about how the Countess was won over and progressively transformed. Unfortunately, no letters from her have been preserved.

However, some traits have not been forgotten. For example, during one visit, the Countess advanced an idea which Mother Mectilde did not approve. She said to her with energetic frankness, "I want you to know that, Countess though you are, and having some power to assist me in the great need to which I find myself reduced with my Sisters, if you continue, I will have no more esteem for you than this." And she showed her a straw under her feet. "I do not regard your person except inasmuch as I know God wants to make use of you to do something great for your sanctification."[2] This audacious firmness, far from offending Madame de Châteauvieux, conquered her.

Marie had entrusted her spiritual direction to the curé of St.-André-des-Arts and was having scruples about an increasing familiarity with

2 MS, p. 268.

Mother Mectilde which was becoming spiritual direction. However the priest told her he did not see any problem with this. Providence willed that the Countess met him one day on a visit to Mother Mectilde. He took the occasion openly to entrust his directee to her, going so far as to say, "I give her to you." She was reassured by this.[3]

If the *Memoirs* are discreet about the Countess's spiritual life, they show well how much she took to heart the cause of the Benedictines of the Blessed Sacrament. She worked to help them from her resources and to find them benefactors, in such a way as to permit them to lodge more comfortably and to obtain, first, the permission to be established in the quarter from the Abbot of Saint-Germain-des-Prés, who had the jurisdiction of the neighborhood, and second, from the Keeper of the Seals, the royal patent letters authorizing the foundation. This was no small matter. Many benefactors arranged their bequests with unacceptable clauses about which laborious negotiations were required. She also had to win over families, often less generous and little inclined to see the inheritance they had anticipated encroached upon by bequests to nuns. Furthermore, in society at that period, women did not have full civic capability. The agreement of the husband was required and was sometimes delayed.

A sufficient sum being gathered, it was the opposition of the Abbot of Saint-Germain-des-Prés and his vicar which they came up against next. It seemed he would not yield, and that they would give in only to the Queen herself, whose favor then had to be gained. Fortunately she was ready to give it, and carried out her cooperation with much fidelity. The patent letters were not, however, obtained from the Keeper of the Seals. The convents were already numerous—too numerous for the available resources, he judged. It was again necessary to convince and have the intervention of important people with whom the Châteauvieux family were connected.

Some proceedings were also necessary for finding a dwelling. First, the house of Madame de Rochefort, rue Férou, served for a time. Then, an area for building a monastery, that of rue Cassette, close to the Church of Saint-Sulpice, fit the bill. Madame de Châteauvieux

---

3 MS, p. 371.

tirelessly pursued these interminable negotiations. It was almost three years before the monastery could merely set up at rue Férou, and another four years before they came to rue Cassette.

Madame de Châteauvieux wanted to give something even better than her resources, her time, and her trouble—she wanted to give herself and take the habit of the order, as a foundress. This did not mean that she would leave her husband, however. He gave his consent. But Mother Mectilde wanted to test at greater length a woman as lively as she was generous, and it was only in 1662 that she received the habit. It was a symbolic clothing ostensibly, since the foundress had to put aside the religious vesture to return to her town mansion. However, at the same time she promised that she would not remarry if her husband died before she did, and that she would be clothed again with the habit on her deathbed.

But Providence gave this first commitment more reality than was supposed: three months later, on November 6, 1662, René de Châteauvieux was called back to God. The couple had been very close and the Countess was distressed. Yet now she was free. The next day, she entered the monastery where her husband was interred. Three days later she pronounced her vows "of victim, of obedience to our Reverend Mother, to which she added perpetual chastity." She took the name of Sister Victim of the Blessed Sacrament.[4]

That a Prioress as clear-sighted as Mother Mectilde was ready for such a commitment may cause surprise and shows her trust in the Countess. For foundresses kept some rights and, in wanting imprudently to impose their views before they had any experience of religious life, often constituted a source of difficulties for prioresses or superiors. The patience of St. Francis de Sales was more than once severely tested by some foundresses of the Visitation. Mother Mectilde knew it; she had experience of the pretensions of benefactresses toward whom gratitude obliged one to be gentle. However, she accepted the entry of Madame de Châteauvieux into the monastery. She entrusted to her the care of the financial books. We find there that in 1663, Sr. Victim changed the sizeable loans, which she had made with her husband, into donations pure and simple. This gesture,

4 *Memoirs*, 205.

observes the *Memoirs,* was the equivalent of the vow of poverty that she had not pronounced in November 1662.

Sister Victim of the Blessed Sacrament bowed to the common rule. The questions she posed to Mother Mectilde—preserved at the end of the *Breviary*—show that she assimilated its teachings perfectly.

On July 7, 1669, she had the sorrow of losing her daughter, her last child, who, however, left her some grandchildren.

She herself wanted to die in order "to avoid the infidelity which I constantly incur," she said. She saw it as a grace "to die suddenly without being sick." Thus, "I would not be occupied with myself, or my pains, or creatures." Every two weeks she confessed and every day she received Holy Communion. She had recently made a "review" with Fr. Guilloré. On Wednesday, as was customary, she confessed. The next day, as was customary also, she had a conversation with the Prioress about Christ's words, "Learn from me for I am meek and humble of heart," at the end of which she fell ill; she had scarcely time to repeat "Jesus, Mary" and went to join the Lord. This was in 1674.

✠

WHEN DID MOTHER MECTILDE SEND TO MADAME DE Châteauvieux the texts which constitute this *Breviary*?

First, let us glean some chronological indications.

Text n. 353 (p. 53) assumes that Monsieur de Châteauvieux is still living. But it is the only one to allude to the recipient's family. Letter 3146 (p. 72) is related to the vow of victimhood Madame de Châteauvieux made soon after the death of her husband. Should the texts on servitude be put in relation to the vow of obedience to which the *Memoirs* assign the same date? That is very doubtful since the obedience to Mother Mectilde and servitude in Jesus cannot be compared.

We find no trace of other dated facts. Did Mother Mectilde never ask her for news, did she never allude to the present interests or events of the family, as she did in the letters which do not belong to this collection? That is difficult to imagine if she was writing to a woman living in the world, and who still remained inquisitive after her entry into the monastery. Would Mother Mectilde have insisted that she turn the page without ever again thinking of her own? Surely the fragment from n. 1815 (p. 171) invites her to a great detachment. But it is inconceivable that Mother Mectilde spoke in such terms to a woman who had just lost her husband. It is exceedingly probable that these texts were, from the very beginning, expurgated of all that could have allowed them to be placed or to recognize the addressee, as is the case with the majority of correspondence from that era, so that they might suit every man or woman who read them.[5] For this they were rendered as impersonal as possible. Indications of dates and places were suppressed and probably also the traits which could give away the recipient. The often loose style lent itself to such excisions. Only if the autographs were discovered could our curiosity be satisfied. And that is unimaginable. Having entered the monastery, Marie de la Guesle was dead to the world. She succeeded in effacing herself. Let us respect her secrecy.

However, there remain to be noted in the content some clue texts, which allow us to situate them in a hypothetical manner. First, we understand correctly that Mother Mectilde would have recourse to writing if the Countess did not yet live in the monastery. Regarding the commitments to which the *Breviary* refers (except for n. 3146 cited above), these are not about personal vows, but about baptism. Wouldn't this be addressed to a woman who had not yet actually made vows?

It is true that Mother Mectilde proposed to her correspondent the prayer of simple regard[6] which is not ordinarily the form of prayer that best fits a beginner. But Francis de Sales had already led through the ways of prayer some women committed to marriage and life in the

---

5 In other words, when the letters were arranged thematically for any reader, most of the strictly personal content was removed, as one can see with other examples of the genre of spiritual correspondence from this era.

6 This type of prayer may be familiar through the writings of St. Francis de Sales. "The prayer of simple regard or *simple remise en Dieu*. Simple attentiveness or simple entrustment to God. This prayer consisted in a hidden and quiet waiting, an expectant attention to the presence of God. It was a virtually imageless and wordless type of prayer" (Wendy M. Wright and Joseph F. Power, OSFS, Introduction to *Francis de Sales, Jane de Chantal: Letters of Spiritual Direction* [Mahwah, NJ: Paulist Press, 1988], 84). St. Jane de Chantal describes it thus: "When the time comes to present ourselves before his divine Goodness . . . simply the presence of our spirit before His and of His before ours forms prayer whether or not we have fine thoughts or feelings . . ." (ibid., 84–85).

world, such as Madame Brûlart, the Philothea of the *Introduction to the Devout Life*. Let us recall that at that epoch parents married their daughters very young and without asking for their opinion, some of whom may have been apt for religious life, just as they sent to the convent others who seemed in no way disposed to it. This explains why cases of extreme piety outside of religious life, as well as cases of some in religious life who were without piety, were more common than today. In 1664, Mother Mectilde invited to the prayer of simple regard beginners and faithful without instruction, as a short way which was appropriate to them (*Easy Practice to Elevate the Soul to Contemplation, in the Form of a Dialogue*, Paris, 1664). The danger was obviously that these beginners might confuse daydreaming or spiritual idleness with prayer. But this risk was less with the Countess: her vivacity and her active temperament immunized her against such a torpor. Mother Mectilde understood she was addressing an exceptional woman. There is nothing which makes it impossible that the texts of the *Breviary* are by and large from the period before the entry of Madame de Châteauvieux into the monastery.

Let us attempt to read its message in light of the theology of the era.

II. THE *BREVIARY* AND THE THEOLOGY OF THE TIMES

God in Himself

From the outset, the reader of Mother Mectilde is struck by her insistence on adoration and one recognizes in this a Bérullian accent. Is this accent more Bérullian than Benedictine? On this point Bérulle only expressed what every Christian lives, any believer who thinks about God, because we can live it without knowing how to talk about it. How can one express the grandeur of God, the infinity of God, the sublimity of God? As with all those who grasped the meaning of God, Mother Mectilde lacks words. She takes up the stuttering, but frank, expression of Isabella of Bellinzaga,[7] spread later by Bérulle: "have a high esteem for God," or "venerate God."[8]

---

7 Isabella Bellinzaga (1552–1624). This discreet Italian mystic helped Charles Borromeo with the administration of the hospitals and monasteries of the diocese of Milan. She also wrote a compendium on Christian perfection.

8 n. 674, n. 2054, pp. 46, 61.

Her insistence on God even before speaking of Christ stems from what is often called "abstract mysticism"—"abstract" as opposed to the concrete representation that the contemplation of Christ permits. Mother Mectilde doubtless knew the masters of abstract mysticism, notably Benet Canfield, whose influence at Montmartre was profound. Moreover, the Prioress's intelligence allowed her to access metaphysical language. It did not frighten her. Now metaphysics is with certain spiritual persons the extreme form of abstraction and provides them with concepts and means of expression about God. With these, Mother Mectilde emphasizes that God is "of Himself"—we would say "through Himself."[9] That is the first divine attribute she mentions.

These means of expression, however, have also a limit. What can be said of God, even by abstraction? Isn't it more prudent to keep silent? Or rather, since it is impossible to stop the succession of thoughts and the flow of interior language, one might at least dispute the fittingness of saying something about God, always remembering that anything it evokes is still not God. Thus apophatic theology, that is, proceeding by negations, is often the result of an abstract mysticism: all that we can conceive or say about God is so far below His reality that it is better to deny than to affirm: nothing of what comes into the mind, nothing that it represents to itself, is God. God remains "incomprehensible," as Mother Mectilde often recalls.

The Son

Was this sensibility for abstract mysticism related to St. Francis de Sales whose *Treatise on the Love of God* speaks so little of Christ? Not exactly. For she also speaks much of Jesus. Mother Mectilde desires "to cleave to Jesus Christ"—yet another Bérullian expression—"to be filled with Jesus Christ, to see only Jesus Christ, and to love only Him" and there she invites her correspondent:

> And if you ask me from what life you must live henceforth, I answer you that it is neither the life of good souls, nor of angels, nor even the life of the saints, but the pure and holy life of Jesus.... May all your actions be, in

9 *de soi* versus *par soi*.

> consequence, the actions of Jesus in you . . . may your thoughts be the thoughts of Jesus, your words the words of Jesus, your works the works of Jesus.[10]

However, Mother Mectilde cannot acknowledge Christ as God without giving to the word "God" a meaning which in itself affords some grip. She adores Christ all the better as God because she can draw up a list of divine attributes which she recognizes in Him. For her thought has a vigorous thoroughness. She is not one of those disciples for whom it is enough to see Jesus as a superman, without seeking to understand what the affirmation of His divinity means.

She remained fascinated by the Trinitarian mystery. She doesn't think of Jesus without at the same time thinking of His relation to the Father and the Spirit, a relation which holds all her attention, whereas the details of Jesus's actions fade into the background.

This explains why Mother Mectilde sometimes seems polarized by Jesus and directs all adoration toward Him, and sometimes speaks only of God, as if she no longer thinks of Jesus. In reality, Jesus is no less present. It is only through Jesus that she addresses God His Father, it is only in Jesus that she speaks about Him. Neither does the apostle Paul enter into more detail about the actions or the words of Jesus: he mentions only the last supper or the cross and the resurrection. But he is constantly united to Jesus, to the point of confiding to the Galatians, "It is not I who live, it is Christ who lives in me."[11] We could schematize by saying he doesn't consider Christ as opposite him, since he knows He is in him. The fourth Gospel displays more the deeds, gestures, and words of Jesus, showing Him in order that in Him the Father may be seen. Mother Mectilde's manner is more akin to that of Paul than to that of John. This is partly due to the fact that, like the former, she writes letters, without trying to make a sustained presentation.

This life in Jesus also explains the small space given in these letters to a rather frequent theme in the seventeenth century (as in many other periods) in spiritual literature, particularly feminine: Jesus as the "divine Bridegroom of the soul." Was it only because she was writing

---

10 n. 530, p. 120. 11 Gal 2:20.

to a married woman that she was little inclined to this language? I do not believe this is the case. Rather, it is because of the orientation of her religious thought. If we distinguish two fundamental types, the mysticism of unity and the mysticism of nuptials, Mother Mectilde seems indisputably to belong to the former.

This fascination with the mystery of the Trinitarian God appears in her manner of envisaging the mystery of the Incarnation. She enters into it by the path that is today called descending: her thought does not lift the man who is Jesus up to God, but, like the Prologue of the fourth Gospel, considers first the Word before the Father, then admires and contemplates His abasement in human nature. Many masters of the seventeenth century proceeded in this way, meditating on the humiliation—the *anéantissement* (being reduced to nothing), as certain of them call it—of the one "who, though he was in the form of God, did not count equality with God a thing to be grasped, but emptied himself, taking the form of a servant, being born in the likeness of men; and being found in human form, he humbled himself and became obedient unto death, even death on a cross."[12]

More than we do, the seventeenth century saw in the childhood of Jesus a surprising abasement. Indeed at that time childhood was not considered as a golden age, but rather as the age of immaturity, ignorance, inconsistency, and errors. The child must be watched and kept in close dependence. And the Word of God, although He possessed all knowledge and all wisdom, accepted being treated as a child.

He was humbled still more, unto death, and death on a cross. Like Condren, Mother Mectilde closely unites the death, resurrection, and ascension of Christ. Jesus rose, less to live again on earth among His disciples than to begin a new life. "We must begin a new life, a life which is not of earth, a life which must be completely detached from the senses, totally purified and raised to God," even "divine," as Jean-Jacques Olier liked to say; but let us allow the Prioress to speak: "St. Paul says, 'If we are risen, let us seek the things which are on high.'[13] A resurrected soul cannot delight in earthly things. Creatures are crosses to such a person, and everything the world regards as most delightful is a hell to him."[14]

12 Phil 2:6–7. 13 Col 3:1. 14 n. 279, p. 215.

The Holy Spirit

Before death, parents leave their goods as an inheritance to those who will be orphaned. Christ promised His disciples He would not leave them orphans: He would remain with them through the gift of the Spirit. This gift signifies that union with God is not a chimerical ideal, or divinization merely a Promethean dream. The believer is not only adorned with graces, namely, God's gifts; he can also be united directly to God. The gift of God is nothing less than God. The plural "gifts of God" should not cause us to forget the Gift of God *par excellence*, the Spirit who is God Himself, the Spirit who lives in our hearts through faith. The seventeenth century in France was the great epoch of the theology of the Spirit. It is Pétau's distinction to have insisted on the indwelling of God in the souls of the just, to have studied why (following St. Paul) the Fathers of the Church attribute this indwelling to the Holy Spirit, and to have emphasized that the Holy Spirit is present in the souls of the just, not only by His gifts, but in Person. However, in order to preserve the word "grace," the theologians speak in His regard of "uncreated grace."

Mother Mectilde echoes this theology in mentioning the Holy Spirit quite frequently, and in writing in a slightly abrupt, but profound, manner: "If grace is the Holy Spirit. . . . "[15]

The last decades of the seventeenth century experienced an especially deep suspicion toward "visionaries," those people who, under the pretext of obeying the Holy Spirit, wandered from the beaten path and from conformity to tradition. Mother Mectilde had a more nuanced position. She knew that one can confuse a movement of nature, which turns one toward creatures and one's own interest, with the movement of grace which causes one to seek "God's pure glory." "It is necessary to distrust oneself very much in this discernment." Such discernment is not, however, impossible, on the condition that one is "in silence and the passions are calm." For "the Spirit of God is peaceful, and it is the sign of His Spirit when He causes us to perform our actions in peace."[16] This truly Benedictine note often underlies what she says. Without allowing herself to be intimidated

15 n. 2477, p. 21.

16 n. 312, p. 96.

by the criticisms to which *illuminati* are exposed, the Prioress advised, "Act as much as is possible for you through the Holy Spirit."[17] She urged, "Give yourself to the power of His Spirit."[18]

ATTITUDES

"Pure faith"

Mother Mectilde frequently invites Madame de Châteauvieux to "pure faith." She finds her correspondent too much of a "rationalist." For lack of documentation about her, and texts where she develops her thought, it is impossible for us to tell if this reproach was justified. In any case, we risk misunderstanding, if we take it to mean what it would in the contemporary context and refer it to the modern dialogue between faith and unbelief. For many of our contemporaries, "faith" implies lack of proofs or at least their limitedness. In modern terms, "faith" consists in making the step that the arguments lack success in making necessary. Those who refrain from taking that step remain unbelieving; those who take it are committing themselves despite a lack of evidence. This isn't at all the outlook of Mother Mectilde. She doesn't preach fideism; she doesn't place faith and rationality in opposition to each other. Like Condren, like Olier, like Jean de Bernières, the contrast for her is between "pure faith" and meditation.

Meditation is an exercise which mobilizes the intellectual faculties. By means of connections properly made, such reasoning puts into relief various aspects of revealed truth, and the imagination "colors" them in some fashion and makes the chosen subject of the meditation more concrete, whether it is a question of a Gospel scene or an invisible reality. Mother Mectilde wanted Madame de Châteauvieux to pass from this meditation to a prayer of "simple regard."[19] Perhaps the Countess's character did not much incline to that way of praying, at least in the beginning.

"Simple regard" means, not that one contests the value of reasoning, but that, for the moment, one proceeds differently. Reasoning can be useful, in the same way that discovering, verifying, evoking something's

17 n. 307, p. 242. 18 n. 1873, p. 58.

19 She seems to be borrowing this expression from Jane de Chantal, whose thought she probably knew through the work of Henri de Maupas: *La vie de la vénérable Mère Jeanne François Frémiot*, Paris, 1644; especially p. 297.

qualities can lead to admiration. Nevertheless to admire is much more than enumerating qualities. It is both more and simpler. Now, the prayer of simple regard consists in admiring God. At any rate, this is how Epiphane Louis presents it when he explains to, or reminds, the Benedictines of the Blessed Sacrament what the prayer of pure faith is.[20] While he only insists on admiration, Mother Mectilde provides a little more detail; to admiration, she adds respect, love, attention, and submission as also forming part of this attitude toward God.

Like several of her contemporaries, and like Jane de Chantal, she uses the expression "simple regard," but less frequently than that of "pure faith." Doubtless this is because the word "regard" evokes an activity of the eyes, or at least of the interior eyes of the imagination, which could lead to misunderstanding. It isn't a question of looking, but of thinking of the one whom we don't see, with a very great humility of mind. Faith alone surpasses everything we can think about Him to go on to encounter Him. You think of this or that, and interiorly tell Him all sorts of things you would like to say to Him. You meet Him and this imaginary chatter completely ceases before the one who is different from all that you imagined. Likewise, the Countess of Châteauvieux was invited to go from inner discourse to the presence of God. It wasn't that she should imagine this presence, localizing God in some way. "Presence" means above all that one is not thinking anything particular about God; a single thought is impressed on the mind: *God is here*. Epiphane Louis pushes this interruption of reasoning so far that he declares:

> I do not even want you to imagine, with regard to God, the Persons of the Father, the Son, and the Holy Spirit, or that you consider Him as a Judge in His tribunal, or as a King on His throne, because in this contemplation [of simple regard] your object is a Being infinite and incomprehensible; and if you have that idea, there should be no distinguishing of the Persons, or placing any distinction between the attributes and the supereminent qualities which we are accustomed to attribute to Him.[21]

20 *Conférences Mystiques*, Paris, 1676, conf. 2.

21 Ibid., p. 14.

This explains what might surprise us: that Mother Mectilde speaks so often about God without mentioning the divine Persons. It isn't that she stops praying through Jesus Christ in order to hold to a wider mysticism where Hindus, Muslims, and Christians, and even all those who only believe in God, would have the same experience. More simply, it is that she experienced what Epiphane Louis described, this ineluctable surpassing of all that is unavoidably verbal and imaginative in the naming and representation of the divine Persons.

Love

We are not surprised to see Mother Mectilde mention faith before love. Love of God assumes that we know that God is, which is properly the affair of faith. This does not mean that faith must necessarily precede love and that we must first of all become aware of God's existence and then go on to love Him. It only means that faith establishes the foundation of love and makes it rest on a certainty.

Love and respect. The Prioress joins love and respect for God in a remarkable manner. Love banishes fear, said St. John, but it doesn't banish respect, taught Mother Mectilde. Why such insistence on respect? One can see here the influence of the social customs of the epoch; the condition of hierarchy was universally accepted and one took into account the "rank" of the person one addressed. But there is much more. For her, respect is a sign that we recognize God's transcendence, His "grandeur," His "incomprehensibility."[22] In human relationships, we can allow familiar expressions with those men and women that we know. But God is "essentially known only by Himself." Far from being opposed to love, as fear would be, this respect is, on the contrary, a courtesy: "the loving satisfaction of seeing one's God [to be] incomprehensible."[23]

"Pure love" is a second quality which must be emphasized. Mother Mectilde frequently uses the expression "pure love." It was common

22 n. 2054, p. 63.

23 What Dupuy contrasts as "fear" and "respect" would be, in the language of St. Thomas Aquinas, "servile fear" and "filial fear"—the former belonging to a slave who serves out of fear of punishment and for his own survival, the latter belonging to a child who wishes to please his parent as one worthy of honor, and fears offending him.

at the beginning of the seventeenth century. Francis de Sales used it freely in his letters and the Capuchin Laurent of Paris makes room for it in his treatise on the spiritual life entitled *The Palace of Divine Love*. But it quickly gave rise to a pressing debate in spiritual theology. This was because many of the faithful were asking themselves what exactly it means to love God. One knows by experience what it is to love men, women, children. It is at least to express affection to them, to enjoy their presence, to desire the good for them. But none of these terms befits God in the same way. What affection is felt for someone who is not seen? How does one enjoy His presence when He is unknowable? How can we desire the good for Him which is His in plenitude already? Based on this, how can the soul be occupied with God, except through a game of imagination which the *illuminati* play, and which one must beware of encouraging? Furthermore, the expression "pure love" could insinuate that one dangerously leaves aside the practice of good deeds and even the hope of blessedness. In the face of this latter ambiguity, many emphasized that we love God if we love our neighbor and keep the commandments. Do we then reduce the love of God to love of neighbor and the observance of the commandments? This would be merely proposing a humanism in which God would fade into the background.

The moral theologians of the seventeenth century were guarded about it. However, in order to avoid discouraging many people who were little inclined to spiritual effusions, some sought to minimize the obligation to make personal acts of love for God. But Jean-Pierre Camus, a great admirer of St. Francis de Sales and a zealous pastor, was not resigned to such concessions. In 1640 he published a treatise entitled, *The Defense of Pure Love against the Attacks of Self-Love*, wherein he emphasized that the love of God is pure only when one loves Him for Himself, and not for the sake of obtaining a reward. The following year, Antoine Sirmond replied to him with a treatise called *The Defense of Virtue*. It attempted to reassure those who did not experience a very personal love for God: "He did not so much command us to love as not to hate."[24] And he criticized Camus, not without cause, for excluding, under the pretext of pure love, the virtue

24 *Treatise* 2, p. 19.

of hope. "Pure love should have no regard to any reward other than God, but it cannot go beyond that one."[25]

Henceforth, the expression "pure love" was heavy with resonances. In his tenth *Provincial Letter*, Pascal becomes, against Sirmond and the like-minded, the advocate of the love of God. Instead of reducing as much as possible the import of the commandment to love God, on the contrary he wants us to love God without measure. However, he seems to avoid the expression "pure love" as if he already foresaw the storms it would yet raise and the obstinacy with which Bossuet, pursuing those he accused of quietism, would attack even Fénelon.

The tenth *Letter* is from 1656. It is certain that this is the period in which Mother Mectilde was writing. Bolder than Pascal, she used the expression "pure love" constantly. How did she use it?

A heart which is not divided between God and creatures has pure love.[26] Creatures have become nothing for such a heart,[27] not arousing any desire or requiring any attention. "Let us live and breathe only in the purity of divine love."[28] With finesse and precision, Mother Mectilde next noted that the soul is then detached even from its own action. "You lend yourself to the action, but you do not give yourself to it." Or again, "Do not become proprietary about your action; have no attachment to it."[29] Of course, the result is that a pure love is completely disinterested. "You must begin to live from pure love, that is, purely for God, without any return to your own interests." However, Mother Mectilde didn't call hope into question; she lived only in the present, or rather, in the presence of God. Charity toward our neighbor is not absent, since loving the neighbor does not divide the heart between God and creatures, when the neighbor is "seen in God."[30]

Love and holiness. To define pure love by disinterestedness is still only to take a negative approach. We don't say what light is only by explaining that it has no areas of darkness. Light is more than the absence of darkness; it is brightness, it is beauty. We don't say what pure love is by explaining only what could contaminate it. It is better to say what it is to love God than to explain it by oppositions and

25 Ibid., p. 97.
26 n. 1014, p. 79.
27 n. 1712, p. 82.
28 n. 1712, p. 83.
29 n. 1712, p. 84.
30 n. 421, p. 234.

comparisons with precisely what it is not. For Mother Mectilde loves God in what He is in Himself. Thus, she gives a particular place to holiness among God's attributes. Many Christians, on hearing the word holiness, think mainly about moral perfection. Our Prioress, like Condren, by whom she seems to be inspired on this point, takes holiness in the biblical sense of separation from everything which is profane or created. Hence, while to call God Creator or Providence or Savior is to qualify Him in relation to creatures, to call Him "holy" is to declare what He is in Himself. This constitutes Mother Mectilde's joy. She says to Him, "I rejoice in Your divine holiness."[31] Could we find a better expression of pure love for God than these words? In order to love your neighbor in a genuine way, you must rejoice not about what he is for you, but about what he is for himself, in himself. It is the same with respect to God. "To love His holiness is to love Him purely for Himself."

To love God's will. Meanwhile, God's holiness remains unknowable. How does one rejoice in what one does not see? We can do this on the condition that we are animated, not by feeling, but by faith.

However, in a certain manner the love of God does find a tangible object.[32] Canfield said that God's will is God Himself. Mother Mectilde takes up this thought again thematically, under various forms.[33] Now, that will is manifest to us particularly "in events."[34] "We must receive them from His hand." In this regard, how can we fail to compare our Foundress with Pascal who, at the same time, allowed himself to be instructed "by events which are a manifestation of God's will" and noted: "If God gave us teachers from His own hand, oh!, how willingly they should be obeyed! Necessity and events are infallibly so." What happens to us and affects us is thus the occasion of God's loving acts, which don't run the risk of being imaginary. If we truly love God, we love what He wants, the reality He sends us.

All the same, however realistic, penetrating, and stimulating the Canfeldian axiom is—"The will of God is God himself"—it must not lead us to identify God's will absolutely with what we know through events. Knowledge of this will remains partial. As with God

31 n. 88, p. 25.
32 n. 1435, p. 39.
33 n. 2531, p. 55.
34 n. 1873, p. 59.

Himself, His will infinitely surpasses us; to accept is to "obey," a word which recurs frequently under the pen of the Prioress, that is to say, to subordinate oneself to the views of another, seeing oneself only partially.

On the other hand, love of God is seen also in the movement which makes one leave oneself to seek Him. Mother Mectilde invites Madame de Châteauvieux to "not focus on herself," in order to "be content with God's good pleasure."[35]

These counsels, by clearing up some illusions, lead us to ask whether it is possible here on earth for the love of God to be absolutely pure.

Toward pure love. We pose the question: can the love of God be absolutely pure? Mother Mectilde doesn't consider it. Further, she does not make psychological analyses; she knows that Madame de Châteauvieux is only *in via*. She invites her to "begin" by making her consider what is before her. If pure love of God didn't have this requirement of absolute purity for us, it would no longer be love *of God*; it would not be God that we are speaking about. That is why, it seems to me, the Prioress insists on this purity so much. At the same time she never presents this purity as something attained, but always as an ideal: "The one who can live solely from pure love and regard all the rest as nothing, I would consider happy!"[36]

However, it is clear that while proposing this pure love as an ideal, she speaks from experience, for otherwise would she dare to predict, "Your present state will not be of long duration; after sorrow comes joy"?[37] She is very discreet about herself. We divine, in spite of this, in what she proposes to Madame de Châteauvieux, what she herself wished to live more fully. She doesn't conjure up transports of love, but the continual duty to begin to love God, to be irreversibly committed in that love: "How happy is a soul who can be irrevocably plunged in the love of God's good pleasure!" "To love Him in every manner, and to find good everything that He does, is approving and consenting to all His hidden and manifest designs concerning us, submitting our whole will to His, and preferring nothing to His love."[38]

35 n. 966, p. 188. 36 n. 1712, p. 82. 37 n. 3057, p. 85.
38 n. 3057, p. 85.

Anéantissement

Mother Mectilde's insistence on the necessity of being "reduced to nothing" may surprise, frighten, and even irritate and shock a modern reader.[39] This term, fashionable in the beginning of the seventeenth century, provided room for criticisms which quickly led to restraint in using it or an attenuation of its meaning. But Mother Mectilde's expressions do not lend themselves to a softened interpretation. "You must allow yourself to be slain."[40] "You are not there to enjoy some consolation, but to bring about your destruction."[41]

On this point, sensibilities have changed. While in sexual matters, the most realistic terms of psychoanalysis which would have horrified the seventeenth century no longer frighten us, on the contrary the vocabulary by which the seventeenth century described the renunciation demanded by Jesus appears excessive and inadmissible today. Yet the language of Mother Mectilde is not the harshest. That of Jean-Jacques Olier is violent in a different manner, and that of Jesus in the Gospels is very strong: "Whoever does not take up his cross and follow me is not worthy of me. Whoever finds his life will lose it and whoever will lose it for my sake will find it."[42] And Paul is not afraid to say that "those who are in Christ have crucified the flesh with its desires."[43] The gospel, however, remains the good news and brings joy. For if we must die to the world with Christ, it is in order to rise with Him.

Once the necessity of renunciation is recognized, the accentuations can legitimately vary. Shortly before Mother Mectilde, Charles de Condren, by whom she was inspired, emphasized above all the differences between this world and the one to come, differences which call for radical breaks: the present world must pass, be destroyed, for the coming of the future world and the kingdom of God. Today, on the contrary, some are pleased to emphasize the continuity of the two worlds, if not to identify them. They observe how the present world prepares, attracts, and already begins the world to come, which shows through in every act of charity. Don't we go so far as to imagine

39 The verb *anéantir* is translated here as "reduce to nothing." A typical translation would be "destroy" or "annihilate."

40 n. 3146, p. 73.

41 n. 844, p. 92.

42 Mt 10:38–39.

43 Gal 5:24.

that we are artisans of the Kingdom or of God's reign and that we construct it? Yet it is not right to move away from Scripture on this point, it seems to me. If the radical pessimism which sees in this creation only a wicked world to be destroyed is unacceptable, we must not substitute an infantile naiveté forgetting death and the obligatory passage through it in order to arrive at the resurrection, at the new heavens and the new earth.

Mother Mectilde is incontestably from the century of Condren and not from that of Teilhard de Chardin. Furthermore, she doesn't mince her words in declaring the *anéantissement* of self. We must only admire the more, I don't say the moderation, but the correctness of her advice. She is in no way calling for delight in some kind of self-destruction. On the contrary, she emphasizes the values that the *anéantissement* of self makes one discover even here below, and the joys to which it is the path. "There are two or three steps which will cost you dearly, but will also bring you an immense happiness."[44] "This death appears cruel and very harsh to nature and to the senses; but it is very sweet to the soul."[45]

After all, it isn't a question of hurting oneself, but of offering no resistance to God. This remark of our Prioress is especially adapted to the feminine psychology of her directee. And she subtly observes that it does not depend on us to reduce to nothing our memory or our understanding. For we cannot forget on command, even in order to forgive. We cannot become stupid and deny what we have understood to be true. However, the will is free in a different way, and abandonment and *disponibilité*—being wholly at the ready to serve or to be made use of by another—constitute the *anéantissement* of the will proper.

Silence is the attitude which sums up *anéantissement*. "Through silence we are reduced to nothing before that adorable Majesty."[46] Very near the same time, Fr. Guilloré, who was confessor for Madame de Châteauvieux, also praised silence and its religious value; since he is less concise and more exact than Mother Mectilde, I quote him.

---

44 n. 1474, p. 146.

45 n. 2258, p. 148. "It is not the work of the creature, but the work of God's omnipotent hand which causes the soul to enter into it."

46 n. 894, p. 161.

"Where are those souls who, through a holy silence, are sacrificed to all accusations and calumnies?... This refusal to justify makes accusation and calumny supremely sanctifying, because in this you offer to God the most noble of all sacrifices, which is that of your reputation."[47] Yes, such silence is an act of humiliation and destruction of one's own reputation. It is not self-destruction, but abandonment to God—and thereby we can better understand the attitude suggested by Mother Mectilde. And yet, what she asks is simpler. There is no need to fear God being led into error by slander. Before God, it is only a matter of accepting the truth, without being blamed for imaginary wrongs and justifying oneself for it by inventing excuses.

We can better understand an *anéantissement* which is in no way suicidal if we find the model for it in Christ. It is true that the spirituality of the cross might stir up some masochistic reactions. However, Mother Mectilde also considers, as one freely did in her era, the *anéantissement*—we would say *kenosis*—of the Word of God in the Child Jesus. In Him, the Word is reduced to silence, God's Wisdom submits to obedience, the Omnipotent God becomes dependent. This silence of the Child Jesus makes us understand what kind of silence Mother Mectilde is requesting: it's a question of living in dependence on divine grace, discovering how much one is at God's mercy, as the Child Jesus was in the hands of adults. For the Prioress, *anéantissement* is the spirit of childhood. Nonetheless, we must not put into this expression what it evokes so often today: naiveté or even the mental diminution of a "return to childhood." Once more, it isn't the intellect but the will which must be reduced to nothing. The Child Jesus, far from being ignorant, possessed all knowledge, for the seventeenth century did not know the modern considerations and speculations on the ignorance of Jesus. Thus the spirit of childhood is not naiveté, but *disponibilité* and humility.

Simplicity

The spirit of childhood is not naiveté, but simplicity. Naiveté implies a lack of judgment. Simplicity requires a correctness of judgment which discerns from the outset what is essential and goes

47 *Maximes spirituelles pour le conduite des âmes*, Bk. 2, Max. 9, ch. 1.

straight to it, without getting lost in a multitude of possible considerations. Simplicity permits openness and trust with respect to others. And it brings a very particular manner to our relationship with God: if we waited until every question is exhausted, faith would always be put off. That is why one must "receive the lights God gives you, through Himself or through another, with great simplicity."[48] And the "thought of the incomprehensible God limits all the mind's curiosities and subjects it to a simple and very respectful belief in what God is."[49]

This simplicity leads to "the prayer of a quite simple unity and unique simplicity in the presence of God, through a complete abandonment of themselves to His most holy will and by the care of His divine Providence."[50] Mother Mectilde borrowed these phrases from Jane de Chantal. The latter saw in simplicity the antidote to falling back into oneself or into reflection on oneself: one must forget oneself, as much as possible, by the continual remembrance of God, and rest in Him alone through a genuine and complete confidence, and especially in prayer, and reject every kind of discourse, busyness, rejoinders, and similar things. Instead of considering what one is doing, has done, or will do, consider God, remaining in this simple view of God and of one's nothingness.[51] Certainly examination of conscience is necessary and salutary, but on the condition that it is less introspection than receiving God's judgment, since reflecting on oneself can poison the spiritual life and close a person in on himself, especially during the time dedicated to prayer.

Mother Mectilde makes Jane de Chantal's teaching her own. "Do not reflect so much on yourself, walk in confidence."[52] "Do not burden your mind with multiplicity." "The first thing I have to do is to leave myself."[53] And speaking about the Magi, she gives them as an example: "Depart from the land of yourself, your own house, and the place of your knowledge. Give up your interests as they did and go to find Jesus in Bethlehem. Follow inspiration, which is the star. Leave the old habits of your senses and your own thinking."[54]

---

48 n. 1873, p. 59.
49 n. 2054, p. 63.
50 n. 2471, p. 99.
51 n. 2471, p. 100.
52 n. 2531, p. 56.
53 n. 1873, p. 59; n. 2054, p. 65.
54 n. 120, p. 211.

PRACTICAL APPLICATIONS

Vows

To better understand the teaching of this collection, it's beneficial to recall the principal debates around the topic of religious vows during the seventeenth century.

At the beginning of the century, the Protestant controversy held the attention of the theologians and stirred up their efforts. Luther had found fault with vows. It was necessary to respond by showing that they were justified. In France, however, there soon arose another controversy among Catholics, between the seculars and the regulars. The seculars were the diocesan priests who did not take vows. They found themselves sometimes in competition with the religious priests for ministry, especially for preaching and the sacrament of penance (for example, with Capuchins or Jesuits). Were the regular priests more competent for such works because they were in a "state of perfection"? Wasn't the priesthood also a perfect state of life? Isn't it also the state of "acquired perfection," while the religious life is only the state of "search for perfection"?[55] The commitments of the priest flow from his ordination, which is a sacrament, rather than from religious profession, which is not a sacrament. This debate was inoffensive, indeed it was salutary for the priests, as long as it only caused them to recall their obligations and their ideal.

Unfortunately, the polemics led the one or the other group to depreciate the religious life in order to oppose it to the grandeur and beauty of the state of the priesthood. In 1638, the Oratorian Séguenot caused a scandal by writing that "vows add nothing to Christian perfection, nor to what was promised in baptism, except with regard to the externals, in which perfection does not consist."[56]

---

55 According to the scholastics (see, e.g., St. Thomas Aquinas, *Summa theologiae*, II-II, qq. 184–85, following Dionysius the Areopagite's *Ecclesiastical Hierarchy*), the religious life is entered for the sake of perfecting oneself in charity, while the episcopal state is for those already perfected, who are appointed to lead others to perfection. Since the presbyterate participates in the work of the bishop and to some extent vicariously represents him, someone might attempt to extend this doctrine to the secular or diocesan clergy as well.

56 *De la sainte virginité*, Paris, 1638, p. 18. In this regard, he reanimated the arguments of medieval seculars against the mendicant orders which had already been refuted by St. Thomas and St. Bonaventure, among others.

Séguenot retracted. However, his calling into question (public) vows was not forgotten. This was because he was not the only one to criticize them. He was participating in a larger current in which are to be found, among others, the disciples of Jean Duvergier de Hauranne, Abbot of St. Cyran, who did not yet have the name of Jansenists. Without calling vows into question, these pleaded for a religious life more separated from the world and closer to what the Church lived in its beginnings, a life not defined by rules, but flowing simply from a deeper understanding of what baptism implies. They liked to think of it as arising in the framework of the Christian community, namely, the parish.

On the other side, the reformers of the clergy started to compare, with regard to the obligation to perfection, not priests and religious but religious and "clerks." For the seminaries—especially the seminary of Saint-Sulpice, in the neighborhood of the monastery of rue Férou as in that of the monastery of rue Cassette—had for lodgers simple clerks as much as and more than they had priests. It's striking to see how Jean-Jacques Olier proposed to them a baptismal spirituality: he linked the requirement of death to self, *anéantissement*, and sacrifice of self, not to vows, or to the priestly ministry, but to the condition of baptism, since baptism is a death and resurrection with Christ and every Christian is called to be perfect as our heavenly Father is perfect.

We are not surprised then, to see Mother Mectilde recall to Madame de Châteauvieux in such a vigorous manner the consequences of her baptism and to insist more on baptism than on an eventual religious profession. However, she refrains from the excesses of Séguenot. She can maintain the traditional values while taking on the challenges of her epoch.

Séguenot took exception to vows insofar as they demanded external actions. Let us remember that under the *ancien régime* the vow of poverty had juridical consequences recognized and sanctioned by civil society, especially the impossibility of possessing property. But Séguenot did not take exception to vows as a firm resolution to be bound to God. He saw in them also an act of perfection. And the Oratorians, after having refused the vows of religion, made various vows with only internal consequences, such as the vow of servitude and the vow of host (or victim). On this point, Jean-Jacques Olier imitated them. Therefore, we aren't surprised that these interior vows assume a great importance in Mother Mectilde's thought.

Servitude

Today this word offends us; we are inclined to emphasize that Christ brought liberty instead. Saint Paul was as utterly convinced of it as we are and boldly recalls that he is a citizen, a free man, and that everything is permitted to him, even if it is not helpful.[57] Nevertheless, in his letter to the Romans, he presents himself as a "slave of Christ." Mary called herself the "servant" of the Lord, but it would also be correct to translate it as the Lord's "slave," since the word she used was also used to designate slaves.

At the end of the sixteenth century, Inés de St. Paul founded in Spain a "Confraternity and Fraternity of Slaves of the Virgin Mother of God." And the Franciscan John of the Angels became the propagandist for this confraternity and the apostle of Marian servitude. The practice passed a short time later into France. Pierre de Bérulle made a vow of servitude to Mary and led the Oratorians and Carmelites of France likewise to pronounce this vow. He formulated a similar vow of servitude to Jesus which he proposed likewise to the Oratorians and Carmelites. This vow promised a particular *disponibilité* with respect to all that Jesus would ask or bring about through His Spirit.

He was censured for having imposed this vow on the Carmelites. A juridical and theological controversy ensued. The theology of the Incarnation underlying the vow was scrutinized, while the critics asked precisely what object a vow had which did not commit one to external actions. To avoid such polemics, when Bérulle spoke of servitude he substituted for the term "vow" the less compromising terms "elevation" and "oblation." Yet there is no doubt that the practice of vows of servitude to Mary and Jesus (whether separate or not) continued to spread. Jean-Jacques Olier made a vow of servitude to Jesus on January 11, 1642.

It seems that Mother Mectilde prepared Madame de Châteauvieux for such a vow. "I entreat you to truly cherish this holy captivity which Our

57 1 Cor 6:12.

Lord causes you enter."[58] And in the lesson which apparently followed, "I have the inclination to write you a word about the blessed slavery that you have the honor to bear."[59] The word "vow" doesn't appear, but the context is exactly that of the vow of servitude. "The slave is so ready to do the will of her Master that at every hour, at every moment, she is ready and willing to carry out His orders in any way He pleases."

The Vow of Victim

The vow "of host" or "of victim" (the two expressions are equivalent) was a practice which followed shortly after the vow of servitude. It doesn't seem to have met with the same opposition. The theological and juridical questions did not arise; the idea of a vow with purely interior consequences had been accepted. We know that Jean-Jacques Olier made a vow of host on March 31, 1644. He explains it thus: it is "the vow to live only for God, awaiting the times and occasions of being sacrificed to Him for the good of the Church. And the disposition in this vow, or rather the secret obligation which we contract in making it, is to die continually to self, to immolate oneself, in the moments when the flesh wants to live and act in you, in such a way that we mortify all that the flesh demands." Of course, it's a matter of the flesh in the Pauline sense—not the body, but egotism, and all that leads to sin. Olier continues: "The vow of host expresses also the obligation to expose to the Holy Spirit all the smallest movements of the flesh, when they arise, in order to consume them in Him."[60]

The victim (or host) is passive in the hands of the one who offers it and of the one who accepts or immolates it. To make the vow of host is to become available to God in a particular manner. One offers oneself, but the offering of self is genuine only if it leads one to leaving the initiative to God. Mother Mectilde indicates how, in fact, human advances and divine requests are united. "God wants me to work with His grace in certain encounters; and in others He wants me to be completely passive and holding completely to the powerlessness He causes me to experience. We must follow Him just as it pleases Him to lead us."[61]

---

58 n. 1374, p. 74. 59 n. 692, p. 75.

60 Unpublished, Archives of Saint-Sulpice, Montreal. 61 n. 1435, p. 40.

The offering implies that we are making a sacrifice of self, here understood as the sacrifice of "returns to self."[62] "Give your own dispositions few backward glances, but give yourself very much to Jesus to be clothed with His Spirit and with His holy dispositions."[63]

Today the word "victim" is not well received. To call oneself a victim is to complain. Action is better. To offer oneself as a victim appears to be masochism. It is better to pull oneself together than to grieve and withdraw into oneself. That is exactly what our Prioress counsels in different words: to complain would not be giving oneself sufficiently. "If you are suffering in the capacity of a victim, [remember that] the victim does not utter a word: it is led to punishment without complaining, notwithstanding that it may be charged with the crimes of the one for whom it becomes a victim."[64]

The Old Testament recognized various kinds of sacrifice. However, in the New Testament it is the passage of Christ through death which fulfills and defines sacrifice. Henceforth, a "victim" only deserves this name in the measure that it is configured to the immolated Lamb. However, as Condren especially emphasized, Christ's sacrifice is both holocaust—that is, the victim is consumed—and resurrection. To make a vow of "victim" is to accept being consumed this way. Mother Mectilde echoes this:

> You must be consumed by the fire of Jesus's pure and divine love. However, the fire burns the victim only after these other effects have preceded it, to show us that the sacred fire of divine charity is lit in the heart only after all the impurities of ourselves, which are in us, are slaughtered and destroyed. Picture yourself as this victim condemned to death in order to receive a new life in Jesus.[65]

In his conferences to the Benedictines of the Blessed Sacrament, Epiphane Louis treated victimhood spirituality in a remarkable way. We quote a passage which synthesizes what the bits and pieces from

62 In French the phrase *retours sur soi*, "returns to (one)self," can have either a positive sense of reflection or self-examination or a negative sense of morose preoccupation with self, dwelling on injuries sustained or losses suffered.
63 n. 3146, p. 73. 64 n. 1815, p. 171. 65 n. 3146, p. 73.

Mother Mectilde's lessons have allowed us to begin to see. He shows us how to be a "victim." Far from leading to complaining, on the contrary it makes one go beyond all withdrawal into self and to despise that as idolatry:

> The quality of victimhood places the person in a state of death, or at least in a continual tendency toward death, since we can consider something as a victim only for the purpose of death and for being sacrificed. This disposition and continual tendency to death goes to the point of not wanting to live for oneself, nor to establish oneself, nor to maintain or support oneself in any fashion whatever for oneself, but only for the glory of the one who has accepted the victim, and depending on his will for the manner of sacrifice. If the victim wants to live for itself, if it acts for itself, from that point on it is leaving its condition of victim for the Son of God, and it becomes a victim for itself; it is sacrificed to itself, and worships itself, giving to the creature what it was obligated by a personal commitment to give only to the Son of God. But unable to live for self, unable to do anything to establish or sustain itself, it is obliged to work ceaselessly at being unoccupied with itself.[66]

Contrition and Confession

In this area we must place Mother Mectilde's teachings in their theological context to better grasp her choices and appreciate the nuances and the balance of her thought.

First of all we must remember the discussion between "attritionists" and "contritionists" which was carried on during the second half of the seventeenth century. The Council of Trent declared that attrition, or imperfect contrition, prepared one to receive the sacrament of penance. However, it had not specified the limits for this. The "attritionists" enlarged them and the "contritionists" restricted them. A whole range of positions unfolded between extreme attritionism (for which regret

66 *La vie sacrifiée et anéantie des novices qui prétendent s'offrir en qualité de victimes du Fils de Dieu* &c., Paris, 1674, pp. 79–80.

for sin could be reduced to the fear of hell, and this would still suffice for the valid reception of the sacrament of penance) and extreme contritionism (for which repentance is genuine only on the condition that it is disinterested, i.e., inspired by the love of benevolence toward God[67]). Jansenius, without denying the role of fear, deemed it insufficient: it didn't produce conversion; "it restrains the hand, but not the heart." He was followed not only by those who are called Jansenists, but also by a number of theologians who conceived the relation to God as animated only by love, and by pastors disturbed by the relaxation of morals and by Confessions of pure formality, without conversion: a too easy means to avoid hell, they dispensed with having to make a conversion of life. Spiritual directors, without entering the theological debate, invited people to convert to the love of God. Thus, Condren drew the attention of his directees to the imperfection in their regret for their sins. If they examined themselves they would discover that they were humiliated, less by having offended God than by having given in to temptation and failed in virtue. It was above all their pride which was wounded and about which they felt stung.

In 1667 Pope Alexander VII, rather than ending the theological debate, called the theologians to stop launching attacks against those who were defending a position different from their own on the subject of attrition.

How did Mother Mectilde offer guidance in the matter of repentance? She could call for a clearer and more attentive examination of conscience, untangling the skein of motivations. But this was not at all what she proposed. She preferred to consider Christ bearing the sins of the world. Then there would not be the risk of sinking into an attrition which is primarily composed of fear or principally motivated by pride. It will not be on my own account, but because of Christ that I will regret my sins. Nevertheless, Mother Mectilde's language may surprise and shock:

> God took vengeance on His Son for all sins, and He was not only rejected as a sinner, but condemned as a criminal

---

67 That is, looking only to God's interests, not to one's own reward or punishment.

> for divine high treason. He condemns Him and in a certain way could not endure Him; not in His capacity as His Word, but in the capacity of a sinner, because He was covered in our sins. And the eternal Father, hating sin with an eternal hatred, treated Jesus Christ as if He had been sin itself.[68]

The Prioress is well aware that these phrases are debatable, since she inserts the prudent reservation "in a certain way." In fact, base human feelings cannot be attributed to the Father, such as rancor, the desire for vengeance, hatred. Paul certainly speaks of "God's wrath,"[69] but never of God's vengeance. Nonetheless, the rhetoric of the seventeenth century didn't lack this element, which excuses Mother Mectilde. And we are fortunate that she did not take this presentation, too common at that period, as her own without reservation. If we are asked not to confuse sin and the sinner, and to detest sin while continuing to love the sinner, we must think that God Himself makes the same distinction, not willing the death of a sinner, but that he be converted.[70] This does not prevent Paul from saying in a sharp formula that Christ "became sin for us, so that we might become in Him the justice of God."[71]

In discussions about the "residue" of sin, theology distinguishes the sin or fault and the punishment due to it. Christ bore the punishment of sin, but not the fault; He could not know Himself to be culpable. But He could be bruised (in Latin, *contritus*) interiorly at the thought of sin and in solidarity with sinners, even to the point of sharing their punishment. Mother Mectilde invites Madame de Châteauvieux to "offer to the eternal Father the contrition of His Son."[72] She echoes Condren (or one of his disciples) when she writes "Our Lord had contrition for us." This is admissible if "contrite" is taken in the sense of the Latin *contritus*, which Psalm 50(51) uses, and which was certainly known by heart by all the nuns—that is, bruised interiorly but also beaten unmercifully.

Keeping these details in mind, we must remain aware of the presentation's vigor which leads into the heart of the mystery of redemption

68 n. 1879, pp. 107–8.
69 Rom 1:18.
70 Ez 33:11.
71 2 Cor 5:21.
72 n. 1879, p. 109.

and reveals the gravity of sin better than any psychological analysis. Then we glimpse that sin is offense against God, "divine high treason." The contemplation of Christ does not free the conscience from being personally culpable:

> Behold Jesus Christ who is your ransom. He suffers for you, He makes satisfaction for you. You must enter into His holy dispositions and do not render useless what He did for you, or vain the grace He merited for you. When going to Confession, you must have whatever disposition makes you have a likeness to those Jesus had and clothes you in His contrition, in His most holy and perfect horror of sin, and His profound humiliation to which He was reduced before the greatness of God His Father—a contrition and humiliation so profound that through it He remains prostrate and as if utterly reduced to nothing. This is how you should be at the feet of the priest who represents Jesus Christ for you. You should bring to Confession a humbled and contrite spirit and a heart broken with horror and regret for your sins.[73]

This regret is not necessarily felt at the sensible level. Mother Mectilde didn't wish it to be, for she did not want to "disturb" Madame de Châteauvieux. Nor should she be "constrained," that is, on the rack (*gênée*). The word *gêne*—stronger in that era than today—was sometimes written *géhenne,* and could make one think of the punishments of the damned. Now, regret does not consist of picturing oneself in hell, as if hope was forgotten; but regret for sin must "humble and mortify."

The distinction between the fault and the pain of sin is therefore illuminating: "Therefore, you must hate your infidelities, because they dishonor God, but not be disturbed or anxious about them."[74] This is because Christ did not bear the fault, but the pain. One can and should love the pain, because He has made it His own. But we cannot dwell on the fault, with which He is not associated. God's pardon frees us from it. In this matter, we see with what sureness

73 n. 1879, p. 109.

74 n. 57, p. 144.

Mother Mectilde directed the Countess. We would say that the feeling of culpability becomes morbid when the sin is reviewed with a sort of masochistic satisfaction. To love not the fault, but the punishment, as our Prioress invites us to do—that is to say, to accept the punishment—is, on the contrary, what makes humility healthy. Then bitterness gives way to peace. Could humility and peace be ignored by a daughter of St. Benedict?

With regard to the examination of conscience, Mother Mectilde is prudent. She does not want to awaken scruples in Madame de Châteauvieux. The judicious text given to this subject by MS N 260 is borrowed thematically from Condren. There is no need to analyze it here.

The Eucharist

The *Breviary* of Madame de Châteauvieux contains some beautiful texts on the Eucharist.

The most developed concern Communion. We aren't surprised by this. The Eucharist was primarily ordered to Communion by the one who said, "Take and eat." We are happy to find in these pages the "theocentric" orientation familiar in Condren, by which I mean envisaging Communion not only from the point of view of the communicant, but also, and first of all, from the point of view of Christ and God. "You must not receive Communion for yourself, neither for this nor that [intention], but only for Jesus Christ.... Begin to enter into detachment and into the void of yourself. Do not see anything except Jesus Christ and His interests."[75]

In this way is justified an unexpected remark: Jesus Himself communicated.[76] Olier did not doubt it. This affirmation—or rather, this hypothesis—allows us to communicate in imitation of Jesus. It places the emphasis less on the meeting with Jesus now than on the contemplation of Jesus at the Last Supper and the union with Him which is manifested there. The detachment from self goes as far as this recentering on Jesus.

The feast of Corpus Christi happily gave Mother Mectilde the occasion to speak also about the contemplation of Christ in the

75 n. 530, p. 120.

76 St. Thomas Aquinas and St. Jerome, among others, held this view. See *Summa theologiae* III, qu. 81, art. 1.

Eucharist. However, we have in the *Breviary* only one rather short text.[77] One expression in it surprises the modern reader: "The divine life hidden and reduced to nothing in the Most Holy Sacrament." Everyone agrees it is hidden. But that it is reduced to nothing causes difficulties. If the Eucharist gives us the presence of Jesus in His humanity, this is neither changed nor "reduced to nothing." This is still less the case with His divinity, so to speak. Some spiritual authors of the seventeenth century were tempted to see in the Eucharist a humiliated state of the Savior, which is debatable. Pascal himself is among these.[78] We prefer to be precise: the Eucharist is indeed the memorial of Christ's humiliation in His Passion and death. But it is not properly said to be a new humiliation, even if the sacred species are shown disrespect by infidels. For the humanity of Christ is now forever glorious and is not affected by what happens to the sacred species; and as for His divinity, it could not in any way be "reduced to nothing." Thus Mother Mectilde can be excused for being carried away for an instant by a language faulty but common.

It seems, however, that what she means (and what the theologians of the period who use this language with her mean to say) is something else and sheds light on this term, *s'anéantir*, which taken literally means to "annihilate," which we have already pointed out causes difficulties today. It is clear that in the Eucharist Jesus is destroyed not in the sense that He ceases to be, but in the sense that He accepts being unrecognized. Likewise, the *anéantissement* to which the Prioress calls her correspondent is not a self-destruction, but consists in withdrawing from the gaze of others and even from one's own gaze. "Your life is hidden with Christ in God."[79] How many times does she quote these words of St. Paul, already dear to Bérulle?

All in all, Mother Mectilde [in this set of letters] doesn't seem to us to speak of the contemplation of the Eucharist as much as we would like and as much as we would expect when we know the place that it holds in the life of her daughters. This is because our Prioress does not separate the Eucharist from what it signifies: communion with the

---

77 For more extensive Eucharistic writings by Mother Mectilde, see the anthology *The Mystery of Incomprehensible Love.*

78 *Pensées*, Br. 553.

79 Col 3:3.

divine life. So her adoration and her love go, through the Eucharist, straight to the divine life. This is the best way to live the Eucharist.

✠

BÉRULLE, JOHN EUDES, CONDREN, OLIER ARE THE MASters of what is called the French School and which it would be more exact to call the Bérullian School. While wholly remaining faithful to St. Benedict, Mother Mectilde clearly belongs to it. The adoration of the Blessed Sacrament was formerly in favor in the Bérullian oratory. It was also in favor at Port-Royal, for which the Countess of Châteauvieux had previously showed sympathy. It is to Mother Mectilde's credit that she could, while preserving herself from the Jansenist deviation, assimilate the best of Port-Royal's thought, for example when it was a matter of calling the laity to perfection in keeping with their baptism, or a question of Eucharistic contemplation, or simply of inviting one to submission to events. The faithful of Port-Royal—above all Nicole—manifested reserve with regard to mental prayer, and had an obsession with quietism. Mother Mectilde, on these points too, kept her independence and her equilibrium, and we rejoice in that. She dares to call one to the prayer of pure faith, in imitation of Jane de Chantal, invokes John of the Cross, pleads for pure love, and urges one to follow the movement of the Holy Spirit.

Was it not the Spirit who granted her the grace to guide her ship, with so much sureness, in the midst of the spiritual currents of the seventeenth century?

APPENDIX II

The History of the "Breviary of Fire"

MSGR CHARLES MOLETTE

DURING THE DISTURBANCES OF THE Fronde, Anne of Austria, "distressed with a mortal sorrow about the revolt of the majority of the kingdom against the King her son . . . then resolved to labor efficaciously in appeasing God's anger by many prayers and vows; she made these herself, and she had them made in her name by several devout persons in whom she trusted."[1] Among the vows she thus had occasion to take upon herself was a properly religious act of a very precise character: it was a question, she was to write, of

> honoring the Most Blessed Sacrament of the altar, in reparation for the sacrileges which were committed during these unfortunate wars. Since it was found that this could not be done better than by establishing a house of nuns whose principal duty would consist in praising and adoring the Blessed Sacrament ceaselessly and praying day and night for the peace of the kingdom and for the preservation of the King, I cast my gaze on Mother Mectilde of the Blessed Sacrament.[2]

Out of the vow of Queen Anne of Austria, therefore, were founded the Benedictines of the Blessed Sacrament of "Sister Mectilde of the Blessed Sacrament, Prioress of the monastery." This foundation was made possible through the substantial help of Marie de la Guesle de Châteauvieux who, on the day after becoming a widow, joined the

1 The archivist of the Rouen monastery notes that this testimony (apparently from 1702), contained in the manuscript P 101 kept at the monastery of Rouen, seems to be attributed to Mother Mectilde's grandniece and goddaughter, Elizabeth-Catherine de Vienville (1660–1747), who died at the monastery of rue Cassette. We know, from other sources, that Elizabeth-Catherine "withdrew, after the death of her mother (1685), to the monastery of Rambervillers" (*Lettres Inédites*, p. 117, n. 17).

2 *Lettres Inédites*, p. 147.

community, where she became "Sister Victim of the Blessed Sacrament, called in the world Marie de la Guesle."[3] The transformation of this woman of the world into a nun resulted in the present manuscript, published by the nuns of Rouen.

THE QUEEN'S VOW

When the political troubles were magnified by spiritual and doctrinal—and even sacrilegious—disorders, a Sulpician, Charles Picoté, without being aware of the projects and proceedings of Mother Mectilde de Bar, thought of the institution of a religious foundation dedicated to reparative adoration. This idea that he had become the content of the vow he made in response to Anne of Austria's request, transmitted to him by the Countess of Brienne, the queen committing herself to carry out the vow that he would accomplish.

If Picoté had then only "a general view of honoring the Most Blessed Sacrament without determining which order of nuns this would be," at least he had a conviction: the realization of this vow was, in fact, likely to bring about

> the true and specific remedy for the woes that one wished to heal, being certain that war does not displease God so much on account of the injustices committed against particular parties whose goods are stolen, as on account of all the crimes and sacrilege that soldiers commit—in churches the majority of which are destroyed, and the profanations against the Most Blessed Sacrament, which one saw often trampled underfoot and put into the feedbox of horses. However, if a war did no other harm than making the Holy Sacrifice of the Mass and divine worship to cease, this would already be a great woe since it would deprive God of the only infinite glory He receives on earth.... The interruption of the sacred mysteries is the most terrible of all chastisements... the cessation

3 These signatures appear this way on the last page of the "Register containing the summary of the state of the temporal affairs of this first monastery of Benedictine nuns of Perpetual Adoration of the Most Holy and Most August Sacrament of the Altar" (National Archives, LL. 1710).

> of the sacrifice is the greatest of all evils: its continual worship is the greatest of goods and the most excellent manner of honoring God.... One cannot thank Him and honor Him better than by the establishment of an institute committed by vow to perpetual adoration day and night, and through union with Jesus Christ, to be victims consecrated to His glory and to make reparation to it, and to pray for the conversion of sinners.[4]

This conviction, which was largely shared in the spiritual milieu of the capital, was further invested sometimes with a rather dramatic expression. Thus one can recall the repeated visions, precisely in Paris in 1652, of a woman known as a mystic: Jeanne de Matel, foundress of the order of the Incarnate Word and of the Blessed Sacrament.

> On the feast of the Visitation, July 2, 1652, she was preparing to enter into the joy of the feast [when] the Blessed Virgin appeared to her, leaving Paris and carrying her divine Son with her. Jeanne threw herself, at this sight, face to the ground.... "Ah, my Queen, ah, my noble one, where are you taking the Child of Holy Love, Love itself, my Jesus, my God?... If you leave Paris, we are doomed! With my tears, I will stop you from taking Him away. He did not despise them when He was mortal. With their tears, the widow of Naim and Lazarus's sister made Him resurrect the dead.... I will not stop praying to you both to give me peace and until I see our King and his court return to Paris!"[5]

And, in her entourage, it was to the prayer and the radiance of Mother de Matel that the end of the Fronde was attributed.

In the case of Mother Mectilde, instead of visions, it seems she had only interior inspirations, dictating to her the path ahead, step by step, to which she strived to be faithful, in "pure faith." Thus, when she dreamed of becoming a recluse in the midst of the miserable situation

4 P 101, pp. 425–26.

5 R. M. St. Pierre de Jésus, *Vie de la révérende Mère Jeanne Chézard de Matel*, Fribourg (Switzerland), 1910, p. 461.

to which she was driven, she fell seriously ill; she was even at death's door, around the end of July until the middle of November 1651. In this situation, it was with a complete surrender to the divine will that she agreed to do what the Lord asked of her. Therefore, returned from death to life[6] and having resolved to do what God was asking of her, Mectilde de Bar was guided by three events which marked her spring of 1652.

On a visit to a charitable lady of the district, the Marquise Anne de Bauves, "she saw a painting... in which was represented a pagan ceremony of priests and priestesses around an altar, in a posture of adoration, torch in hand. This caused her to say to the Marquise that those infidels, who were shown so imbued with reverence for their idol, would be the condemnation of Christians before the Blessed Sacrament." And the Marquise offered financial help to her "if she would accept it for a foundation toward the Blessed Sacrament in her chapel."[7] From that time on, Anne de Bauves joined together with some "pious persons, who, moved with a great desire to make the Most Blessed Sacrament continually adored," worked to gather the necessary funds to "begin this pious work" and soon "to buy a house in order to establish a monastery for the purposes described."[8]

There were still some months to go, however, before attaining this goal. Around the time when she observed the painting which was at Anne de Bauves's house, another interior suggestion deeply affected Mectilde de Bar: "One day at Holy Communion," she noted, "I understood the dignity and holiness of this perpetual adoration."[9]

Nevertheless, it was another factor which was decisive, while she remained very hesitant to undertake the work in view of which she was being solicited—in fact, she could only submit to "the authority of a bishop who, hearing my Confession, commanded me not to resist."[10] The Keeper of the Seals, president Mathieu Molé, to whom she turned in order to ask for "patent letters for a new house of nuns

6 Cf. Letter of Mother Mectilde to Jean de Bernières, November 25, 1651.

7 Account of Fr. Pierre Berrant, P 108 bis, p. 64.

8 Letter of Mother Mectilde to Bernières, January 2, 1653; *Lettres Inédites*, p. 357.

9 Letter of Mother Mectilde to Mother Benedicta of the Passion, January 28, 1652; *Lettres Inédites*, p. 143.

10 Mother Mectilde to Berniéres, January 2, 1653; *Fondation de Rouen*, p. 357.

which she wished to establish in Paris . . . answered her . . . that for this it was necessary that she have a contract of foundation in the forms and permission from the ecclesiastical superior."[11] For this foundation she asked the agreement of the Sisters: nine of them gave it to her without reservation in a letter from August 2, 1652.[12] And the contract of foundation was signed on August 14, 1652.

When and how did Fr. Charles Picoté hear about these projects and proceedings which corresponded so precisely to the vow he himself had made in the Queen's name? Perhaps it was through one or another of the charitable ladies devoted to Mother Mectilde and solicitous to see the project they had made their own succeed. It was shortly after the entry of the King and Queen into Paris in October 1652 that Picoté

> was informed in depth, to the full, about the motives and the project of the establishment proposed between the Ladies whom we have mentioned and Mother Mectilde of the Blessed Sacrament. So much resemblance was found between what God's light had made him conceive in his prayer and it, that he resolved to have the vow he had made apply to it. He then put the proposal about it to Mother Mectilde to know for himself what this work involved. The venerable Mother told the pious founding ladies what this good priest had told her, and asked them if they approved of their foundation being applied to it.[13]

From that point it remained for Picoté to find a favorable occasion to obtain an audience with the Queen. This may have taken place on December 8, the Queen having anticipated the step that she had planned to take in Val-du-Grace.[14] The Queen inquired about the circumstances of his vow, the motives which had urged him to make it, the sentiments he had had in prayer, and who these nuns were whom she would be setting up in a monastery "where perpetual adoration of the Most Blessed Sacrament of the Altar would be taking place day and night." After she had "satisfied her pious

11 P 108 bis, p. 66. 12 *Lettres Inédites*, p. 142. 13 P 101, pp. 426–27.
14 P 101, p. 427.

curiosity, he gave her to understand that in applying her vow to Mother Mectilde's plan, she would be fulfilling her obligation before God without any expense, and that he had the word of the founding ladies that they would gladly consent to it." Although the Queen had not long before rejected the project in question, "she ratified this vow which she regarded as her own and promised to do everything that depended on her for its success."[15] Further, knowing the opposition of the Abbot of St.-Germain, it was she who wrote to him immediately to ask him to grant "the necessary permissions for this establishment."[16]

While waiting until it was possible to construct a real monastery (this would be at rue Cassette in the following years), a house to rent was found at rue Férou which belonged to the Countess Catherine de Rochefort. The lease was signed on Wednesday, November 4, 1653.[17] The work progressed rapidly, and Mother Mectilde hoped that "we will be in complete enclosure in time for Christmas or Epiphany."[18]

It was thus that, on March 12, 1654, perpetual adoration was officially inaugurated. In the very small chapel installed in the house at rue Férou, Anne of Austria was present, and beside her were Mectilde of the Blessed Sacrament, Prioress, and the first nuns; behind the Queen, Madame de Châteauvieux, foundress, and Anne de Bauves (or Catherine de Rochefort, in whose house the ceremony took place). The Queen and the nuns were holding a candle in their hands and wore a cord around the neck.[19]

---

15 P 101, p. 427–28.

16 Letter that the Queen sent to Fr. Picoté to forward to the Abbot of St.-Germain, Monsieur de Metz, December 12, 1652; *Lettres Inédites*, p. 147.

17 Cf. Letter of Mother Mectilde to the Countess of Rochefort, November 6, 1653.

18 Letter of Mother Mectilde to M. de Roquelay, friend and secretary of Berniéres, November 25, 1653.

19 These are the symbols of the *amende honorable*, a punishment that required the offender to be led barefoot by the public executioner into a church or other public place in his shift, with a torch in hand and a rope around his neck, to beg pardon on his knees of God, his King, and his country. The phrase *amende honorable* came to have the meaning of reparation or sufficient apology. The Queen offered this gesture of reparation to God on behalf of France.

The scene was immortalized in a painting attributed to Philippe de Champaigne. At present, however, there are two versions: one in the monastery of Mas-Grenier, the other in the monastery of Rouen. These two pictures are reversed to right and left, as when an engraving is made, and this specific engraving exists and is found at the abbey of Limon. The painting preserved at the monastery of Mas-Grenier belonged to the nuns of the community at rue Cassette who, after the Revolution, ended by arriving at rue Tournefort, or at least the majority of them. The dispersion of the monastery at rue Tournefort in 1973 resulted in the painting being brought to the recently founded monastery (1922) at Mas-Grenier. At Rouen, a monastery founded in 1677, to date no document has been discovered which gives the origin of the painting now hanging close to the entry of the priory church, at the bottom of the side aisle. With regard to the engraving kept at Limon, its origin so far seems not to have been determined.[20]

20 Erected as an abbey in 1932, the community of Limon, although it had ceased to be part of the institute of the Benedictines of the Blessed Sacrament, still preserved some souvenirs of its relation to the Institute, notably some documents concerning the Warsaw monastery. The community now at Limon was founded in 1816 by the princess Louise-Adélaïde de Bourbon-Condé, who having fled the Revolution in France made her profession in the monastery in Warsaw founded in 1687. Upon returning to Paris, King Louis XVIII granted her the property

The engraving preserved at Limon (several copies of it were handed over to the monastery of Rouen) matches the painting from Mas-Grenier: the features, the expressions on faces, the postures of personages corresponding to what is known; the design is sober, with the emergence of low vaults on the lateral wall, which limits the space. This corresponds to the arrangement still found today in the cellar of the house on rue Férou. In the painting from Rouen, reversing the layout, in order to convey the greatness of the ceremony, the artist placed the scene in a much larger design by substituting for the proximity of the lateral wall a certain depth that the chapel of rue Férou could not have had, putting the view of the vaults above and beyond the Queen, at the same time distorting the altar in such a way that the monstrance is presented to the spectator rather than to the adorers, whose profiles are seen.

In this exaltation of the royal foundation, there is indeed a sign of the importance attached to the work of reparative adoration which was inaugurated in this way. It is not only a fine votive marble admirably sculpted which testifies to this royal vow, nor is it merely a votive painting evoking the scene. No, that which bears witness to this vow is the Institute itself which came from it and which perpetuates what it recalls; it is the reparative perpetual adoration which this Institute has continued for more than three centuries.

Here we cannot pass over in silence the page of the history of this Institute which is written in letters of fire and blood in the heart of the dramas of our twentieth century.[21] It was through the fulfillment of the vow of Queen Marie Casimire that the monastery of Warsaw was founded in 1687 as an *ex voto* of the victory won at Vienna by King John Sobieski III, a victory which delivered Christendom from the peril of the Turks.

However, in 1944 it was from the conjunction of two contemporary state totalitarianisms that this monastery of Warsaw was martyred. In 1943, the uprising of the Ghetto of Warsaw occurred 250 meters from this monastery. In August 1944, under the impassive eyes of

---

of St. Louis-du-Temple. In 1848 the nuns resettled at rue Monsieur, and finally to Limon in the aftermath of World War II. These letters from Warsaw were given to the monastery of rue Tournefort.

21 This essay was published in French in 1989.—*Trans.*

the Russian army encamped opposite on the right bank of the river Vistula, the Warsaw uprising brought a pitiless German repression. On August 6, the community of the Benedictines of the Blessed Sacrament, whose monastery dominated the left bank of the Vistula, went down into the cellars where little by little a thousand people, wounded, hunted, etc., were taking refuge.

Out of the forty-seven nuns, there were at least seventeen who went to ask the Prioress—who felt overwhelmed by this élan in which she discerned a heavenly inspiration—the permission to make an offering of their lives for the survival of Catholic Poland, for the Church, and for peace. On August 31, around 3 PM, a raid hit the Church. The cupola collapsed, crushing the thirty-four Benedictines who surrounded the tabernacle (including all those who had made the vow of victimhood), hundreds of refugees (there were only twenty survivors), and four priests. A fire broke out in the rubble whose size and flames prevented rescuing the victims, thus buried alive. In the midst of the cries and the terror there rose from the ruins the chant, "*Adoremus in aeternum Sanctissimum Sacramentum,*" the sounds of which became, hour by hour, more and more feeble until the third day when silence reigned...

From the foundation produced by a royal vow in the troubles of the Fronde and formalized on March 12, 1654 in a little oratory in the Saint-Sulpice quarter, to the voluntary oblation accomplished August 31, 1944 in a royal monastery, at the hour when contemporary man was crushed to the point of degradation and annihilation by the totalitarianisms of the State, there was the permanence of the reparative adoration of the Benedictines of the Blessed Sacrament, present in each period amidst the dramas of its time.

A SPIRITUAL FRIENDSHIP IN THE *GRAND SIÈCLE*

The foundation of the institute of the Benedictines of the Blessed Sacrament was not the result of a royal vow alone. In fact, the foundation was made possible by the spiritual friendship, quite exceptional, which developed between Mectilde de Bar and Marie de la Guesle de Châteauvieux. Indeed, the latter not only brought substantial help—both material and administrative—to the institute's origin, but had so much entered into the project that, beginning on the day after her husband died, she went to join the monastery then established at rue Cassette, where she became "Sr. Victim of the Blessed Sacrament, known in the world as Marie de la Guesle."

It is perhaps helpful here to summarize briefly the beginning of the ties which united Mother Mectilde to the Countess of Châteauvieux. It is not necessary here to go over Mother Mectilde's life again, as was done by Pierre Marot in the preface to *Documents Historiques*, which deals with the foundress (called the *institutrice*, leaving the name of *fondatrice* for the Countess of Châteauvieux) of the congregation of the Benedictines of Perpetual Adoration of the Blessed Sacrament. In that work, published by the monastery of Rouen in 1973, the notices, biographies, or studies which appeared previously are listed. In its section on Mother Mectilde's connection with Lorraine it "recalled the importance of the Lorraine tradition in Mother Mectilde's work. She was driven away by the invasion of Louis XIII's troops but protected by the French apostle of charity, Vincent de Paul. Her virtues bore fruit in Paris and enriched the spiritual patrimony of France." Moreover, it was this feature which had to be remembered in 1979, and then 1981, by Joseph Daoust, in the rich little books which he prepared with the nuns of Rouen, and in which he was careful to evoke the momentous life of Mother Mectilde, while bringing to light some selected extracts from the writings—even unpublished—of the spiritual master that Mother Mectilde was and remains, whose radiance, as well as Eucharistic message, is ultimately very great.[22]

Louis Cognet, in the introduction he wrote in 1965 to certain extracts of Mother Mectilde's writings addressed to the Countess of Châteauvieux, wanted to place the spiritual personality of Mother Mectilde in the religious currents of the seventeenth century: an "exemplary nun" with the Annunciades of Bruyères (1631–1638; Prioress in 1633), then with the Benedictines of Rambervillers (1639), at Montmartre (1641–1642), in Normandy (1642–1643). During this latter sojourn, Mother Mectilde became acquainted with the Company

22 For a translation of Joseph Daoust's selection of Mother Mectilde's Eucharistic writings, see the aforementioned book *The Mystery of Incomprehensible Love*, which also contains a biography of her by Canon G. A. Simon.

of the Blessed Sacrament; and, having become friends with Jean de Bernières, she was to remain in epistolary contact with him until his death in 1659. Having returned to Paris in 1643, Mother Mectilde was lodged with some refugee nuns at Saint-Maur-des-Fosses where she met a boarder who, in providing some resources to her community, introduced her to Parisian high society. Elected Superior in 1646, she was also quickly requested at Caen (1647), and at the end of her three-year term, she was elected Prioress at Rambervillers (1650), the monastery of which she remained part. However, the war in Lorraine brought her back to Paris, with four nuns—"the youngest, since they were the most in danger in such a wretched time"[23]—in March 1651 to the community at St.-Maur, then taking refuge in Paris in the St.-Germain suburb, on account of the disturbances of the Fronde. It was to a house in the rue du Bac called "*Le Bon Amy*" that they arrived on "the vigil of Our Lady in March," that is, March 24, 1651.[24]

Mother Mectilde and her seven "little Sisters from Lorraine" knew there "the most complete destitution," as Fr. Michel Dupuy reminds us in his essay in this volume. To this situation, dire from the material point of view, must be added Mother Mectilde's falling gravely ill in the month of July. Such was the material situation of the monastery and the state of her health when she received in August the visit of two charitable ladies from the neighborhood: Charlotte de Ligny, *présidente* de Herse (a relation of Jean-Jacques Olier, the priest of Saint-Sulpice), accompanied by the Countess of Châteauvieux, who was not "from the same parish." Her town mansion (which she had inherited from her family) was situated a short fifteen minutes away in the rue Saint-André-des-Arts.

Born Marie de la Guesle half a century earlier, she became Countess of Châteauvieux on June 8, 1625, in the church of Saint-André-des-Arts. From her marriage with René de Châteauvieux were born two children: the elder, a son, died young; a daughter, Françoise, who married Charles de la Vieuville on September 25, 1649. Thus it was two years after her daughter's marriage that the Countess of Châteauvieux became acquainted with a gravely ill Mother Mectilde.

Having come to the *Bon Amy* for a very short charity visit, Marie

---

23 *Documents Historiques*, p. 69.

24 Ibid., p. 70.

de la Guesle Châteauvieux returned several days later to "talk of spiritual discourse about which she was extremely inquisitive."[25] Soon she opened her soul to Mother Mectilde, who initiated her into the spiritual life. Henceforth, the Châteauvieux family set about helping as efficiently as possible the one who would become the foundress of the Benedictines of the Blessed Sacrament, since it was upon recovering from that grave illness that Mother Mectilde renounced her desire for the life of a recluse to give herself completely to every task God wanted of her. Such was the demand of "pure faith" whose experience she would hand on to Marie de la Guesle Châteauvieux.

In any case, in the midst of the material and moral disorder of the times Mother Mectilde was soon entreated to "undertake something important for honoring the Blessed Sacrament."[26] Certainly from various sides was emerging the need to respond to "the many profanations of the Eucharist, instigated by the lure of profit and by the hatred of Protestants, who were numerous among the mercenaries of the various armies."[27] We have already observed how much this need was felt in the spiritual milieus of the capital.

However, as Mother Mectilde gradually went forward in the project of a foundation in view of honoring the Blessed Sacrament, in the same proportion obstacles seemed to develop.

From the material point of view, to think of thus establishing a new monastery of nuns, and in the St.-Germain suburb, wasn't that a risk? However noble and generous were the intentions of the donor ladies and of the Prioress and of the nuns around her, how could such a monastery survive, since at that time in the St.-Germain area alone six communities had been forced to leave their monasteries, and "the majority had withdrawn to their parents' houses"?[28] The abbot of Saint-Germain-des-Prés might not be inclined to grant his permission as ecclesiastical superior.

Another difficulty arose from the spiritual point of view. The devotion to the Eucharist seemed to be tarnished by the use being made of it by the Jansenists; the monastery of Port-Royal was dedicated to

---

25 Ibid., p. 81.
26 Ibid., p. 84.
27 Dom Yves Chaussy, *Les Bénédictines et la Réforme catholique en France au XVIIe siècle*, Paris, 1975, p. 373.
28 *Documents Historiques*, p. 88.

perpetual adoration in 1646.[29] Now, precisely Port-Royal undertook to gather the nuns who had taken refuge in Paris and whose situation was precarious; and, what was more, in that program, the "Gentlemen of Port-Royal wanted her [Mother Mectilde] as director in a house of women of this same Port-Royal order, which they wanted to set up at the gate of Saint-Marceau." And they offered her "six hundred crowns as payment for this, in addition to her food." However, accepting their offer would have imposed on her some conditions of infeudation which her conscience could not accept. She preferred not to owe them anything that was an alienation. On March 5, 1652, at the time when her project was taking shape, she wrote to Bernières's secretary [Roquelay]:

> I am glad that he [Bernières] is working for the destruction of Jansenism. Our Lord granted me the grace to work for it according to my little scope also, and gave me the consolation of withdrawing some souls from it who were quite hindered by it; and divine Providence wanted to make use of us, though very unworthy [Mother Mectilde speaks of herself], to place these souls in liberty of spirit and Our Lord has given them very great graces since they left those opinions. That is how Providence has made use of us since the great malady in August.[30]

This abandonment to Providence in the midst of the trials which overtook her, this spiritual and doctrinal fidelity in the face of subtle solicitations which, though scarcely noticeable, could have caused her to stray from pure rectitude by leading her to give in to some temptation of her own will—this is what she experienced daily in "pure faith," in a constantly renewed stripping of self through "pure love." This inner attitude, this spiritual forward march was the soul of the project which she brought to maturity in a total deprivation of self. This was also the way she initiated Marie de la Guesle Châteauvieux into the interior life, who day by day shared in the cares

29 Louis Cognet, Introduction to *Mère Mectilde du Saint-Sacrement. Ecrits spirituels à la Comtesse de Châteauvieux*, IX–X.
30 Letter to M. de Roquelay, March 5, 1652.

of that foundation, about which we have recalled some stages up to the ceremony in the little chapel of rue Férou on March 12, 1654.

There is an additional feature which would have its place once the foundation was properly established. Mother Mectilde, who during the whole preparation for her foundation had always sought to efface herself solely in favor of God's will, would do the same in the exercise of her responsibilities: she refused to establish the office of abbess; this she left to the Virgin Mary on August 22, 1654. As for her, she wanted to use her term as Prioress for the formation of her daughters, for the consolidation and extension of her foundation according to God's good pleasure. Marie de la Guesle Châteauvieux was a witness to this inner demand that Mother Mectilde experienced, through the occasional notes she was led to address to her.

Thus trained in the spiritual ways, the Countess of Châteauvieux on the day after her husband's death (November 6, 1662) withdrew, until her death (March 8, 1674), into the monastery which she had had built at rue Cassette—thus always in the same quarter of Paris—and where the Benedictines of the Blessed Sacrament were settled on March 21, 1659.

The spiritual exhortations Mother Mectilde addressed to the one who became Sister Victim of the Blessed Sacrament were part of the solicitude which the foundress had for the spiritual formation of her community. This was the solicitude that she had shared with the woman who, after having supported her foundation, and having thus entered into the intimacy of her religious plan, had then taken her place in the community.

The spiritual blossoming of Marie de la Guesle Châteauvieux led her to collect "for her personal use" some of Mother Mectilde's letters or conferences having to do with the various liturgical feasts. This is where the name of "breviary" comes from, given to the manuscript at that time, which seems at rue Cassette to have been subsequently added to. Mother Mectilde herself reviewed the copy and allowed those among her daughters who desired it to copy it for their own use. That is why there are a certain number of copies of the *Breviary of Fire of Madame the Countess of Châteauvieux.*

THE PRESENT EDITION

Now, what does this manuscript represent? First of all, we must recognize that this is not the original text. This is a way of proceeding which, when it becomes systematic, we must be honest enough to denounce. In some extreme cases, respect for persons led to certain things being destroyed; indeed, in certain cases there was a "duty" requiring that something be placed in the fire (the text of a completed Confession, for example); this is obvious. But why, when the originals have been recopied, systematically destroy the original? Everyone knows that even with "revisions from the original," copies are deprived of the freshness of the original text.

We recall how the manuscripts of St. Thérèse of Lisieux (another victim of love) were handled, for a goal of edification, no doubt, for being put into print. If the initial documents had been erased, written over, etc., at least they were not destroyed. When things are like this, it's usually possible now to arrive at a correct reading and to restore the original text, even if only by having recourse to a "Wood's lamp," but of course, the condition being that one can refer to the original.

It is not at all a question of suspecting the copyists of some manipulation of the text. All the same, it's permissible to ask what happened to Mother Mectilde's original manuscripts, and why they were—it seems—destroyed, and how the copies were made which are recognized as official. Further, in the present case, the question can be posed all the more freely since there is a certain favorable presumption regarding the quality of the copies. If it's true, as the oral tradition has it, that Mother Mectilde authorized the copying of this manuscript to those among her daughters who wanted it, it's certain that she did not find her thought had been distorted.

However, it remains that this *vademecum* for the use of "Sister Victim of the Blessed Sacrament, called in the world Marie de la Guesle," deprives us of a direct contact with the freshness of Mother Mectilde's thought. We can only regret it, and this, for several reasons.

First of all, we must recognize that the concrete circumstances which suggested a thought, even one of general scope, are not in themselves indifferent for finding the meaning the author gives to it and the scope of his purpose. Let us take an example close to us:

to recall the inalienable rights of every human being at the precise moment when, a few steps away, the Gestapo shipped away the Jews to an unknown destination; to pray explicitly in Holy Week 1943 for those who were being exterminated 250 meters from the monastery, as the Warsaw monastery did when the neighboring ghetto was being annihilated—is the one insignificant for grasping the other? Were not the cardinal virtue of fortitude and the theological virtue of charity concretely entangled?

There is still more. There is an idea about spiritual writings with which we must state that we cannot agree. This is because if it is held, the result is that one succeeds in veiling the personal holiness of the spiritual master, for whose reality one substitutes in some way one's own veneration. Certainly we cannot forget St. John of the Cross's very penetrating reflection about founders: "By giving these heads of families the firstfruits of His Spirit, God entrusts to them treasures and grandeurs in connection with the succession of children, more or less great, who must embrace their teaching and their spirit."[31] Nevertheless, what constitutes each man's and each woman's personal sanctity is not directly their ministerial graces or the charisms they were given for the service of their brethren—it is their personal correspondence to grace, even unto the heroic practice of the virtues. It is their heroic response to their own vocation through the spiritual progress of their life, step by step, until the final consummation. In other words, to use St. Paul's expression: "We all who, with unveiled face, beholding the glory of the Lord, as in a mirror, are being changed into his likeness from one degree of glory to another; for this comes from the Lord who is the Spirit."[32] Therefore the questions we can legitimately pose are of this kind: through what purifying stages did the servant of God, whom we venerate, pass? How did God progressively lead him or her to be configured to His Son? etc. In short, what was, for each such man and woman, his or her "journey of faith," following the expression John Paul II continually used regarding the Virgin Mary in the encyclical *Redemptoris Mater*? Moreover, if God willed that, taking a human nature, His Son would enter into human time and creation and that

31 *The Living Flame of Love*, stanza 2.2.

32 2 Cor 3:18.

He had to "grow in wisdom, in age and grace, before God and men"[33] and that, "Son though He was, He learned obedience through what He suffered,"[34] how could any human being, even exceptional, do without such spiritual growth? Even if such a person attained in each state of his life the corresponding perfection, didn't his perfection also grow in proportion as he advanced in his human and spiritual life? An exacting spiritual discernment bringing to light the heroic progress of spiritual masters and founders, all along the rigorously historical journey of their life as men and women among the men and women of their time: this is the best way to approach the truth of their personality, such as God—submitting to the time of men—wanted it to develop concretely in time.

These reflections having been made, and which it was undoubtedly necessary to make given the character of the manuscript which is the subject of the present volume, it still remains to touch upon this edition.

Recopied in each age, the copies of the *Breviary of Fire of Madame the Countess of Châteauvieux*, as with all the copies of documents coming from the origins or concerning them, were thus transmitted in the communities. Now we must underline the importance of this living transmission, since, in the Revolution, and at the time of the dispersal of religious houses in 1792, each nun left with her concealed manuscripts. Mother Mectilde's texts were not for them talismans or museum pieces; they were truly the source of their religious life which they had to keep alive by making it their own life on the roads or hiding places of their exile, at least when that was not in prison.

After the Revolution, the two Parisian monasteries, the one from rue Cassette—in large measure—and the one from rue St. Louis-au-Marais, were united, after some vicissitudes, at rue Tournefort, where the preserved manuscripts were collected: some autographs from Mother Mectilde, some copies from the seventeenth and eighteenth centuries, "reviews from the original." These are copies from the hand of Mother Monica of the Angels de Beauvais (1653–1723): a member of the group of foundresses of the monastery of Rouen,

33 Lk 2:52. 34 Heb 5:8.

this nun was to return to the monastery of rue Cassette, of which she became Prioress in 1713.[35]

The same thing was done elsewhere. That is why other copies from the seventeenth century are now kept in Rouen. Certain of these came from Rouen, others from Paris, others from Bayeux, and among these certain ones are from various monasteries of Lorraine. Others are preserved at Crâon, copies from the seventeenth century originating in Rouen; at Caen also; and for various reasons, at the Bibliothèque nationale or the archives of the town of Sens. Which leads us to observe that, apart from these last exceptions, explicable if not justified, these diverse copies were used in accordance with their reason for existence: in fact, in the various monasteries, these copies served to nourish the nuns' spiritual life according to the spirit of their foundation, as they were handed down from age to age. It was a family heirloom used to give glory to God for the graces of the foundation and for the spiritual nourishment of the nuns of the Institute.

It was in this spirit that the Arras monastery, the first new foundation of the Institute in France after the Revolution, received in 1823 some manuscripts coming primarily from rue Cassette. How was this transmission made? Mother Catherine of Jesus Heu, who belonged to the monastery of rue Cassette where she had made profession in 1775, and who had preserved some of its legacy, was judged to have a responsibility vis-à-vis the foundation's memory, and thus of the Institute's spirituality. She brought therefore

> to Arras some belongings which the venerable foundress of perpetual adoration had used, her authentic portrait, and some of her more important works which were still in manuscript. She was herself a precious treasure for the house she adopted. She had known nuns who had lived

35 "She remained close to twenty years in the monastery of rue Cassette before being elected Prioress of it. In this lapse of time it was easy to revise her own copies according to the originals which should still have existed, since she mentions them. That is why the manuscripts copied by Mother Monica of the Angels de Beauvais are regarded in the Institute as deserving complete confidence" (note from the archivist of the Rouen monastery). Regarding Mother Monica of the Angels, see *Fondation de Rouen*, p. 43, n. 31 and *Lettres Inédites,* p. 392.

> with Mother Mectilde of the Blessed Sacrament; therefore she knew perfectly the history and the primitive customs of the Institute.

Mother St. Francis de Sales Bernierre

> found in her [Mother Catherine's] memories, as well as in the belongings and in the manuscripts she was eager to entrust to her, precious help for establishing a regularity which extended to the smallest details in her monastery. In addition, there was help for answering the thousand questions which came to her from all the houses of the Blessed Sacrament to provide to each the features they needed for regularization.[36]

There was, therefore, truly a living tradition, a transmission animated with fidelity. And this monastery of Arras had also a rather exceptional fruitfulness throughout the nineteenth century, not only because of the number of vocations, but also because of its various foundations: one at St.-Omer (1841), which made a foundation in its own turn in Germany, then a foundation in Scotland at Dumfries (1884) and one in Milan (1892).

On November 24, 1904, in virtue of the Law of Separation, the nuns were expelled from France. Those from Arras took refuge in their foundations in other countries: seven went to Milan and fifty-five to Dumfries, which then had only twenty-five nuns. That is why the precious manuscripts of the house of the monastery from rue Cassette were exiled to Dumfries with the majority of the Arras community. In 1919, when the French sisters, free to return to their native land, returned to Tourcoing, they left at Dumfries, in the community of the Scottish sisters, the oldest French nuns with a certain number of original manuscripts. Now, among these manuscripts there was the copy made in the seventeenth century in the rue Cassette monastery, which had the inscription, "Breviary of Fire of Madame the Countess of Châteauvieux, original of our Mother

36 *Life of Mother St. Francis de Sales Bernierre*, professed at the Rouen monastery in 1808 and foundress of the monastery of Arras in 1815, pp. 781–82 (MS preserved at the monastery of Tourcoing).

institutrice, who gave to this lady many instructions according to her spiritual attraction and dispositions, transcribed from the original." Such then is the manuscript now being published.

Finally, why was this manuscript, so important because of its age, at Dumfries? An heirloom of rue Cassette transmitted to Arras by Mother Catherine of Jesus Heu, it was quite natural that, rather than leaving it to be confiscated, the nuns driven from France took with them the manuscripts from the origins, to continue to nourish their spiritual life. This was all the more natural since it was on the monastery of Arras that the duty of preserving the living memory of the Institute had devolved. When the French nuns were able to come back to the soil of their native land, on whom would it devolve to preserve alive the memory of the community? Tourcoing, the community resurrected from that of Arras, after fifteen years of exile, or Dumfries, the daughter house of Arras? Was it sensitivity toward the older French sisters who remained on foreign soil that led to some of the oldest manuscripts, which had nourished their monastic youth, being left at Dumfries? However respectable they may be, these sentimental reasons were not always the most advisable...

However, since in October 1957 the prioresses of the Institute, meeting in Milan, decided to publish the writings of Mectilde, it is in service of that publishing project, destined to keep alive the Institute's memory, that henceforth all manuscripts must be placed. Such an edition cannot be the desiccated publication of the dead testimony of a bygone past; it is even necessary to specify that the edition can be alive only insofar as it is nourished by living fidelity. Obviously, if a monastery were to leave the federation, at the same time it would inevitably renounce this living fidelity and disqualify itself from serving this living memory of the Institute, since it would have renounced it.

On the occasion of the publication of the *Breviary* of Madame the Countess of Châteauvieux we must rejoice in the determination of the Institute of the Benedictines of the Blessed Sacrament. We must thank them for allowing a greater number of people to be able to benefit from these substantial texts. Through their determination to undertake the publication of Mother Mectilde's writings, these nuns demonstrate their will to "*servata tradere viva*" (hand on alive what has been preserved), according to the motto of the Archivists of the Church of France. Thus we must congratulate the Benedictines of the Blessed Sacrament on their enterprise.

If we might be allowed to lengthen these pages with one more reflection?

Perhaps the work decided upon in 1957 will be completed only when, beyond the manuscripts whose publication they have courageously undertaken, the Benedictine Sisters of the Blessed Sacrament will have fully rediscovered and made to be discovered, in all its vitality, the life of Mother Mectilde and her spiritual growth through the concrete circumstances which marked it out; for it is in this way that God wished, step by step, to make their foundress progress and blossom on our human pathways.

If, beyond the documents and testimonies, we try to scrutinize Mother Mectilde's life itself, it seems already possible to have a presentiment of her spiritual itinerary, the trials through which she had to pass. Think, for example, of those months from July to November 1651; for it was indeed through trials of health, which brought her to the last extremity, that she acquired that total *disponibilité* to God, which was the condition for the Institute's foundation. Let it be remembered that it was also in the midst of a particularly difficult trial of health that she made a six-week retreat from November 21, 1661 to January 6, 1662, where she matured her thoughts on the Institute—a trial from which emerged the nineteen chapters of the work *The True Spirit of the Perpetual Adorers of the Most Holy Sacrament of the Altar.*

Does not such a spiritual itinerary, such a journey of faith illuminate, from the inside, the foundation of the Institute? And would this consideration not at least incite us to examine the possibility of a process of beatification? The renown of Mother Mectilde's holiness was obvious and undisputed. Will it not have room to go further?

Must we not also give thanks to God for this life of Mother Mectilde which He raised up among us? For, throughout her life, step by step, she learned to let herself be led by God, to accomplish His will in His Church. Would it not also renew in their vocations all the nuns who are nourished with the spirit of Mother Mectilde? For, through reparative adoration, the Institute assists the Church to lay hold of a better awareness of its own identity and to be renewed in its sacramental mystery!

Beyond the Institute and indeed even beyond the Church, would it not render a service to the world of today, as to the world of yesterday? For today as yesterday, it is important to denounce and refute the "gnosis which is falsely called knowledge," to take up St. Paul's expression,[37] which inspired St. Irenaeus.[38] Who could say that it is not important to exorcise this intellectual terrorism and this degrading conformism which, celebrating new knowledge, new powers, new myths, new lusts, invents in each age some "pagan ceremonies of priests and priestesses around an altar, in a posture of adoration, torch in hand"? The vow which Queen Anne of Austria fulfilled, kneeling, rope around her neck, candle in hand, by establishing at 11 rue Férou in Paris, on March 12, 1654, the Benedictines of the Blessed Sacrament—has it truly lost its burning relevance?

---

37 1 Tim 6:20.
38 This is the title of the book which we now call *Adversus Haereses*.

Made in United States
North Haven, CT
16 June 2024

53686793R10211